# The Lost Messiah

# The Lost Messiah

## In Search of the Mystical Rabbi Sabbatai Sevi

THE OVERLOOK PRESS

WOODSTOCK & NEW YORK

First published in the United States in 2003 by
The Overlook Press, Peter Mayer Publishers, Inc.
Woodstock & New York

WOODSTOCK:
One Overlook Drive
Woodstock, NY 12498
www.overlookpress.com
[for individual orders, bulk and special sales, contact our Woodstock office]

NEW YORK:
141 Wooster Street
New York, NY 10012

Library of Congress Cataloging-in-Publication Data

Freely, John.
The lost Messiah : in search of the mystical rabbi Sabbatai Sevi / John Freely.
p. cm.
Includes bibliographical references and index.
1. Shabbethai Tzevi, 1626-1676. 2. Rabbis—Turkey—Biography.
3. Sabbathaians. I. Title.
BM755.S45 F74 2003    296.8'2—dc21    [B]    2002034626

Printed in the United States of America
ISBN 1-58567-318-8
FIRST EDITION
1 3 5 7 9 8 6 4 2

For
Nikos Stavroulakis, who started me off on this quest,
and for
Toots, who, as always, was with me all the way.

# Contents

# Acknowledgements

I am grateful to Anthony E. Baker for the photographs he has supplied for the book. I would also like to acknowledge the assistance of Dr Anthony Greenwood, director of the American Research Center in Istanbul; Professor Gün Kut, librarian of Boğaziçi University; Eran Lupu, for help in Hebrew translations; Korkut Özgen, for assistance with Turkish sources; Professor Jak Deleon, for introducing me to the staff of the Istanbul Jewish newspaper *Shalom*, who kindly allowed me to use their archives; Erol Çoskun, for information about the Sabbatian community in Istanbul; Mario Rodrik, for an introduction to the community, a number of whom generously shared their family reminiscences with me; Emin Saatçi, who helped with our trip to Albania; and the Honourable Ahmet Rifat Ökçün, Turkish ambassador to Albania, who made our visit to Tirana such a pleasure. I would also like to thank Eleo Gordon for her invaluable advice on my manuscript.

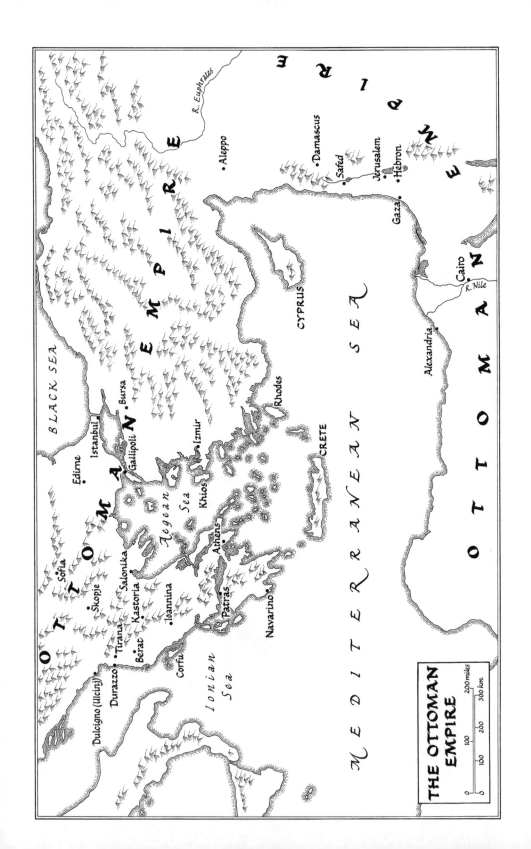

THE OTTOMAN EMPIRE

# Prologue

This is the story of my search for Sabbatai Sevi, known to history as the False Messiah. But I prefer to call him the Lost Messiah, for though he died more than three centuries ago his followers remain as a distinct group, some of them perhaps still waiting for his return.

The chapters that follow tell the story of Sabbatai Sevi, interwoven at the beginning and end with an account of my own travels on the trail of the Lost Messiah. These journeys took me around the eastern Mediterranean and into the southern Balkans, ending when I travelled into the remote interior of Albania in search of Sabbatai's grave. But what I found only deepened the mystery that surrounds the memory of Sabbatai, whose enigmatic character fascinated me from the moment I first learned of him. My travels have been in time as well as space, and I have tried to recreate the period in which Sabbatai lived – actually a hidden microcosm within an age, for the esoteric Jewish mysticism that enveloped him made his world utterly different from that of his contemporaries in western Europe: within the Islamic Ottoman Empire, where he spent his entire life, the rationalism of the seventeenth-century Scientific Revolution did not penetrate.

My search for Sabbatai Sevi was made difficult because of many missing pages in his story – lacunae due both to the total secrecy of his followers and to the censorship of orthodox Jewry, not to mention the layers of myth that form a palimpsest upon every incident in his life, right down to the circumstances of his death and burial. Throughout, I was deeply dependent on the pioneering works of Gershom Scholem, particularly his magisterial *Sabbatai Sevi: The Mystical Messiah*, which was my principal source of information, particularly of quotes from contemporary figures in this strange and seemingly endless story.

converted to Islam, forming the secret sect known to the Turks as the Dönme. The Dönme survived as a religious group into the twentieth century, moving from Salonika to Istanbul in the population exchange following the Greek–Turkish war of 1919–21. Because they did not marry outside their sect until recent years, the Dönme remained a distinct group, separate from the Jews and the Muslim Turks around them. Although to all appearances they were practising Muslims, some of them were said to be keeping the faith with Sabbatai Sevi, their Messiah, whom they believed would one day return and lead them to redemption.

On Monday I was pleased to find a copy of Rycaut's work in the rare-book room of the Near East Collection at Robert College. I immediately turned to page 201, the point I had left off at in Eliza's shop, and read Rycaut's account of Sabbatai's birth at Izmir and his life until 1666 – a year that ended with his conversion to Islam under pain of death, an apostasy in which he was eventually joined by many of his followers. Rycaut ends his digression on the Jews at that point, commenting in the last paragraph on page 219, 'Since we have so long insisted on the phrensie of the Jews, let us return to matters of greater Consequence, and more general concernment . . .'

I was by now curious about Rycaut himself, and I read what I could find about him and how he came to write about Turkey and Sabbatai Sevi.

I learned that his involvement with Turkey began in London in 1660, when he was engaged as private secretary by Heneage Finch, second Earl of Winchilsea, who had been appointed ambassador to Constantinople (known to the Turks as Istanbul). The salary of the ambassador and his secretary were paid by the Levant Company, a group of English merchant adventurers also known as the Company of Turkey Merchants. This firm had been founded through an agreement between Queen Elizabeth and Sultan Murat III, who in September 1581 granted a charter to the Company, giving it a monopoly in maritime trade with the Ottoman Empire, and allowing the English merchants to establish factories at Istanbul, Aleppo and Izmir (known to the Greeks and other foreigners as Smyrna).

Rycaut's intent from the very beginning of his appointment was to write about the Ottoman Empire: as he later remarked in his history, 'I resolved from my first entrance into these Countries, to note down in a blank Book what occurred in that Empire, either as to civil or military affairs; with what Casualties and Changes befel our Trade, so that both one and the other might serve for Examples and Precedents to future ages.'

Rycaut remained with the embassy in Istanbul until the end of August 1667, when he left to take up a new post as acting British consul in Izmir. The previous year he had completed work on *The Present State of the Ottoman Empire*, which was published in London by John Starkey and Henry Brome in August 1666, though the title page was postdated 1667. According to Samuel Pepys, all but about twenty-two copies of the print run were destroyed in the Great Fire that ravaged London in the first week of September 1666. Nevertheless, the book attracted much attention, and a second edition was published the following year.

On 3 September 1667 Rycaut arrived in Izmir, where he would serve as British consul for eleven years. During the months before his arrival he had been receiving reports about the extraordinary progress of Sabbatai Sevi since his triumphal reappearance at Izmir in 1665, after he proclaimed that he was the Messiah. The Jews had been waiting since biblical times for the apocalypse, a cosmic cataclysm in which God would destroy the powers of evil and bring the righteous into their messianic kingdom. The declaration that Sabbatai was the Messiah had sent a wave of apocalyptic fervour throughout the Jewish world.

As soon as Rycaut settled down in Izmir he began gathering information about Sabbatai, with the intention of publishing a pamphlet about him. His principal informant was Thomas Coenen, a Dutch chaplain who had been in the city when Sabbatai returned from his enforced exile, and who would in 1669 publish his own account of the episode. Sabbatai still had many disciples in Izmir, so Rycaut thought it best to publish his account anonymously. He did so with the help of John Evelyn, who included Rycaut's story along with two others by Pietro Cesii in a book entitled *The History of the Three late famous Impostors, viz. Padre Ottomano, Mahomed Bei, and Sabbatai Sevi . . . the suppos'd Messiah of the Jews*, published in London by Henry Herringham in February 1669. Rycaut finally included his account of Sabbatai's messianic movement in the 1680 edition of *The Present State of the Ottoman Empire*, the one that I had read in the Kohen Sisters' Bookshop, beginning my obsession with the strange figure whom I began to think of as the Lost Messiah.

The following Saturday I stopped in again at the Kohen Sisters' Bookshop, for I was interested in learning more about Sabbatai Sevi and his followers, and wondered whether he still had believers in Istanbul. When I asked Eliza Kohen about this, she said there were still a few thousand Dönme left in the city. She pointed out one of them in her shop, but when he felt our eyes on him he abruptly departed.

Eliza then sold me a book about Sabbatai Sevi and his followers. This was Abraham Galanté's work on the Dönme, published in Istanbul in 1935. Galanté, a Turkish Jew of Sephardic ancestry who died in 1961, had been the leading authority on the history of Turkish Jewry, and had spent much of his life in search of Sabbatai, tracking down documents on him and his followers.

Galanté had identified a number of places associated with the Sabbatian sect, including the house in Izmir where Sabbatai was born. During the years that followed, I found this house, as well as other places associated with the history of Sabbatai Sevi and his followers, and read whatever I could find on the subject – most notably Gershom Scholem's magisterial *Sabbatai Sevi: The Mystical Messiah*. I also read Scholem's work on *The Messianic Idea in Judaism* and his book *Kabbalah*, on the Jewish mysticism from which the Sabbatian sect emerged.

Messianic mysticism was incomprehensible to me at first, for my training as a physicist was definitely a handicap in trying to understand the Kabbalah. Only when I began to look upon the Kabbalah as a form of cosmology, though based on mystical beliefs rather than the laws of mathematical physics, did I begin to make some headway.

Shortly after I read Scholem's books for the first time I met Nikos Stavroulakis, founder of the Jewish Museum in Athens, who shared my fascination for Sabbatai Sevi. Nikos invited me and my wife to spend a summer with him in Khania, the ancient capital of western Crete, where he had restored a thirteenth-century Venetian tower-house in the former Turkish quarter. He had also rebuilt an abandoned synagogue in the old Jewish quarter, although, as he said sadly, he was the only Jew left in Khania, where in Ottoman times there seems to have been a community of Sabbatians. They were mostly Sephardic Jews, he said, and up to the early twentieth century they still spoke Ladino, the medieval Spanish their ancestors brought with them when they were driven out of Spain in 1492. Nikos was deeply versed in the Kabbalah and had an insider's feeling for seventeenth-century Jewish mysticism. He communicated some of this insight to me, and gradually I began to part the veils that separated Sabbatai's era from mine, entering into the apocalyptic spirit of his times.

Such was the manner in which I began my search for the Lost Messiah, a quest that took me into the vanished world of Sabbatai Sevi, though the man himself – shrouded in myth, mystery and ambiguity – continued to elude me right to the end.

# 2. Izmir

The harbour of Izmir lies at the inner end of a deeply indented gulf on the Aegean coast of Asia Minor, and is Turkey's principal outlet to the Mediterranean. Ships dock under the western slope of Mount Pagus, the focal point of the landscape for those approaching the city by sea, its summit crowned with the ruins of the ancient fortress known to the Turks as Kadifekale, the Velvet Castle. This was the scene that met us when my wife, Dolores, and I first sailed into Izmir in 1962, at the beginning of my search for the Lost Messiah.

Modern Izmir has spread out to the horizon around the inner end of the gulf, but its heart is still the ancient bazaar under Mount Pagus, a market quarter known as Kemeraltı, 'Under the Arches'. The old Jewish quarter was beyond the western end of Kemeraltı, where the gold merchants have their shops.

We looked for the shop of Jacob Benveniste, which we found halfway along the street of the gold merchants. I had been given his name by friends in Istanbul, and had written to tell him of my interest in Sabbatai Sevi and his origins in Izmir. He had agreed to help me. One of his ancestors, Hayyim Benveniste, had been chief rabbi of Izmir at the time that Sabbatai had declared that he was the Messiah, and two others had been on the council of rabbis which had been summoned to deal with the ensuing controversy.

Jacob said that he would take us to the quarter from which Sabbatai Sevi had originated. We followed him down a narrow alley off the main market street of Kemeraltı, and then into a cul-de-sac ending in a wooden fence. When we reached the fence, he pulled aside some loose boards and motioned for us to make our way through. We found ourselves in the courtyard of a huge old Ottoman caravanserai, whose portico had been converted into a slum tenement of ramshackle wooden buildings. The courtyard and its surrounding shacks were crowded with people who looked more Spanish than Turkish, and when I heard them speaking

Ladino I knew that we were in the heart of the old Jewish quarter.

Jacob led us through the courtyard and into a labyrinth of narrow cobbled streets beyond, bringing us to an ancient stone building that seemed on the verge of falling into ruins. This was the house in which Sabbatai Sevi was born, he said, though his sceptical tone indicated that he was not convinced that this was really so.

We followed him up three flights of tottering wooden stairs to the top floor, and there we found a number of old people kneeling in front of a niche in the crumbling front wall, all of them mumbling repeated phrases in Ladino that I took to be prayers. Jacob whispered that these were followers of Sabbatai Sevi, known to the Turks as Dönme, a derisive term meaning 'Apostates' or 'Turncoats', and he said that they were praying to their Messiah. We watched them in silence for a while before departing. None of them seemed aware that we were in the room, though others whom we passed on our way out of the building looked at us curiously, and Jacob averted his gaze.

We followed Jacob again as he led us further down the street, to a walled enclosure where he used a huge rusted key to let us into a courtyard paved in large flagstones rutted with the marks of wagon wheels. The domed building at the inner end of the courtyard, he said, was the old Portuguese Synagogue, which had been built by the Sephardic Jews soon after they had arrived in Izmir in the seventeenth century.

He led us inside and introduced us to the rabbi, a biblical figure with a long white beard, who bowed to us gravely. Jacob spoke to him in Ladino, and when he mentioned the name 'Sabbatai Sevi' the rabbi looked at me with suspicion. He spoke heatedly to Jacob, and then abruptly broke off the conversation, bowing to us as he indicated that we must leave, for it was time for him to close the synagogue.

After we left, Jacob apologized and explained that the rabbi was angry that he had brought to the synagogue foreigners who were interested in Sabbatai Sevi, whom he and others in the Jewish quarter of Izmir still despised for having disgraced their community. This was one of the synagogues where Sabbatai had worshipped in his youth, before he was banished from Izmir for his unorthodox beliefs. Though Sabbatai had been all but forgotten elsewhere, he was still remembered vividly in Izmir, though three centuries had passed since he had turned the Jewish world upside down with his messianic claims.

But when I returned to Izmir thirty-six years later I found that Sabbatai had been forgotten there too – or so it seemed.

I knew that Jacob Benveniste had long ago left Izmir and moved to Israel. None of the gold merchants in the Kemeraltı market quarter now had a Jewish name, but by asking around I found that one of them was in fact a Jew, though he had taken a Turkish name. He said that the Jews who still lived in Izmir had for the most part moved to more modern parts of the city, the few who remained in Kemeraltı being old people. He did not know if there were any Dönme left in Izmir, he said in answer to my question, although he doubted it, for he had heard that they had all, such as they were, moved to Istanbul.

When I walked through the old Jewish quarter I heard not a word of Ladino, only Turkish and Kurdish. I found that the house in which Sabbatai Sevi had been born had disappeared, replaced by a modern commercial building. No one I questioned knew anything about the house, nor had any of them ever heard of Sabbatai Sevi.

Sabbatai's own testimony gives the date of his birth as the Ninth of Ab in the Hebrew year 5386 – 1 August 1626 in the Gregorian calendar. The Ninth of Ab is the day on which Jews commemorate the destruction of the First and Second Temples. The First Temple, built by Solomon, was destroyed by the Babylonians in 586 BC, and the Second Temple was demolished by the Romans in AD 70, both catastrophes occurring on the Ninth of Ab, according to tradition. The Ninth of Ab fell on the Sabbath in 5386. Boys born on the Sabbath were often called Sabbatai. According to a Midrash, or ancient rabbinic tradition, the Ninth of Ab would be the birthday of the Messiah. Sabbatai's detractors claimed that he had altered his birthday to fit in with this tradition, but Gershom Scholem was of the opinion that the date was correct.

At the time of Sabbatai's birth, most of southern Europe, Turkey, the Middle East and North Africa was ruled by the Osmanlı sultans, known to the West as the Ottoman Turks. The name of the dynasty came from Osman Gazi ('Warrior for the Faith'), who at the beginning of the fourteenth century took the title of Sultan as his warriors began expanding westward into the domains of the declining Byzantine Empire. By the middle of the following century the Byzantine Empire had been reduced to little more than its capital, Constantinople, which was surrounded by the lands of the rapidly expanding Osmanlı Turks. Byzantine history effectively ended in 1453, when Constantinople was captured by Mehmet II, the seventh Osmanlı sultan, who then made the city capital of the Ottoman Empire.

Sultan Mehmet – thenceforth known to the Turks as Fatih, or the Conqueror – repopulated Constantinople/Istanbul with both Turks and non-Muslims from elsewhere in his empire. This was in keeping with the Ottoman system known as *sürgün*, or resettlement, which allowed the sultan to move his subjects around to suit his needs – sometimes for punitive reasons in the case of rebellious elements, at other times, as in the case of Istanbul in Fatih's time, to repopulate a city that had greatly decreased in numbers during the latter Byzantine era.

Fatih organized the non-Muslim inhabitants of his realm into separate ethnic communities, with each *millet*, or nation, directed by its own religious leader. The Greek millet was headed by the the Orthodox patriarch of Constantinople, the Armenian *millet* by the Gregorian patriarch, and the Jewish *millet* by the chief rabbi. The Jews in Istanbul at the time of the Turkish Conquest were predominately Romaniote, or Greek-speaking, though there were also a small number of Karaites, members of a schismatic sect that emerged in Babylon in the eighth century. During the next four decades the Romaniotes and Karaites were joined by refugees from Spain, Portugal, Provence, Italy, Sicily, Germany and Austria. The Iberian Jews were called Sephardim, and those from central and eastern Europe were called Ashkenazim.

Jewish immigration to the Ottoman Empire increased dramatic- ally in 1492, when the Jews were expelled from Spain by King Ferdinand and Queen Isabella. The order of expulsion was signed by Ferdinand and Isabella on 31 March, and all the Jews were gone from Spain by 31 July of that year. This was the Seventh of Ab in the Jewish year 5232 – just two days before the anniversary of the destruction of the First and Second Temples. And so the expulsion of the Sephardim was considered to be a third *huban*, or destruction, another landmark in the woes of the Jewish people.

Most of the expelled Sephardim settled in the Ottoman Empire, considerably increasing the size of the Jewish communities in Istanbul and Salonika. The Jewish community in Izmir developed only in the seventeenth century, when the city first emerged as a major Ottoman port. One reason for the rise of Izmir was the founding of the Levant Company, whose factory there generated a great increase of trade between Turkey and England. Another was the outbreak of war between Venice and the Ottoman Empire, in which the Venetians blockaded the Dardanelles in 1646, cutting off Istanbul and leaving Izmir as the only major harbour. Louis Deshayes, Baron de Courmenin, who landed at Izmir in 1621, wrote of the busy commerce there, much of which was in the hands of European merchants: 'At present, Izmir has a great traffick in wool, cotton and silk, which the Armenians bring there rather than to Aleppo. It is more advantageous to go there because they do not pay as many dues. There are several merchants, more French than Venetian, English or Dutch, who live in great freedom.'

Unlike the older Jewish communities in Istanbul and Salonika, most of the Jews who came to Izmir were not foreign exiles but were drawn from other parts of the Ottoman Empire by the commercial opportunities in the newly developed Turkish port. At the beginning of the seventeenth century Izmir had only one synagogue, which in the following century was taken over by the Turkish authorities and converted into a mosque. By the time of Sabbatai's birth there were five Jewish congregations, each with its own synagogue. The number of congregations and synagogues had increased to six by the 1640s, and by the end of the century there were nine. The first census of Ottoman Izmir was not taken until 1831, but from various sources one can estimate that the population in the mid seventeenth century was about 80,000, of whom some 2,000 were Jews, though foreign travellers tended to overestimate the size of the Jewish community. At that time the other non-Muslim minorities in Izmir probably included about 2,500 Greeks and 500 Armenians, along with a less permanent population of several hundred European merchants and their families, known to the Turks as 'Franks'.

The Jews in Turkey were obliged to dress somewhat differently from Muslim Turks, as the French traveller Jean de Thevenot remarked in 1687: 'The Jews in Turkey are clothed as the Turks are, save that they do not dare wear green, nor a white Turban, nor red Vests; they wear commonly a violet colour, but are obliged to wear a violet Cap, shaped like a Hat, and of the same height; and such as can afford the price of a Turban, have one round their cap below.' Thevenot also noted that the Jews and the Christians were forced to pay a yearly head tax known as the *haratch*.

The Jews in the Ottoman domains were left in peace, and many of them prospered, but when the Empire began its long decline in the seventeenth century the situation of the Jewish communities declined too, though they suffered no repression. Things were very different in Christian Europe, where animosity against the Jews reached its peak during the Cossack riots of 1648–9 in Poland and the Ukraine under the leadership of Bogdan Chmielnicki. The Jewish chronicles say that 100,000 were slaughtered and 300 communities destroyed during the Chmielnicki massacres, adding still another *huban* to the list of Jewish tribulations.

The Chmielnicki massacres had a profound emotional effect upon Jewish communities everywhere, giving rise to fears that an apocalyptic cataclysm was approaching, along with hopes that the Messiah would soon appear. Messiahs had appeared periodically in Jewish history, arousing the hopes of the dispersed Jews and in the end leaving them in desolate disappointment. But still they continued to hope, encouraged by the predictions of the mystical movement known as the Kabbalah, whose masterwork, the *Zohar*, prophesied that one day the Messiah would appear and lead the Jews back from their Galut, or Diaspora, to redemption in the Land of Israel. But this would not happen all at once, according to the *Zohar*:

At the time when the Holy One . . . shall set Israel upright and bring them out of the Galut, He will open to them a small and scant window of light, and then He will open another that is larger, until He will open to them portals on high to the four directions of the universe. So shall it be . . . and not for a single instant, for neither does healing come to a sick man at a single instant, but gradually, until he is made strong.

Sabbatai's father, Mordecai Sevi, is thought to have been from the Morea, as the Peloponnese was then known – perhaps from Patras (present-day Patrai), which at the time had the largest Jewish community in southern Greece. A Samuel Sevi is known to have been in Patras in 1614, when he was listed as a witness at a wedding there. The family was probably Ashkenazim, since the name 'Sevi' is unknown among the Sephardim.

Mordecai Sevi was originally a poulterer in the Morea, and sometime after 1614 he moved to Izmir and continued making his living in the same way for a time. Then, probably in the 1630s, he gained employment as a commercial agent for an English merchant in Izmir, which soon made him quite prosperous.

Mordecai's wife, Clara, bore him three sons: first Elijah, then Sabbatai and finally Joseph. Elijah and Joseph followed their father's profession and prospered as commercial agents in Izmir. Both of them became followers of Sabbatai after he proclaimed himself the Messiah, but returned to orthodox Judaism after their brother's apostasy. Solomon Kohen, a Sabbatian rabbi from Volhynia in Poland (now Volynska in Ukraine), mentions Elijah Sevi in a letter dated 1672, part of a biography of Sabbatai, now lost. He writes that he had spoken with Sabbatai's brother, 'the learned and very wealthy rabbi, who is Our Lord's senior by a few years. He told me about the life of his brother – whose majesty be exalted – from his youth to this day, and I wrote down everything.'

Sabbatai's parents had died before the messianic movement began, Mordecai in 1663, Clara some years earlier. The tombstones of Mordecai and his brother Isaac, who also died in 1663, could still be seen until 1918 in the ancient cemetery of Bahri Babi in the Karatash quarter of Izmir, but after the First World War the burial ground was covered over and became a park. Clara would have been buried in the same cemetery, but her gravestone disappeared much earlier. According to a letter written in 1665, and now preserved only in a Polish translation, upon his return to Izmir in 1665 'Sabbatai Sevi resuscitated his mother who had died twenty years earlier.' This statement is contradicted by the fact that Sabbatai wrote to his followers after his return to Izmir and recommended that they visit his mother's grave and touch it with their hands, telling them that this was equivalent to a pilgrimage to the Temple in Jerusalem. Thomas Coenen writes that at Sabbatai's request, Nathan of Gaza, the great prophet of the Sabbatian movement, visited Clara's grave before he left Izmir in 1667, and that afterwards he drank from a nearby well, probably an *ayazma*, or holy spring.

At that time the houses of the European merchants were concentrated along the shore north of the port, along with the mansions of the English, Dutch, French, Genoese and Venetian consulates. The consulates lined a street known as the Rue de Francs, which from the description of a local merchant seems like an enclave of western Europe in Turkey: 'Turks pass along it but rarely . . . nothing is spoken but Italian, French English and Dutch . . . Provençal is the dominant language . . . the cabarets are open day and night where one plays, makes good cheer and dances after the French, Greek and Turkish styles.'

When Paul Rycaut first arrived at Izmir in 1667 he disembarked at Sanjakburun, the customs control station, where the merchants of the Levant Company had already prepared a house for him. He described his arrival in a letter to Winchilsea: 'The whole factory next morning met me, and made a handsome collation, conducted me with about a hundred horse and six trumpeters before, through the streets of Smyrna . . . and in all our nation I observed that cheerfulnesse at my reception, that from thence I gather, and conjecture a happy omen to all my designes, and successes here.'

Almost all the foreign merchants in Izmir employed Jewish agents, who were usually fluent in several western-European languages as well as Turkish and Greek. Jews often also served as customs collectors. The English merchants who employed Mordecai Sevi and his sons Elijah and Joseph would have been members of the Levant Company. The only one of Mordecai's three sons who did not become a commercial agent was Sabbatai, who was evidently better suited for a life of study than for a career in commerce. Rycaut writes briefly of Sabbatai's father, noting that he was 'an Inhabitant and natural of Smyrna, who gained his Livelihood by being Broker to an English Merchant in that place; a person who before his death was very decrepit in his Body, and full of the Gout and other infirmities'. He goes on to remark of Mordecai that 'his Son *Sabatai Sevi* addicting himself to study and learning became a notable proficient in the Hebrew and Arabick Languages; and especially in Divinity and Metaphysicks'.

Aside from Paul Rycaut and Thomas Coenen, there are very few sources for Sabbatai's early years, particularly his studies. He appears to have had a traditional Jewish education, and his evident intelligence led to his being encouraged to pursue rabbinic studies. His first teacher has been identified as the rabbi Isaac di Alba, who died in 1681. The source for this is Moses Pinheiro, who knew Sabbatai from the time of their youth, and who became one of his devoted followers. Pinheiro writes of 'Rabbi Isaac, who for six years laboured with AMIRAH in the spiritual life, and AMIRAH first studied with him'. Here 'AMIRAH' comes from the initials of the Hebrew words for 'Our Lord and King, his Majesty be exalted', the name by which Sabbatai's followers referred to their master.

Isaac di Alba was later a member of the court of rabbis which sent out a circular letter announcing the excommunication of all Sabbatians after Sabbatai's apostasy. According to Gershom Scholem, this letter – now lost – contained a biographical account in which mention is made of Sabbatai's 'strange and immoral behaviour as a youth'. There is a reference to this behaviour in a fragmentary work called the *Vision of R. Abraham*, which appears to have been forged by Nathan of Gaza. This work, which purports to be an ancient document written by a seer named Rabbi Abraham, who foretells the life story of the coming Messiah, seems to be based on actual biographical episodes of Sabbatai's early years that he himself supplied to Nathan. Its last paragraph mentions Isaac di Alba, and goes on to tell of the sexual torments that will be endured by the young Messiah. According to Rabbi Abraham, the first of these erotic traumas will literally brand him: 'When he is six the Shekhinah, which has revealed herself to us, will appear to him in a dream as a flame, and cause a burn on his private parts, but he shall not tell anybody.' The Shekhinah referred to here is the Presence of God, or, in a deeper Kabbalistic sense, the feminine principle of the Godhead, exiled from her divine husband.

Rabbi Abraham goes on, 'And the sons of whoredom will accost him so as to cause him to stumble, and they will smite him but he will not hearken unto them. They are the sons of Na'amah, the scourges of the children of man, who will always pursue him so as to lead him astray.' In the Kabbalah the 'sons of whoredom' are the demons who are given birth by the sperm released in masturbation and nocturnal emission, and Na'amah is the Queen of Demons, who seduces men through the uncontrollable sexual desires she excites in them.

Coenen and other sources report that at the age of fifteen or sixteen Sabbatai began to live a solitary existence, renouncing all pleasures of the flesh. Scholem quotes two letters sent to the Yemen in the mid-1660s, in which it is stated that after 1642, when Sabbatai was sixteen, 'he began to accept discipline, to renounce all pleasures because of their sinfulness, and to reject . . . frivolity'.

Sabbatai continued his studies with the rabbi Joseph Eskapha, the most renowned Jewish scholar in Izmir at the time, and at the age of eighteen he was accredited as a *hakham*, or rabbi. Moses Pinheiro, who pursued talmudic studies alongside Sabbatai, said that there was 'none like him' in his knowledge of the subject – one of a number of contemporary testimonies to his brilliance.

Apparently Sabbatai began to study the Kabbalah somewhere between the ages of eighteen and twenty. Both Coenen and Pinheiro report that he studied it without a teacher, at first working by himself, then later joining Pinheiro. According to Leyb ben Ozer, a non-Sabbatian who was notary of the Amsterdam Jewish community in the late seventeenth century, Sabbatai 'lived in his father's house during those years, secluded in a special room and completely given over to his studies, so that in a short time he became proficient in Kabbalistic learning'.

# 3. Kabbalah

Sabbatai's Kabbalistic studies focused on the *Zohar*, the *Book of Splendour*. This is the core work in the literature of the Kabbalah, composed mainly between 1280 and 1286 by Moses ben Shem Tov de Leon. It summarizes the ancient traditions of the Kabbalah, the esoteric teachings and mysticism of Judaism, dating back to antiquity.

Sabbatai also studied the *Qanah*, a huge work on the 'meaning of the commandments'. The *Qanah* was held in high regard by the followers of Isaac Luria of Safed, whose interpretation made the Kabbalah a powerful force in the subsequent development of Jewish mysticism.

Isaac Luria was born in Jerusalem in 1534 and died in 1572 in Safed (present-day Zefat), where his grave is still a place of pilgrimage. The knowledge that came to him from his meditations and visions he revealed orally to his students and never published. His only writings are a commentary on the *Zohar* and three Sabbath poems, one for each meal of the day.

Some of Luria's students, most notably Hayyim Vital, committed Luria's teaching to writing, though guarding them jealously from their contemporaries, whom they did not consider worthy to receive them. Only at the end of the sixteenth century did copies of parts of Vital's writings begin to circulate, first in Palestine and then further afield. By then a complete account of Luria's teaching by another of his followers, Moses Jonah, had reached Europe in manuscript copies. This was entitled *Kanfey Yonah*, or *Wings of a Dove*.

Although Sabbatai claimed to have rejected Lurianic Kabbalah, it is evident that he and his followers, most notably Nathan of Gaza, were deeply influenced by Luria's ideas, particularly the doctrine of creation and its relation to the significance of exile and redemption.

The doctrine of creation in Lurianic Kabbalah is based on three main concepts: *zimzum*, or 'contraction'; *shevirah*, the 'breaking of the vessels'; and *tiqqun*, or 'restoration', all of them adapted from earlier Kabbalistic ideas.

The concept of *zimzum* comes from the *Sefer ha-Iyyun*, a work from thirteenth-century Provence ascribed to Rav Hama Gaon. This deals with the question of how God, the Infinite, created the universe despite His omnipresence seeming to leave no space for the world. The *Sefer ha-Iyyun* asks the question and gives *zimzum* as the answer: 'How did He produce and create this world? Like a man who gathers in and contracts his breath, so that the smaller might contain the larger, so he contracted His light into a hand's breadth, according to His own measure, and the world was left in darkness, and in that darkness He cut boulders and hewed rocks.'

The notion of *shevirah* concerns the 'vessels' that are supposed to contain the *sefiroth*, the ten stages of the primal divine light that ultimately makes the Godhead manifest. The first three *sefiroth* managed to contain the light that flowed into them, but when the radiation reached the seven lower *sefiroth* they proved too weak to confine it and were shattered. Sparks of the divine light were trapped in the shards of these vessels, some of which ascended while others fell. The fragments that fell are the *qelippoth* or husks, which were transformed into the forces of impurity and evil, becoming the source of the material world. The strength of the *qelippoth* stems from the sparks of divine light which are trapped within them, exiled and subjected to evil. Thus even Shekhinah, the Divine Presence, is in exile and the universe flawed, all due to the catastrophe caused by the shattering of the vessels.

The process of *tiqqun* began immediately after the catastrophe. When the sparks that are trapped in the broken vessels are redeemed, the exile of the divine light will be at an end and redemption will come about, both for humanity and for the cosmos.

Two remarks that Luria made to his disciples suggest that he thought himself to be the Messiah, though he never said so directly. Both of these allusions are quoted by Israel Zinberg in his history of Jewish literature, the first having been preserved in a Lurianic legend and the second in a story by Hayyim Vital.

The story told by Hayyim Vital is as follows, where the rabbi he refers to is Isaac Luria:

Once we stood with the rabbi near the grave of Shemaya and Avtalyon [leading Jerusalem rabbis of the first century BC]. The rabbi said to us, 'My children, Shemaya and Avtalyon command me to request that you pray for the Messiah the son of Joseph, that he may not die.' But we did not understand and did not dare to ask who the Messiah the son of Joseph really is. But the Messiah the son of Joseph was our rabbi himself. A few days later he died.

According to the legend, every Friday before sunset Luria and his disciples would leave Safed clothed in white garments, and in the open fields they would welcome the 'queen Sabbath' by singing 'Lecha Dodi' by Solomon Alkabetz, which Luria considered to be the most beautiful of Sabbath hymns. Once when they were singing this song Luria asked his disciples if they would like to go to Jerusalem at once and welcome the Sabbath there. Some said they were willing, but others said that they would first have to tell their wives that they were going. At this Luria exclaimed, 'Woe to us who have not the merit! If all of you had agreed to my proposal, an immediate end would have come to the exile and the Messiah would have appeared in Jerusalem.'

Sabbatai was undoubtedly influenced deeply by Isaac Luria, though he was reluctant to admit it. Moses Pinheiro, who became one of the leading Kabbalists of his day, writes that Sabbatai never practised any Lurianic meditations, but that he attained his knowledge of the Mystery of the Godhead through meditation 'on the plain meaning of the words, like one praying before his King'. He also remarks of Sabbatai that 'In the science of truth he never studied any books but the *Zohar* and the book *Qanah*.'

Pinheiro's statement that Sabbatai did not practise Lurianic meditations is somewhat surprising, given Luria's profound influence on seventeenth-century Kabbalism. Abraham Miguel Cardozo, one of the leading Sabbatian theologians of the seventeenth century, quotes Sabbatai as saying, 'Isaac Luria made a beautiful chariot, but he did not say who was riding in it.' Cardozo also reported that

Sabbatai 'rejected the Lurianic Kabbalah, though he admitted its truth, because it caused him confusion and profited him naught in his pursuit and knowledge of God'. Elijah Sevi and other disciples told Cardozo that Sabbatai relied mainly on the Talmud and the Midrashim, the literature of rabbinic tradition, which at that time would have included the *Zohar* and the *Qanah* as ancient 'Midrashic' texts. As Cardozo writes of Sabbatai, 'He used to kiss the Talmud and the Midrashim, and would say that the talmudic teachers were his fathers and masters in the doctrine of the Mystery of the Godhead, and that through their word he had been aroused to seek God and that through them he had found Him.'

En-Sof, the Infinite, is the Kabbalistic term for the 'Hidden God', remote from all creation, known only through the emanation of His power. The ten stages of this emanation, the *sefiroth*, make this power manifest as a personal God who can be apprehended through meditation. The tenth and last *sefirah* is the Shekhinah, the Presence of God, of which a talmudic proverb says, 'Wherever Israel is exiled, the Shekhinah goes with it.' According to the Kabbalah, the Shekhinah is like a bride who has been separated from her husband, the Holy One Blessed Be He. Only with the coming of the Messiah will the perfect unity of the *sefiroth* be permanently restored, with the Shekhinah rejoined in eternal unity with her husband.

While Sabbatai was studying the Kabbalah he began acting strangely, as several sources note in writing about his early years. Tobias Rofe Ashkenazi, who collected anecdotes of Sabbatai's life in Turkey, published in 1707, writes, 'In spite of his knowledge and learning, he always used to do foolish things . . . so that people used to talk about him and call him a fool.'

When Sabbatai was somewhere between the ages of twenty and twenty-two he was married for the first time, to an unidentified girl from the Jewish quarter of Izmir. But he did not consummate the marriage, and after a few months his father-in-law complained to the rabbinic court and a divorce was arranged. Soon afterwards Sabbatai married again, his new bride, also unidentified, being 'of a highly respected family in Smyrna' according to Coenen. The result was the same, and after Sabbatai failed to approach his wife her father complained to the rabbinic court and again there was a divorce. Divorce was rare enough among Jews at the time, but two such cases in rapid succession would have caused intense gossip about Sabbatai's manhood.

Coenen reports that the Jewish community of Izmir attributed Sabbatai's failure to consummate the two marriages to his saintliness and purity. But Leyb ben Ozer notes rumours of a statement made by Sabbatai after his second wedding, in which he reported that the Holy Spirit had appeared to him and said that the woman was not his predestined mate.

It is possible that the two failed marriages may have been at least partly due to Sabbatai's mental state, for at about this time he began to show signs of what many thought to be madness. Coenen reports that before his first marriage Sabbatai had delusions of levitation, at which times he would quote Isaiah 14:14, 'I will ascend above the heights of the clouds; I will be like the most High', and on one occasion he recited this verse with such ecstasy that he imagined himself to be floating in the air. Once Sabbatai asked his friends whether they had seen him levitate, and when they denied that they had he said imperiously, 'You are not worthy to behold this glorious sight because you are not purified like me.'

One of his most devoted followers, Abraham Cuenque of Hebron, also reports on Sabbatai's eccentric behaviour at this time. He says that when the Jewish community in Izmir ridiculed Sabbatai as a fool 'He would retire to the mountains or caves without his brothers or family knowing his whereabouts; at other times he would withdraw to a miserable little room where he locked himself in and from which he emerged only occasionally.' Cuenque goes on to write of how this upset Sabbatai's family: 'His brothers were grieved by his behaviour and were greatly ashamed but could not prevail upon him to change his ways. Being wealthy they felt disgraced by his behaviour; they upbraided him but to no avail.'

Sabbatai later spoke of his psychic experiences during this period to his disciple Solomon Laniado, whom he first met in Aleppo in 1665. Four years later Laniado wrote about this conversation to two rabbis in Kurdistan, telling them that Sabbatai's strange actions stemmed from the nature of his messianic mission.

Sabbatai told Laniado that the spirit of God descended upon him one night in 1648 while he was walking in solitary meditation about two hours from Izmir. The voice of God said to him, 'Thou art the saviour of Israel, the Messiah, the son of David, the anointed of the God of Jacob, and thou art destined to redeem Israel; to gather it from the four corners of the earth to Jerusalem . . .' From that moment on, according to Laniado, 'Sabbatai was clothed with the Holy Spirit and with a great illumination; he pronounced the name of God and performed all sorts of strange actions as seemed fit to him by reason of the mysterious *tiqqun* intended by them.'

Those who did not understand the reasons for Sabbatai's behaviour looked upon him as a madman, and one of his teachers in Jerusalem, where he studied in 1662–3, repeatedly flogged him for his 'many deeds which appeared repugnant to reason, until he retired, away from men, to the wilderness'. Sabbatai told Laniado that 'Sometimes he beheld the splendour of the Shekhinah, and sometimes God tried him with true temptations, all of which he withstood until in 1665, when he was in Egypt, God tried him with a very great temptation but he – praise be to God – withstood it.' Sabbatai went on to say that he prayed to God 'not to tempt him again, and since the day he made this adjuration the Holy Spirit has forsaken him and so has his illumination, and he has become like an ordinary man. He also repented all his "strange acts", since he could no longer understand their significance which he had understood when he originally performed them.'

According to Coenen, Sabbatai at first told only his family and close friends of the revelation that he was the Messiah. Coenen goes on to say that, when Sabbatai proclaimed in public that he was the Messiah, 'various factions arose', but Scholem is of the opinion that this did not happen before 1665.

Coenen remarks that after 1648 Sabbatai began to exude a fragrant odour, which other sources also mention, noting that his disciples later believed this to be the scent of the Garden of Eden. This aroused gossip among a number of people in the Jewish community of Izmir, who were scandalized by what they thought to be the use of perfume by a rabbi. Coenen states that a Jewish physician named Dr Barut, having heard these rumours, confronted

Sabbatai, who invited him home and stripped down so that he could prove that the odour was not perfume. Sabbatai explained to the doctor that he had had a vision of the patriarchs, who had anointed him with fragrant oils and commanded him not to reveal this to anyone until the appointed time. The doctor kept the secret for eighteen years, until Sabbatai publicly announced that he was the Messiah.

Moses Pinheiro also told of this anointment in his reminiscences of Sabbatai's early years. He recalled Sabbatai telling him of 'a voice calling out three times, night after night, "Do not touch my anointed Sabbatai Sevi," and at the third time he was visited by the patriarchs who anointed him'.

The anointment of Sabbatai was later commemorated by his followers, along with the other significant dates in his messianic career. According to the Sabbatian calendar, on the Twenty-first of Sivan Sabbatai was 'anointed by the prophet Elijah'. (That would be 21 Sivan 5408, or 11 June 1648.) This suggests that Sabbatai had changed the story by the time he announced himself as the Messiah, having himself anointed by the prophet Elijah rather than the patriarchs. The Dönme of Salonika continued to commemorate this day into the twentieth century, as they may still in Istanbul. One of the hymns that was sung on that day in honour of Sabbatai has been preserved:

> Truly God is good to Israel.
> This is the day on which AMIRAH was anointed.
>
> .   .   .   .   .   .   .
>
> On the day of his anointing
> The Shekhinah found relief.

Coenen learned from Elijah and Joseph Sevi that after their brother's anointment his face shone brightly during his ecstasies: 'After being anointed by the patriarchs, his face was exceedingly bright and shining, like the face of Moses after the giving of the Law.'

All but one of the contemporary sources seem to say that Sabbatai made no public messianic claims before 1665, the single exception being Jacob Sasportas, who became a relentless enemy of the Sabbatian movement. Sasportas, writing around 1669, notes that

some twenty years ago, he [Sabbatai] opened his mouth, saying, 'I am the Messiah' and uttering the Ineffable Name of God, so that the great rabbi Joseph Eskapha, who was his principal teacher, rebuked and outlawed him, and announced, 'Whoever strikes him down first deserves well, for he will lead Israel into sin and make a new religion.' He [Eskapha] also wrote to Constantinople about this matter.

The statement by Sasportas is suspect, since he often rewrote earlier accounts in the light of subsequent events. It is true that Sabbatai spoke the name of God in public, several times, as he later told Laniado. But otherwise Sabbatai does not seem to have done anything to offend the sensibilities of the Jewish community in Izmir at this time, although his two divorces and his suspected use of perfume would have led many to be suspicious of him. Sasportas, however, says that Sabbatai was 'outlawed' immediately after his 'strange actions' in 1648, and that 'he and his friends who supported him were exiled and harassed until he went away, driven out and exiled to Salonika'.

Sasportas is evidently compressing the events of several years, for there is clear evidence that Sabbatai and his followers were still in Izmir as late as 1650, studying the Kabbalah without any trouble between them and the Jewish community. The principal source for this is Abraham Cardozo, who gives the names of several young rabbis who were studying with Sabbatai in Izmir in 1650. Cardozo mentions Moses Pinheiro and the rabbis Abraham Barzillay, Moses Calameri, Isaac Silveira and others, writing, 'And when I came to Smyrna I heard [the testimony of] their faith from their own mouth.' This seems to indicate that Sabbatai was then instructing his followers in the Mystery of the Godhead rather than claiming that he was the Messiah.

Coenen writes that Sabbatai and his disciples used to meet in Sabbatai's father's house, and two or three times a week they would make excursions in the environs of Izmir, fasting during the day and taking ritual baths in the sea. On one of these occasions they were swimming in the Aegean off the end of the Cheshme peninsula, opposite the Greek island of Khios. Suddenly Sabbatai was caught in a whirlpool and almost drawn down into the depths, but at the last moment he was saved from drowning by his companions, who attributed his salvation to a miracle. This incident was commemorated in the religious calendar of the Sabbatians, and became one of their most important feasts. The oldest extant copy of this calendar records that this miracle was commemorated on 'Sixteen Kislev – the day on which he [Sabbatai] rose from the sea and was saved: it is like the day of Purim.' The hymns for this festival sing of the miracle as a symbol of the rising of the Messiah's soul from the depths of the abyss, where he beheld the 'crooked serpent'. (The 'crooked serpent' is in the Sabbatian Kabbalah a symbol of the Messiah.) One of these hymns mentions Abraham Barzillay:

His disciple Barzillay was strong, till evening he cried.
He brought new clothes from his home, and rejoiced with the son of David.

The Sabbatian calendar notes that the Fifteenth of Kislev is a fast day, the most important of the year, and in the prayer that begins the liturgy then it is stated that the custom was initiated by '*Hakham* Barzillay, the disciple of Our Lord [Sabbatai]'.

A number of sources refer to the severe depressions that Sabbatai suffered periodically during the early years of his manhood. His followers describe the anguish of these depressions in Kabbalistic terms, writing of the times when 'God hid his face' from Sabbatai, which alternated with periods of 'illumination'. Nathan of Gaza, writing in 1665, tells of 'the severe afflictions, too immense to be conceived, which R. Sabbatai Sevi suffered on behalf of the Jewish nation'. In Nathan's *Treatise on the Dragon*, written in 1666, he compares Sabbatai with Job:

All the sufferings of Job really refer to him who has suffered many great afflictions by all kinds of *qelippoth* . . . Many times when he stood in the height of heaven, he fell again into the depth of the great abyss . . . But when the illumination came over him . . . then he emerged from the realm of the *qelippah* where he had sunk in the days of darkness.

His followers also give many accounts of Sabbatai's glowing appearance when he was in a state of illumination. One of his disciples, Israel Hazzan, of Kastoria in northern Greece, writes that at such times Sabbatai's face was 'like the face of Moses which was like the face of the sun'. Abraham Yakhini writes in Kabbalistic terms of Sabbatai's alternating states of illumination and darkness being what one would expect of the Messiah: 'When the messianic king comes, he will not reveal himself by complete redemption, but he will appear first in all manner of pain and suffering, as our very eyes have seen it with Our Lord [Sabbatai] in whom there is at some times darkness and at others light.'

According to Gershom Scholem, an apocalyptic Yemenite work called *Gey Hizzayon, The Valley of Vision*, appears to be based on events in Sabbatai's life in the period 1642–50. After 1642, according to this work, Sabbatai began 'to accept discipline' while he rose seven *sefiroth* on the mystical ladder. Then 'God laid his hands on him and he came to understand the Mystery of the Godhead.' This would have been around 1650, by which time all Jewry was in a state of shock from the Chmielnicki massacres of the previous two years.

Then, sometime between 1651 and 1654, Sabbatai was driven out of Izmir by the elders of the Jewish community. The rabbi Joseph ha-Levi of Livorno, on the north-west coast of Italy, reports that Sabbatai 'proclaimed himself a prophet and the whole congregation persecuted him. He and his friends were thoroughly beaten, and banished from the district.' According to Sasportas, Sabbatai was 'opposed' by his teacher Joseph Eskapha and Aaron Lapapa, one of the most renowned Jewish scholars in Turkey. Sasportas remarks that he heard of Sabbatai's banishment soon after the event from 'truthful reporters who had been there when Eskapha outlawed him . . . saying, "This one will entice you to serve the Baals." ' Coenen writes that the 'Grand Rabbi Eskapha' advised that Sabbatai be killed secretly, but no one was willing to do this and so it was agreed to banish him instead. Nathan of Gaza, writing in 1665, says that

Sabbatai 'suffered exile for eighteen years, hunted from pillar to post, and sometimes his blood was declared free for all'.

The reasons for Sabbatai's banishment are obscure. One possible reason is that, as all sources agree, he used to speak the unutterable name of God. This is the Tetragrammaton (or 'Four Letters') usually spelled 'YHWH', from which the Christian form 'Jehovah' derives. According to Israel Hazzan, 'Our Lord [Sabbatai], before his kingdom became manifest, used to pronounce the holy name when reciting the blessing during his illuminations . . .' Pinheiro told Abraham Cardozo that in 1650 Sabbatai revealed to him that the Mystery of the Godhead was nothing more than the sixth *sefirah*, *Tifereth*, the 'attribute of mercy and the name YHWH'.

Sabbatai's own doctrine concerning the Tetragrammaton is preserved in a Sabbatian work entitled *Raza'de-Razin*, a long and detailed treatise concerning the Mystery of the Godhead: 'the Tetragrammaton is our God and He is superior to the whole emanation; He is also signified by the letter W of the Tetragrammaton YHWH and is called the husband of the Shekhinah'.

Another possible reason is suggested by the poet Emanuel Frances of Livorno, who with his brother Jacob wrote a series of satirical anti-Sabbatian poems entitled *Sevi Muddah*, or *The Chased Roe*. (The title is a pun on the name 'Sevi', which in Hebrew means 'roe'.) Emanuel Frances also wrote a short work entitled *The Story of Sabbatai Sevi*, as an appendix to *Sevi Muddah*. According to the latter work, Sabbatai once assembled his friends early one morning in the fields outside Izmir, 'and they went up into the mountains and Sabbatai cried to the sun with a mighty voice to stand still, and so did his disciples, until they were ashamed'. *The Story* goes on to say that when Joseph Eskapha and the elders of the Jewish community in Izmir heard of this incident they summoned Sabbatai, who refused to appear before them. The rabbis then threatened to excommunicate him, but Sabbatai 'returned the ban', adding the insulting message 'that his little finger was bigger than [Eskapha's] loins'. *The Story* concludes by telling how the rabbinic council suggested killing Sabbatai, but Eskapha persuaded them that they should limit themselves to 'castigating him, so that he should not return to his foolish ways, and banishing him from the city'.

This story supports the claim, made by some of Sabbatai's supporters as well as his enemies, that he was engaged not only in theoretical Kabbalah but also in practical Kabbalah, in which a study of the holy names could give adepts the power to work miracles. Sasportas writes that Sabbatai 'devoted himself to both the holy and the unclean names', by which he meant that Sabbatai was engaged in black magic – another factor that may have led the rabbis of Izmir to ban him from their community.

Rycaut gives a brief account of the circumstances surrounding Sabbatai's banishment from Izmir, his principal source undoubtedly being Coenen. He writes that Sabbatai 'was so cunning a Sophister, that he vented a new Doctrine in their Law, and drew to the profession of it so many Disciples, as raised one day a tumult in the Synagogue; for which afterwards he was by censure of the Kockhams (who are the Expounders of the Law) banished out of the City'.

Thus Sabbatai was forced to leave his birthplace and to go into exile, beginning a phase in his life known as his 'years of darkness'. As Nathan of Gaza wrote of Sabbatai in the *Vision of R. Abraham*, 'his soul was in the depth of the great abyss. Darkness, clouds, and thick darkness were round about him, and when he issued as if out of the womb, thick darkness was a swaddling-band for him . . .'

# 4. Years of Darkness

The first stage of Sabbatai's journeys during his 'years of darkness' took him into exile in Salonika. He appears to have left Izmir unaccompanied by his followers or by any attendants. Leyb ben Ozer writes that Sabbatai had a servant named Yehiel, who travelled with him up until the time of his apostasy, but Gershom Scholem makes a convincing argument to the contrary.

An Ottoman census in Salonika in 1478 indicates that there were virtually no Jews left in the city, the Romaniotes who had been there since Byzantine times having been moved to Istanbul by Mehmet II soon after his conquest of Constantinople in 1453. Mehmet's son and successor, Beyazit II, re-established the Jewish community of Salonika by welcoming the Sephardim to the Ottoman Empire after they were expelled from Spain in 1492. By 1519 the number of Jewish households in Salonika was 3,143, besides which there were 930 tax-paying Jewish bachelors, together comprising more than half the city's population.

Sabbatai would have arrived in Salonika in the mid-1650s. By that time nearly two-thirds of the city's population was Jewish, a ratio that would be maintained until the end of the Ottoman Empire. Thus Salonika had the largest concentration of Jews in south-eastern Europe, and was the only city in the Ottoman Empire in which they were a majority.

Whereas in Izmir the Jews were all in one quarter, in Salonika their large numbers led them to spread throughout the city, though their densest concentrations were in the port area on the inner side of Iskele Kapısı, the Gate of the Landing Place. The three oldest Jewish congregations had been made up originally of Romaniotes, to whom were added immigrants from Bulgaria as well as Ashkenazi refugees from central Europe in the mid fourteenth century. These were followed by Italian Jews, including many from Calabria and Sicily. After the exodus of Jews from Spain and Portugal in the last

decade of the fifteenth century the Sephardim became predomin-
ant, with the Catalans, Castilians, and Portuguese forming their
own congregations along with those from other regions of the
Iberian peninsula. Each group formed a *kahal*, a community gathered around a synagogue, of which there were thirty-six large ones
in Salonika by the seventeenth century, in addition to a number of
smaller places of prayer.

Leyb ben Ozer reports that Sabbatai was received kindly when
he first arrived in Salonika. Sabbatian tradition preserves many
details of his stay in the city, which he visited again after his apostasy.
During Sabbatai's first residence he prayed in the Synagogue of
Kehal Shalom and lived in the house of Joseph Florentin, one of
the founders of the Sabbatian sect that came to be known as the
Dönme.

Sabbatai apparently made a number of friends among other
young scholarly rabbis after his arrival in Salonika, for he had
an engaging personality and was a talented musician and singer,
particularly when he was in one of his manic 'illuminate' states,
according to the sources for this and subsequent periods of his life.
As Abraham Kokesh, a Sabbatian from Vilna (now Vilnius), told
Leyb ben Ozer, 'When Sabbatai Sevi chanted psalms, as he would
do frequently, it was impossible to look into his face, for it was like
looking into fire. This has been attested by many others, and even
by his opponents.' Leyb ben Ozer had heard from another person
who had met Sabbatai that 'his countenance was beautiful and that
there was none like him', and that 'his cheeks were red all the time'.

Abraham Cuenque, who first met Sabbatai in 1663 and was ever
after his faithful disciple, writes of the Master's striking appearance.
He reports that Sabbatai was tall and imposing, and that 'his face
[was] very bright, inclined to swarthiness, his countenance beautiful
and majestic, a black round beard framed his face, and [he was]
dressed in royal robes; he was very stout and corpulent'. Coenen
quotes an unnamed Dutch source in Izmir as saying that Sabbatai
was 'corpulent, but otherwise of beautiful bodily appearance'. Israel
Hazzan describes the uniformity of Sabbatai's whiskers: 'the hairs
of his beard stood in one equal row from his upper jaw to his chin,
not one hair protruded beyond the others'. All these features are

evident in the portrait that appears at the beginning of Coenen's book on Sabbatai Sevi. Coenen notes that the portrait was by a Christian who saw Sabbatai in Izmir late in 1665, and who drew the picture that same day. All other portraits are either copies of this or purely imaginary.

Despite Sabbatai's attractive appearance and personality, recurrences of his bizarre behaviour and wildly unorthodox religious practices soon alienated the Jewish community in Salonika. According to Leyb ben Ozer, Sabbatai 'returned to his evil ways and resumed his former habit of uttering the divine name'. When Sabbatai was admonished for this, he replied that he was the Messiah and had the right to do so, which led the rabbinic court to banish him from the city.

A somewhat different version is told by the Chevalier de La Croix, whose memoirs of his years as secretary to the French ambassador in Istanbul were published in 1684. La Croix says that Sabbatai invited the leading rabbis to a banquet at which he married himself to the Torah, shocking them so profoundly that they banished him from Salonika. 'Instead of attributing this action to his great holiness, they accused him of madness. And as they were afraid that this and similar innovations might have dangerous consequences, they forced him to leave the city.' This report is confirmed by letters that Sabbatai wrote in 1666, in which he identifies himself as 'the bridegroom coming out of his chamber, the husband of the dearly beloved Torah, who is the most beauteous and lovely lady'.

Sabbatian tradition held that the first stage of the Messiah's ministry began in 1648, when he had his first messianic vision – commemorated by his followers as the date of the Shekhinah's 'rising from the dust'. The second stage began in 1657, when Sabbatai 'uplifted the Shekhinah'. This probably refers to Sabbatai's abolition of the Service of Rachel, a nocturnal liturgy of mourning for the Shekhinah that had been instituted in the sixteenth century by the Kabbalists of Safed. According to a Sabbatian tradition, 'it has been handed down that the Service of Rachel is not to be recited as from 1657'.

After his banishment from Salonika, according to Coenen and

La Croix, Sabbatai travelled through Greece, visiting Athens and the Peloponnese. Other than these two sources, which are not reliable, there is no definite information on the itinerary that Sabbatai followed in Greece. He would have stopped at a number of the towns along the road between Salonika and Athens, particularly those with large Jewish communities, such as Larissa and Thebes. He is mentioned in connection with Larissa by Edward Browne, an English traveller who passed through the town in 1669, three years after Sabbatai's apostasy. Browne writes that 'In this town I also heard some Turkish songs, but especially concerning Sabatai Sevi, the famous Jewish impostor, who had made a great noyse in the world, and how Cussum Basha so handled him that he was glad to turn Turk.' The Cussum Basha mentioned by Browne is Kasım Pasha, son-in-law of Mehmet IV, who would subsequently become deputy to the Grand Vizier, the Sultan's chief official.

Sabbatai is known to have had followers in Thebes, even after his apostasy. A Greek relative of Sabbatai, Abraham Azarah Sebi, is mentioned as being one of the leading Sabbatians in Thebes during 1666–7.

At the time of Sabbatai's journey in Greece, Athens had only the ruins of its ancient monuments to remind the traveller of its glorious past. It was then just a small town with a population of about 7,000 huddled under the north cliff of the Acropolis, comprising little more than the quarters now known as Plaka and Monastiraki. The Jews would have been in Monastiraki, near the ancient Kerameikos cemetery, where the old synagogue of Athens is still in use.

After passing through Athens, Sabbatai travelled around the Peloponnese, where he would have visited Patras, the probable birthplace of his father. During the Ottoman period Patras had the largest Jewish community in southern Greece, numbering 1,812 in a census taken in the mid sixteenth century. When I first visited Patras in 1967 there were only nineteen Jews still living in the city, the rest of the community having perished in the Holocaust or emigrated to Israel. At the time of my most recent visit, in 1993, just a single Jewish family remained, the last vestige of a community that had dwelt here since antiquity.

After wandering around the Peloponnese, Sabbatai travelled back eastward through Greece to Istanbul, where he arrived in 1658 and remained for about eight months.

Istanbul at the time was one of the largest and most important cities in the world, capital of the Ottoman Empire, still the most powerful nation on earth, though it had passed its prime and was beginning to decline. The oldest part of the city, known to the ancients as Byzantium and to the Greeks as Constantinople, is on the European shore at the lower end of the Bosphorus, the incomparably beautiful strait that separates Europe and Asia between the Black Sea and the Sea of Marmara. The city is further divided on its European side by the Golden Horn, a scimitar-shaped estuary that flows into the Bosphorus between the port quarter of Galata, on its left bank, and on its right the first of the city's seven hills, crowned by the pavilions and gardens of Topkapı Sarayı, the great palace of the Ottoman sultans.

According to La Croix, whose informant was a former Sabbatian, Sabbatai arrived in Istanbul with sufficient means to devote himself to his studies, and at first he was well received by the local scholars and other notables of the Jewish community.

There had been a Jewish community in the city since at least the early Byzantine period of Constantinople, and in Sabbatai's time there were three Jewish quarters there. The oldest of these was in Balat, on the south bank of the Golden Horn, just inside the ancient city walls. The other two were on the north bank of the Golden Horn, at Galata and Hasköy, the latter including a number of Karaites.

The oldest Jewish congregations in Istanbul were those of the Karaites and the Romaniotes, whose ancestors had been in the city since early Byzantine times, while the Sephardim and Italian Jews began arriving in the last decade of the fifteenth century. A census in 1623, three years before Sabbatai's birth, recorded that the number of 'Old Jewish Congregations' measured by households was 1,217, as compared to 970 for the 'New Congregation'. The 'Old Congregations' comprised 1,147 households of Romaniote Jews and 70 of Karaites, while the households of the 'New Congregations' were categorized as Sephardim 593, Italians 218, Ashkenazim 62, Unidentified 97.

The seventeenth-century Turkish traveller Evliya Chelebi, writing in his *Narrative of Travels*, describes Hasköy as it was in Sabbatai's time:

Hasköy consists of three thousand houses with gardens, in some of which lemons and oranges are cultivated, the houses look to the sea and belong to Jews . . . Hasköy is a Jews' town, like Salonika, or Safed in Palestine . . . The heights of Hasköy are the general burying-place of the Jews. They are all laid out horizontally and their graves covered with heavy white stones, in a way which is to be seen nowhere else.

A large section of Evliya's *Narrative of Travels* is devoted to a description of the extraordinary procession of the guilds that Sultan Murat IV ordered in 1638, in preparation for his campaign to reconquer Baghdad from the Persians. As Evliya describes it, for three days representatives of 735 guilds paraded past Murat in the Alay Kiosk, or review pavilion, putting on spirited displays of their trades and enterprises, each group trying to outdo the others in entertaining the Sultan. The Jewish tavern-keepers were the last to pass, as Evliya writes:

The last of all the guilds are the Jewish tavern-keepers, two hundred men and one hundred shops, who, in spite of the Greeks and Armenians, are all masked and wearing the most precious dresses . . . Other bearded Jews pass also in precious dresses, bedecked with jewels, carrying in their hands crystal and porcelain cups, out of which they pour sherbet instead of wine for the spectators.

The story of Sabbatai's stay in Istanbul is much the same as that of his time in Salonika, in that his eccentric behaviour eventually alienated the Jewish community and led to his expulsion. The incident that particularly provoked the community in Istanbul is described by La Croix. It seems that Sabbatai bought a very large fish, which he dressed up as if it were a baby and put into a cradle, inviting all the rabbis of the city to see it. Sabbatai explained that the fish symbolized the astrological prediction that the Messiah would appear under the sign of Pisces, with the cradle evidently signifying the nurturing of Israel's redemption. La Croix writes that when the rabbis realized 'that some new sect, which might confuse minds, was fermenting in his brain, they did not act like the rabbis of Salonika who expelled him, but dispatched an officer of the rabbinic court who gave him forty stripes, and forbade his company to all Jews on pain of a penalty'.

A supplement to Nathan of Gaza's apocryphal *Vision of R. Abraham* 'prophesied' a number of apocalyptic events for 1658, and though the author used the future tense he was actually writing of incidents that must have occurred during Sabbatai's first visit to Istanbul. He writes that 'In the year 1658 he [the Messiah] will celebrate the three festivals of pilgrimage in one week, so as to atone for all the sins ever committed by Israel. Then God will give him a new law and new commandments to repair all the worlds. In the year 1658 he shall bless "Him who permits that which is forbidden".'

The institution of new commandments and festivals was a far more serious matter than the incident involving the cradled fish, particularly the blasphemous notion that actions that had been forbidden could now be permitted. This would explain the severity of the punishment imposed on Sabbatai by the rabbis of Istanbul. Israel Hazzan and other sources write of additional heretical incidents involving Sabbatai in 1658, evidently a year in which his messianic mission became truly revolutionary. Hazzan also makes an obscure reference implying that Sabbatai suffered a term of imprisonment in Istanbul that year, probably because of his unconventional behaviour and radical religious practices.

During his stay in Istanbul Sabbatai is known to have been befriended by two prominent Kabbalists, Elijah Carcassoni and David Habillo. According to La Croix, Sabbatai studied 'practical Kabbalah' with Carcassoni, 'a master of the Name', who exorcised evil spirits. Tobias Rofe Ashkenazi reports that Sabbatai 'was versed in practical Kabbalah and the incantation of spirits'. Habillo was one of the leading Lurianic Kabbalists of the day, and he probably tutored Sabbatai in the works of Isaac Luria, which he may not have learned thoroughly until then. At the time Habillo was collector of charities for the Jews of Jerusalem, a post that frequently brought him to Istanbul and the other principal cities of the Ottoman Empire.

It was probably while he was in Istanbul that Sabbatai also came to know Abraham Yakhini, a famous preacher, poet and Kabbalist, who later became one of his most devoted followers.

Sabbatai left Istanbul for Izmir early in 1659, accompanied by David Habillo. The following year Istanbul was devastated by a great fire, in which the Jews of the city suffered grievously. According to La Croix, Sabbatai was pleased by this, 'not because of the insults he had suffered in Constantinople, but because he saw in it the finger of God, calling His people in repentance'.

Sabbatai had been away from Izmir for some five to eight years. One of the reasons that he was able to return at all is that he was accompanied by David Habillo, whose position as collector of charities for Jerusalem was equivalent to that of an ambassador among the Jewish community, giving protection to his companion. And, by the time that Sabbatai returned, the memory of his earlier transgressions had probably faded from the memory of all but those who were most directly concerned. The chief rabbi Joseph Eskapha, who had banished Sabbatai from the city, was now old and infirm. He would pass away early in 1662, aged ninety-three.

La Croix says that Sabbatai now remained in Izmir for three years, leaving in early 1662. One of the few sources for Sabbatai's life in this period is the memoir of his disciple Abraham Cuenque. Cuenque writes of Sabbatai that 'at times he would hide himself in a miserable room in Smyrna'. Cuenque was told by 'trustworthy people' that they had seen Sabbatai in this room 'wallowing in the dust and his bed turned upside down'. But Cuenque's account must be taken with more than a grain of salt, for his informants, who were like him devoted Sabbatians, added that they had also seen two angels supporting Sabbatai between them in his room, saying to him, 'Shake off your dust, arise, and return, O Jerusalem.' According to Cuenque, Sabbatai's brothers, Elijah and Joseph, were ashamed of his 'strange actions', which 'were a burden and scandal to them'.

Cuenque goes on to report that Sabbatai's brothers suggested that he travel to Palestine, which he did, refusing to take money from them and leaving 'by himself, and with nothing but his garment'. La Croix tells quite a different story, saying that Sabbatai's brothers provided for him generously when he decided to go to Palestine, a version verified by subsequent events.

The date of Sabbatai's second departure from Izmir is based on an eyewitness report recorded by Hayyim Segré, a Sabbatian from Vercelli, in northern Italy. Segré collected information from followers of Sabbatai who came to Italy after their Messiah's apostasy. One of his sources was Solomon ben Moses de Bossal, whose father was the rabbi of Rhodes. Bossal reported that 'three years before AMIRAH revealed himself, that is, in the year [5]422 [1662], he passed through Rhodes on his way from Smyrna to Jerusalem. He stayed at his [Bossal's] father's house for one month and studied with him the book *Zohar*.'

The Jewish community on Rhodes had been greatly augmented after the capture of the island in 1522 by the Ottoman Turks under Süleyman the Magnificent. The Sultan had 150 Sephardic families moved there from Salonika, adding them to the small community of Romaniote Jews that dated back to Byzantine times. Both of these Jewish communities would have lived within the walled city, according to Jean de Thevenot: 'None but Turks and Jews live in the City of Rhodes; for Christians are not suffered to be there, though they keep Shops in the town, but at night they must retire to the Villages in the Country about, being only allowed to come to Town in the day-time.'

The Jewish community in Rhodes survived until the Second World War, when all but four families were shipped off by the Germans to Auschwitz, from which only a handful returned. The four families who were not sent to Auschwitz owed their salvation to the possession of Italian passports, as I was told by a member of one of them at the time of my first visit to Rhodes, in 1967. He led me through the old Jewish quarter, in the south-eastern part of the town by the harbour. The vanished community of this quarter is now commemorated by a plaque marking the Square of the Jewish Martyrs. The synagogue where Sabbatai studied for a month with Rabbi Bossal would have been on the square.

In 1658 Rhodes was besieged by a Venetian fleet commanded

by Francesco Morosini, who became Doge of Venice in 1684. This siege occurred during the long war between Venice and the Ottoman Empire that began in 1645, when the Turks invaded Crete, and which ended in 1669, when the Venetian garrison under Morosini finally surrendered Candia (modern Iraklion), the island's capital. That Sabbatai remained on Rhodes for a month may be due to the fact that the war was still raging in the eastern Mediterranean when he was there.

After his stay in Rhodes, Sabbatai went on to Egypt, probably taking a ship to Alexandria. The ship would have been a large caique, a cumbersome wooden vessel that carried both cargo and passengers – a type that remained in use up until very recent times. Thevenot describes his voyage from Rhodes to Egypt aboard just such a ship, which he calls a Saique:

These Saiques are like great Barks, having a round hulk, and a very big and high Main-Mast. They carry great cargoes of Goods, but they sail not fast, unless they go before the wind . . . The Greeks make use of no other vessels for sailing the White [Aegean] and Black Seas, and that's the reason there are so many of them; though the Christian Corsairs pick up several of them now and then.

Thevenot describes the miseries of his own storm-tossed voyage from Rhodes to Egypt in 1656: 'We suffered much from the storm. For my part I strained my very Guts out with Vomiting and Reaching, and when that was over, I had such violent pains in my Side, that I thought they would have killed me . . .' He goes on to tell how a fellow passenger tried to help him ease his seasickness: 'A Turk taking pity on me, gave me Opium to eat, not knowing what it was, I swallowed it down, but when he would have made me take another dose, I asked him what it was and he made answer, Eat it, it is good for you, it is Opium. Then I told him that he had Poysened me, and straining a little, I vomited again . . .'

Thevenot later writes of how his ship repelled an attack by Spanish corsairs: 'We lost but two Men, both killed by one Cannon Bullet, that going through and through the Gun-Room where they were, carried off one half of their heads, and dashed their blood and brains upon the Tillar. We also had two men wounded in the Leg with small shot . . .'

Such were the discomforts and perils that Sabbatai would have had to endure on his voyage from Rhodes to Egypt in the spring of 1662, when his 'years of darkness' were finally coming to an end.

# 5. The Wife of Whoredoms

After his voyage from Rhodes, Sabbatai went on to Cairo, where he probably arrived late in the spring of 1662. He would have settled into the Jewish quarter in Old Cairo, in the ancient district sometimes spoken of as Misr al-Qadimah, or more often as Fustat.

During Ottoman times the orthodox Jewish community in Cairo was divided into three groups: Arabic-speaking Jews known as Mustaribs, who had been living in Egypt long enough to be considered indigenous; North African Jews called Maghribis, also Arabic speakers, who had first immigrated to Egypt in the eleventh and twelfth centuries; and the Ladino-speaking Sephardim. The Sephardic Jews had settled in Cairo after the Ottomans under Selim I conquered Syria, Palestine and Egypt in 1516–17. The Sephardic immigrants, there and elsewhere, brought with them a level of culture higher than that of the Jews among whom they settled, so that the Ladino-speaking exiles became the intellectual elite among the Jewish communities in the Ottoman Empire.

Fustat was on the site of the ancient Roman fortress of Babylon, known to the Arabs as Qasr al-Sham. The oldest of the Jewish communities there was that of the 'Jerusalemites', or 'Palestinians', who had been established in the Byzantine period, before the Islamic conquest. Another community consisted of Jewish immigrants from Persia and Iraq, known as the 'Iraqians' or 'Babylonians'. There was also a third community consisting of the Karaites. When Sabbatai arrived in Cairo in 1662 the Jewish population in the city amounted to perhaps 10,000, of whom the great majority were orthodox, the rest Karaite.

Sabbatai would have worshipped in the Synagogue of Ben Ezra, for it served the 'Jerusalemite' community with whom he became involved after his arrival in the city. According to Jewish tradition, this is the oldest synagogue in Cairo, founded by the prophet Jeremiah, who is believed to be buried there in a crypt. It is also where the Holy Family are supposed to have found refuge in their flight to Egypt. The Coptic Christians obtained the site in the early Islamic period and erected a church dedicated to St Michael the Archangel, which was closed by the Caliph al-Hakim, who ruled from 996 to 1021. The site was then purchased by Rabbi Abraham Ben Ezra, who built a new synagogue there in the twelfth century.

Before the Ottoman conquest, when Egypt was ruled by the Mamluk sultans, the Jewish community was headed by a rabbinic official known as the *nagid*. By the end of the eleventh century the *nagid* had become independent of the chief rabbi in Palestine and took the Arabic title *rais al-yahud*, 'head of the Jews'. After the Ottoman conquest the office of *nagid* was abolished and the head of the Jewish community was called *chelebi*, Turkish for 'honourable' or 'lord'. Under Ottoman rule the *chelebi* was a government official rather than a rabbinic authority, holding the official title of *sharaf bashi* as head of the Egyptian treasury and mint, besides which he supervised all banking activities. The *chelebi* was also responsible for seeing that the Jewish community paid its taxes to the imperial treasury.

At the time of Sabbatai's arrival in Cairo the head of the Jewish community in Egypt was Raphael Joseph, who had been appointed *chelebi* earlier that year. He was the last *chelebi* of the Egyptian Jews, for after his murder in 1669 the office was abolished.

The hospitality of Raphael Joseph Chelebi was renowned, and a rabbi from Livorno noted in 1666 that 'fifty ordained rabbis were eating at his table'. Joseph Sambari, who was a guest of Raphael Joseph for several months, writes of the Chelebi in his chronicle *Dibrey Yosef*: 'There was no king like him before him who turned to the Lord with all his heart and all his soul and all his might . . . And the whole nation was obedient to him, so that in his days every man of Israel lived under his vine . . . And I, the unworthy author, was one of his servants; I ate his fruit and drank his water.'

Sambari would almost certainly have met Sabbatai at the house of Raphael Joseph. But the pages of *Dibrey Yosef* that would have described him have evidently been torn out of the only two surviving copies of Sambari's manuscript, undoubtedly by anti-Sabbatian fanatics. At the bottom of the page before the missing ones, Sambari writes, by way of introduction, 'And now we shall report matters of controversy, strife and discord ... in the market places and streets.'

The removal of these pages is a great loss, because the other sources for this period in Sabbatai's life are very sparse. Abraham Cuenque and an unnamed Dutch source both report that Sabbatai was on close terms with Raphael Joseph and would have been a guest in the Chelebi's home. Sabbatai was to renew his acquaintance with Raphael Joseph in 1664, when he returned to Cairo on a mission from Jerusalem.

Sabbatai seems to have left Cairo for Jerusalem in the summer of 1662. He would have made the journey by camel caravan, as most travellers did until the early years of the twentieth century. Passengers were carried in wicker baskets called *counes*, a pair of which were balanced on either side of a camel's back. Thevenot, who made this journey at about the same time as Sabbatai, describes this conveyance:

These Counes are Hampiers like cradles carried upon Camels Backs one on each side, but they have a back, head and sides, like the great Chairs that sick people sit in. A man rides in each of these Counes, and over them they lay a covering, which keeps them both from the Rain and the Sun, leaving as it were a Window before and behind upon the Camels back.

He goes on to describe the supplies that were brought along for the passengers:

We had biskets made for us, French Bread, Wine in Flasks, Rice, Lentils, and other Lent Provisions; carrying with us a Tent, Pot or Skillet, and in short, all that was necessary, not forgetting Candles, Candlesticks and Leather buckets to draw Water with. All this was carried upon a Camel over and above the Bargain.

At the time there were perhaps 300 Jewish families in Jerusalem, amounting to about 1,500 people. They would all have been living in the old Jewish quarter, in the south-central sector of the city.

The majority of the community were Sephardim, who worshipped in the Hurva Synagogue.

Abraham Cuenque reports that Sabbatai 'came to Jerusalem without servants and attendants. He lived alone in one room, fasting throughout the week and on Sabbath eve buying Sabbath provisions himself.'

According to Leyb ben Ozer, Sabbatai at first attended the *hesger*, or talmudic academy, of Jacob Hagiz, studying there daily with the other scholars after their morning prayers. Hagiz, a distinguished rabbinic scholar, had founded his academy with the financial support of the wealthy de Vega family of Livorno. Among the distinguished rabbis and scholars who studied there with Sabbatai were Joseph Almosnino, who became rabbi of Belgrade, and Moses ben Habib of Jerusalem.

After a few months Sabbatai acquired a house – probably one that had belonged to his friend David Habillo, who had died in 1661. Sabbatai sequestered himself within a single room of this house, though several sources say that he would occasionally leave to spend a few days wandering alone in the countryside outside Jerusalem, visiting the tombs of sainted rabbis, where, as he later told Solomon Laniado, he would hear 'voices from the graves'.

During his stay in Jerusalem, Sabbatai met a number of rabbis who would subsequently become leaders of his messianic movement, including Samuel Primo of Bursa, Judah Sharaf of Jerusalem and Cairo, David Yishaki of Salonika, and Sabbatai Raphael of Mistra, the first three of whom were renowned scholars, the fourth a charlatan. Sabbatai Raphael, speaking to Jacob Sasportas in 1667, said that when he came to Jerusalem in 1663, at the age of twenty, he had heard that 'Sabbatai Sevi was in the Holy Land and studied with a few disciples, though he was not yet called Messiah. He [Sabbatai Raphael] went to him and became a member of his circle.'

The Jewish community of Jerusalem was often subject to extortionate taxes by Ottoman officials. The most notorious of these officials was the *vali* (governor) Muhammad ibn Farukh, who in his short term of office, 1625–7, taxed the Jews of Jerusalem so mercilessly that many of them fled from the city. In 1663 one of his successors, unnamed in the sources, imposed a new tax which was so high that the community could not pay and many were again forced to flee.

The community decided to send an emissary to Cairo to appeal for financial aid from their Jewish compatriots there to help pay the tax. They chose Sabbatai Sevi because of the personal bond he had formed with Raphael Joseph, the wealthiest and most influential Jew in Egypt. Sabbatai agreed to make the journey and plead the community's case before the Chelebi, the first position of responsibility he had ever held.

On the first stage of his journey to Cairo, which he began late in the autumn of 1663, Sabbatai made a pilgrimage to Hebron. There he prayed in the cave of Machpelah, where Abraham had buried his wife Sarah, a place revered as the tomb of the ancient patriarchs. It was there that the young Abraham Cuenque saw Sabbatai for the one and only time in his life; the memory remained with him for the rest of his days. Cuenque writes in his memoirs of his first sight of Sabbatai:

I did not take my eyes off him from the moment of his arrival, both when he said the afternoon prayer with us in the synagogue, and when he recited the evening prayer in the cave of Machpelah, together with the crowd that had accompanied him . . . most of the night I kept near the house where he stayed, observing his behaviour. The other citizens spent a sleepless night too, watching him through the windows.

Cuenque goes on to tell how he stayed up all night watching Sabbatai and listening to him singing:

He strode up and down in the house, which was illuminated at his command with many candles. All night he recited psalms with . . . a most agreeable and pleasing voice, until the light of the morning dawned and we went to attend the morning service. I testify that his demeanour was awe-inspiring, different in every respect from that of other men, and my eyes were not satisfied with seeing him.

Cuenque concludes his account by describing Sabbatai's departure. He says wistfully, 'After the morning prayer he travelled alone to some place six miles away, accompanied only by one Jew on foot. While he was among us he neither ate or drank, nor did he sleep at all. He left, as he had come, fasting, and my eyes have not seen him since then.'

After leaving Hebron, Sabbatai continued on to Cairo, passing through Gaza. According to Cuenque, one of those who saw Sabbatai as he passed through the town was Abraham Nathan Ashkenazi, later to be famous as Nathan of Gaza, the prophet of the Messiah.

Nathan was born in Jerusalem, most probably in 1644. His father, Elisha Hayyim ben Jacob, was from Germany or Poland, and when he settled in Jerusalem he was given the surname 'Ashkenazi', since most of the Jewish community at the time were Sephardic. Elisha Ashkenazi, as he came to be known, became a highly respected member of the community in Jerusalem, for whom he spent many years travelling as an emissary to the Jews of Germany, Poland, Italy and Morocco, where he died in 1673. During the latter years of his life Elisha's travels were on behalf of the Sabbatian movement, of which his son had become the principal spokesman.

Nathan's father enrolled him at the talmudic academy of Jacob Hagiz, where Sabbatai was also studying at the time. It is not clear whether the Messiah and his prophet met while studying at the *hesger*, but it is probable that the much younger Nathan, who was then only about half Sabbatai's age, would at least have been aware of the charismatic rabbi from Izmir, who as usual was attracting devoted followers, though he had not yet announced his messianic mission.

Nathan seems to have been an exceptionally gifted student: his writings show greater literary and intellectual ability than any of his contemporaries, including Sabbatai himself. But Sabbatai was the Messiah, and Nathan was to be his prophet, as an angel would soon tell him in an apocalyptic vision.

When Nathan was nineteen he married the daughter of Samuel Lissabona, a wealthy Jew from Damascus who had come to live in Gaza. Lissabona had gone to Jacob Hagiz to ask him if he could recommend one of the students at his academy as a groom for his daughter, who 'was perfect in beauty, although with a defect in one eye'. Hagiz recommended Nathan, and, when the marriage agreement was made, Lissabona promised to support his son-in-law financially so that he could devote himself to a life of scholarship. Nathan then set up house with his bride in Gaza, where he was living when he saw Sabbatai Sevi passing through on his mission to Cairo.

Soon after his marriage Nathan began to study the Kabbalah, which he had neglected when he was a student of Jacob Hagiz. As Nathan later told Moses Pinheiro, he already knew most of the Talmud by heart, for he had for many years 'applied himself diligently to talmudic casuistry'. Then he had a series of visions that he described to Pinheiro: 'He used to see a sight like unto a pillar of fire that spoke to him, and sometimes he would see a sight like unto a human face. He would always know the nature of the soul that spoke to him, but he would never speak of it, so as not to appear presumptuous.'

These visions led Nathan to study the Lurianic Kabbalah, which he did by himself, assisted on notable occasions by an angel, a celestial mentor known to Kabbalists as a *maggid*. As Gershom Scholem explains, '*Maggidim,* holy angels or the souls of departed saints, speaking either *to* the kabbalist or *through* his mouth (often in a voice different from his usual one), had their counterparts on the "other side" in the dibbuks, demons, or evil souls that possessed some unhappy or mentally sick people.'

One of the works that Nathan is known to have consulted is a manuscript describing revelations that had come in dreams to the Safed Kabbalist Eliezer, a follower of Moses Cordovero, the sixteenth-century Kabbalist. Another that he probably read, for his father had a copy, contained the revelations of the Spanish Kabbalist Joseph Taitsatak, who settled in Salonika around 1490. Nathan told Pinheiro that during his Kabbalistic studies he was told in a vision to expect a 'great light', and once, 'as he was attired in his prayer-mantle and phylacteries, all his senses were extinguished, though his eyes remained open and his reason was more lucid than ever. And he beheld all the stages [of creation], and the *merkabah* [the sphere of the divine *sefiroth*], and the countenance of AMIRAH.' This vision lasted for a whole day, and during that time everything was illuminated by the 'light of the seven days of Creation', and he beheld the entire universe 'according to its order, first the heavens, and then ascending higher in the scale of being'.

Early in 1664 Sabbatai arrived in Cairo, where he stayed in the house of Raphael Joseph while he was raising funds for the Jewish community in Jerusalem. He eventually collected more than a thousand gold ducats, undoubtedly due to the aid and beneficence of his host.

Soon after his arrival in Cairo, Sabbatai began to hear stories of a beautiful young woman in Livorno who did 'strange things', and who had been saying for years that she would be the bride of the Messiah. Her name was Sarah, and she had come to Livorno from Amsterdam. Jacob Sasportas, who had seen Sarah in Amsterdam in 1655, writes that she was 'a girl devoid of intelligence, who in her madness said she would marry the messianic king. Everybody laughed at her, and she betook herself to Leghorn [Livorno] . . . But as she continued to say these foolish things and was, moreover, beautiful, she was reported to Sabbatai Sevi, who was in Egypt with Raphael Joseph.' It is not clear if Sabbatai sent for Sarah or if she came to Cairo on her own in search of him, having heard stories about him. In any event, Sabbatai and Sarah were married in Cairo on 5 Nisan 5424 – that is, 31 March 1664 – undoubtedly in the house of Raphael Joseph.

Little definite is known of Sarah's background, and the mystery of her origins is compounded by the many apocryphal tales that circulated about her life before she arrived in Cairo, including scarcely credible stories she told about herself.

The only part of the story of Sarah's origins that is generally accepted as true is that she was orphaned in the Chmielnicki massacres of 1648. The only other member of her family who survived was her brother, Samuel ben Meir, who became a tobacco-sorter in Amsterdam. Leyb ben Ozer mentions him in his account of Sabbatai's career, noting that after his brother-in-law's rise to fame he was popularly known as 'Samuel Messiah'. Jacob Ragstatt de Weile, in a book he published in 1671, tells of seeing Sarah and her brother many years earlier when he set out for Hanau from his birthplace of Kleve, in north-western Germany. Ragstatt saw him again when Samuel passed through Kleve on his way to Istanbul, where he expected to have a dukedom conferred upon him by Sabbatai, who, after he declared himself the Messiah, began ennobling all his relatives and friends. Later, after Sabbatai's apostasy, Samuel seems to have returned to Amsterdam and his job as a tobacco-sorter.

Gershom Scholem records four separate accounts of Sarah's early years: those of Ragstatt, Leyb ben Ozer, Baruch of Arezzo, and the Chevalier de La Croix, all of which have apocryphal elements in common.

According to Ragstatt, after the Chmielnicki massacres Sarah was adopted by a Polish nobleman. When she came of age her father's spirit appeared to Sarah and informed her that she was Jewish, commanding her to return to the faith of her ancestors. After her stepfather died his family wanted Sarah to marry a Polish Catholic, but she was miraculously carried away to Persia, where her father had fled to escape the massacres. After seeing her father's tomb there, she was just as miraculously transported to 'Asia' and left in a Jewish cemetery, where an angel gave her a '*pergamentum*', or 'coat of skin', inscribed with divine names. According to Ragstatt, the *pergamentum* was generally believed to be the garment that Adam had worn when he and Eve were in the Garden of Eden. The angel then revealed to Sarah that she would be a queen and the wife of the Messiah.

Leyb ben Ozer based his story of Sarah's early years on what he had heard from 'reliable reporters and rabbis, and also from my late father'. He said that his informants, all of whom had known Sarah, had heard from her that she had been taken into a Polish convent at the age of six, after she had been orphaned. She remembered that her father had been a rabbi in Poland. At the age of sixteen Sarah's father appeared to her in a dream and carried her away from the convent to a Jewish cemetery in some unknown land. He left her there, instructing her to travel through the world until she found the Messiah, who would make her his bride. She was found in the cemetery, dressed only in a shirt, and eventually she was brought to Amsterdam. There she was reunited with her brother Samuel, who had fled from Poland to Amsterdam to escape the massacres.

According to Baruch of Arezzo, Sarah had been brought up by a Polish noblewoman, who had forcibly baptized her. When Sarah came of age the woman wanted Sarah to marry her son. The day before the wedding, Sarah's father appeared to her in a dream and gave her a 'garment of skin' inscribed with the words 'She will be the Messiah's wife.' Sarah fled that same night and found herself in a Jewish cemetery, where she was discovered by strangers the next morning, clad only in the garment of skin. She then began her wanderings, which in Baruch's account, took her to Livorno, where she remained for some years before going on to Cairo.

According to the Chevalier de La Croix, after Sarah was orphaned she was adopted by a famous rabbi, who subsequently brought her to a Polish nobleman who wanted to convert her to Catholicism and raise her in his house. One night Sarah's father appeared to her in a dream and miraculously carried her back to the house of the rabbi, whom he commanded to have his daughter sent away to a safer place. Thus she began her travels, which took her first to Amsterdam and then in turn to Mantua, Livorno and Cairo.

All the sources agree that Sarah lived a scandalous life before she met Sabbatai, particularly in Mantua and Livorno, and some of them report stories of licentious behaviour by her after her marriage, although at least some of these tales were told in order to blacken the reputation of Sabbatai and his wife, particularly after his apostasy.

The brothers Emanuel and Jacob Frances were the authors of particularly scurrilous attacks, which were widely circulated in Italy and later elsewhere in Europe. Emanuel Frances, who lived in Livorno while Sarah was there, wrote that she had been a serving maid in the house of David Jessurun; in one of his works he called her a 'witch' and wrote a satirical poem on her 'whoredoms'.

In 1667 the Livorno rabbi Joseph ha-Levi composed a book on the Sabbatian movement which is now lost except for material quoted by Emanuel Frances and Jacob Sasportas, Sabbatai's most relentless enemy. Sasportas, in writing of 'the harlotries of the adulterous Ashkenazi woman', quotes ha-Levi in saying that in Livorno Sarah had prostituted herself to everyone.

Thomas Coenen reports on rumours concerning Sarah that had

been circulating in Izmir: 'She was a maid-servant in a charitable institution in Mantua, which housed all sorts of people and which she did not leave without damage to her reputation; I refrain on purpose from enlarging on the subject. Later she travelled through the country without any company except those she met on the road, and so she went from place to place.'

Baruch of Arezzo was told by Isaac ha-Levi Vali, a Livorno rabbi, that Sarah, before her marriage, had been known as a fortune-teller and spiritualistic medium. Vali had consulted Sarah to gain insight into 'the root of his soul' and other spiritual matters, 'and she answered all of his questions'. When Vali came to see Sarah her landlady said to him in her presence, 'Does your reverence know what this girl says? That she will be the Messiah's wife?' Sarah made no objection to this, remaining silent.

Scholem, writing of Sarah, quotes an anonymous French source 'who not only says that her reputation as a harlot preceded her to the East, but also that Sabbatai married her precisely for that reason, so as to imitate or fulfill the words of the prophet Hosea'. Here Scholem is referring to Hosea 1:2, which begins the story of the prophet's marriage to Gomer, daughter of Diblaim: 'The beginning of the word of the Lord by Hosea. And the Lord said to Hosea, Go, take unto thee a wife of whoredoms and children of whoredoms: for the land hath committed great whoredom, departing from the Lord.'

Sabbatai and his bride lived in Cairo for nearly a year before he resumed his messianic wanderings. Absolutely nothing is known of their life during that first year of their marriage, when they would probably have been living in the house of Raphael Joseph or in one of his properties in the old Jewish quarter in Fustat.

The only Jewish monument that remains in this quarter is the Synagogue of Ben Ezra, which I visited during my first stay in Cairo, in 1962. The synagogue was rebuilt shortly before 1890, using much of the original structure. At the time of my original visit I learned that there were still forty-two Jewish families living in Fustat, and they were the only ones who then used the Ben Ezra Synagogue; the rest of the Jews in Cairo went to the new synagogue in the modern part of the city. When I returned most recently, in

1999, there appeared to be no Jews left in their old quarter in Fustat, and, although the Synagogue of Ben Ezra has been refurbished, it seemed to be principally a museum.

One part of the synagogue that was lost in the rebuilding was the geniza, a chamber used for the storage of documents. The Jewish community here followed a custom which was widespread throughout the Middle East: of depositing all their writings in a special chamber known as the geniza, which means 'storehouse'. They did so to prevent the desecration of any writings that might contain the name of God, the accumulated documents then being ritually destroyed from time to time. But the papers in the geniza of the Ben Ezra Synagogue piled up for nearly nine centuries without being destroyed, and they came to light when the synagogue was rebuilt. The papers have since been collected and studied by a number of scholars, most notably Professor S. D. Goitein of Princeton University, who published a multi-volume collection of the geniza documents.

When I first came across Goitein's works I had the naive hope that one of the documents reproduced there would mention Sabbatai, for the geniza was part of the synagogue in which he worshipped. But I was disappointed, for none of the documents from the Cairo geniza yet published by Goitein or other scholars mentions Sabbatai. Nor is there any other record of Sabbatai's marriage to Sarah, apart from a recently published document certifying that they were divorced on the seventh anniversary of their wedding, 5 Nisan 5431.

But Sarah was subsequently reunited with Sabbatai and remained with him until her dying day, his Wife of Whoredoms.

# 6. Nathan of Gaza

After their wedding, Sabbatai and Sarah remained in Cairo for nearly a year, presumably as guests of Raphael Joseph Chelebi. During that time Sabbatai would have continued to raise funds for the Jewish community of Jerusalem to pay its tax to the Turkish governor.

Meanwhile Nathan of Gaza lived in obscurity with his wife while he continued his studies in the Kabbalah. By this time his researches had taken him into the realm of practical Kabbalah, which Gershom Scholem describes as being 'that of purely motivated or "white" magic, especially as practiced through the sacred, esoteric Names of God and the angels, the manipulation of which may affect the physical no less than the spiritual world'.

Nathan seems to have studied practical Kabbalah on his own, using one of the handbooks then circulating in Palestine. This is suggested in a story told by Moses Hagiz, whose father, Jacob, had taught both Sabbatai and Nathan in his talmudic academy in Jerusalem. The story concerns a book on practical Kabbalah that had belonged to Abraham Hananiah, a prominent scholar who had been forced to flee from Jerusalem in 1663 to escape the extortionate tax imposed by the Turkish governor. Moses Hagiz accuses Nathan of having stolen this book, but the charge is almost certainly untrue.

Early in 1665 Nathan had a vision that he was to describe later in his *Book of Creation*: the revelation that Sabbatai Sevi was the Messiah. During this vision he suddenly saw the image of Sabbatai engraved on the *merkabah*, the sphere of the divine *sefiroth*, and a prophetic voice issued forth: 'Thus saith the Lord, behold your saviour cometh, Sabbatai Sevi is his name. He shall cry, yea, roar, he shall prevail against his enemies.'

Nathan described the revelations that led to his prophetic awakening more fully in a letter written around 1673. According to this, he first began to study the Kabbalah when he was about twenty, reading the *Zohar* and some of the works of Isaac Luria and his school, his meditations assisted by God, who 'sent me some of His holy angels and blessed spirits who revealed to me many of the mysteries of the Torah'. That same year, 'stimulated by the visions of the angels and blessed souls', while fasting in the week before the feast of Purim he had an overpowering vision that made his knees shake and his hair stand on end. 'I beheld the *merkabah*, and I saw visions of God all day long and all night, and I was vouchsafed true prophecy . . . as the voice spoke to me and began with the words: "Thus speaks the Lord." And with the utmost clarity my heart perceived towards whom my prophecy was directed.'

The person whom God had spoken of in the vision was Sabbatai Sevi, but Nathan says that his identity 'remained hidden in my heart until the redeemer revealed himself in Gaza and proclaimed himself the Messiah'. At the conclusion of his letter he writes that 'only then did the angel permit me to proclaim what I had seen'. He explains that he recognized that Sabbatai was the true Messiah 'by the signs which Isaac Luria had taught, for he has revealed profound mysteries in the Torah and not one thing faileth of all that he has taught. And also the angel that revealed himself to me in a waking vision was a truthful one, and he revealed to me awesome mysteries.'

Nathan's mystical vision changed him from a reclusive scholar into a charismatic prophet, although he had not yet revealed the name of the emergent Messiah. As Abraham Cuenque reported of Nathan, 'The inhabitants of Gaza noted a change in his deportment. He began to preach repentance, and gave proof of the indwelling of the Holy Spirit by telling people their secret sins and the like.'

By the spring of 1665, reports of Nathan's activities had reached Cairo, and Raphael Joseph sent a series of emissaries to investigate. The first of these, whose name is unknown, reported that Nathan had all Gaza under his spell, having imposed penances on everyone in the town to help them to achieve a *tiqqun*, the reformation of their souls, and that indeed 'he was worthy of being called a man of God'.

The second visitor was the scholarly Samuel Gandoor, who was sent to see whether Nathan was really a man of God and not a magician or charlatan. Gandoor was immediately entranced by

Nathan and became a devoted disciple, later accompanying him on most of his travels. The glowing report that Gandoor sent back to Raphael Joseph convinced the Chelebi and his circle that Nathan of Gaza was indeed a man of God, and a prophet as well. Gandoor's report came to the attention of Sabbatai, who thereupon returned to Palestine, presumably with his wife, though the sources do not mention her during this period. Sabbatai's return to Palestine is noted in a contemporary letter from Egypt, which says that when Sabbatai heard of the letter from Samuel Gandoor 'he abandoned his mission and repaired to Gaza in order to find a *tiqqun* and peace for his soul'. The letter goes on to say that when Nathan beheld Sabbatai 'he fell to the ground before him, and asked his forgiveness for not having done homage to him when he had passed through on his way to Egypt. He also announced to him that he was a very exalted soul.'

Apparently Sabbatai really did go to Nathan in search of 'a *tiqqun* and peace for his soul'. As Sabbatai confessed to Solomon Laniado at Aleppo in the summer of 1665, he had earlier that year, through his knowledge of practical Kabbalah, performed a great exorcism upon himself in a supreme effort to be rid of the 'illuminate' states to which he had risen in his mystical ecstasies, only to be plunged into the depths of profound depressions when 'God hid His face' from him. As he told Laniado, he wanted to be 'like one of the people', a rabbi like any other, which was why he had gone to Nathan to find spiritual repose.

Sabbatai went on to tell Laniado of his first meeting with Nathan in Gaza. When Nathan addressed him as the Messiah, Sabbatai laughed at him and said, referring to his messianic mission, 'I had it, but have sent it away.'

Sabbatai's first meeting with Nathan took place in the spring of 1665. They then spent a few weeks together privately, in intense conversations, wandering together to Jerusalem and Hebron, where they visited the tombs of the patriarchs and saints, but 'their intent was unknown' to the world, according to a Sabbatian letter. The same letter says that wherever they went Nathan 'taught the people knowledge', undoubtedly preaching repentance and helping them to find *tiqqun*.

At some time in May 1665 Nathan announced that he had discovered a leaf from an ancient apocalyptic manuscript. The manuscript is supposed to have described the mystical vision of a sainted rabbi named Abraham, who around 1200 prophesied that Sabbatai Sevi would be the Messiah and would bring about the redemption of Israel. It has now been established that this document, which came to be known as the *Vision of R. Abraham*, was written by Nathan himself; it was a forgery that Scholem describes as 'the first of what was to be a long series of messianic pseudo-epigrapha'.

Shortly before Pentecost in 1665, Sabbatai and Nathan returned to Gaza, where Sabbatai apparently stayed in the house of the rabbi Jacob ben Moses Najara. On the eve of Shavout, or Pentecost, Sabbatai was suddenly stricken with one of his uncontrollable fits of depression, and was unable to continue with the reading of the liturgy together with Nathan and the other assembled rabbis. According to Samuel Gandoor, 'R. Sabbatai Sevi was suddenly overcome by anxiety and he remained in his house, like a man sick with worry, for he could not even go to read [the liturgy].'

The story of what happened then is told by Baruch of Arezzo, who heard it from Meir Rofe, one of the rabbis present. After Sabbatai had retired, the assembly began singing hymns and Nathan started whirling around the room in an ecstatic dance, throwing off his clothes as he did so before suddenly collapsing on to the floor in a trance. According to Baruch, Meir Rofe examined Nathan and 'felt his pulse as physicians do, and said there was no life in him. Thereupon they covered his face, as one does with the dead, but soon afterwards a low voice was heard, whereupon they removed the veil, and behold a voice came out of his mouth but his lips did not move.'

Nathan himself related what happened then to Mahallallel Halleluyah of Ancona, in north-east Italy, whom he met in 1668. According to this account, a *maggidic* voice said, 'Heed ye, Nathan my beloved, to do according to his word. Heed ye Sabbatai Sevi, my beloved. For if ye knew the praise of Rabbi Hamnuna the Ancient [one of the mystical heroes of the *Zohar*]: ". . . and the man Moses was very meek [Numbers 12:3, possibly referring to

Sabbatai's reluctance to declare himself the Messiah]". The voice repeated this exhortation thrice.'

After Nathan emerged from his trance the other rabbis gathered round and asked him for an explanation. He responded by saying that Sabbatai Sevi was the Messiah and was worthy to be king of Israel. Sabbatai himself did not immediately respond to this prophetic utterance, for after his self-exorcism he could no longer elevate himself to an 'illuminate' state. But then, according to an unnamed Sabbatian source, 'on the third day after the prophet Nathan's utterance, the illumination and the holy spirit returned to Our Lord with redoubled power, and his spirit revived . . . for since the aforementioned exorcism his spirit had been dead within him. But now on the third day after Nathan's prophecy, his spirit was renewed and Our Lord had strength.'

Then a few days later, while at prayer with Nathan and the other rabbis in Gaza, Sabbatai proclaimed that he was the Messiah, 'anointed of the God of Jacob'. According to Solomon Laniado, Sabbatai took an elevated seat in the synagogue so that he 'was higher than any of the people'. His face shone with such radiance that the entire congregation was awestruck, gazing for hours upon the Messiah, who chose twelve of the rabbis present to represent the Twelve Tribes of Israel. Letters written from Egypt say that the rabbis from Gaza and Jerusalem paid royal honours to Sabbatai, who 'went forth like a king in the city of Gaza, mounted on a horse with a man walking in front of him, but no one knew his intention in this'.

Emanuel Frances quotes a letter from Gaza announcing the appearance of the new Messiah: 'Know ye, our brethren, the House of Jacob, that God has visited his people and has sent us a redeemer and saviour, our king Sabbatai Sevi, who has been anointed by the prophet Nathan according to the word of our Lord.' The letter goes on to say that 'And now, by the decree of our king and prophet, call a fast and a solemn assembly, turn from your evil ways, gather yourselves together and come to worship before your king.' Gershom Scholem is of the opinion that this letter is fictitious, and that Frances is either summarizing messianic reports or paraphrasing a letter from Palestine. He notes that the summons for the believers to come and worship the Messiah is suspicious, since by that time Sabbatai had already left Palestine, early in July 1665.

Sabbatai had become an adept in gematria, or numerology, in which the numerical value of the letters in words gives the words' mystical meaning. Israel Hazzan reports that on his first visit to Sabbatai he saw a number of gematria manuscripts that 'he had written concerning himself'. The numerical value of the name Sabbatai Sevi is 814, which he found to be the same as that of the divine name Shadday. This is one of a number of cases in which gematria had indicated to Sabbatai that he was the Messiah. Another was the fact that the first word of the Bible, which in English becomes 'In the beginning', contains the same Hebrew letters as the word 'Sabbatai'. Sabbatai also found that the numerical value of the Hebrew words for 'the true Messiah' equalled that of his own name.

Israel Hazzan says that Sabbatai had two rings on which were engraved combinations of letters of the Tetragrammaton and the divine name 'Shadday'. He goes on to say that Sabbatai also had a third ring, which Scholem suggests may have been engraved with the figure of a crooked serpent after his name. This was the 'sacred serpent', the numerical value of which was equal to that of the Hebrew word 'Mosiach', or 'Messiah'. At least in his later years, Sabbatai used the sign of this serpent as a seal on his correspondence, as evidenced by a recently discovered letter dated 1676.

The testimony of Solomon Laniado dates Sabbatai's messianic proclamation to the Seventeenth of Sivan, the third month of the Jewish year, or 31 May 1665. This date is noted in a manuscript of the late seventeenth century: 'the Seventeenth of Sivan, the day on which AMIRAH's kingdom began to grow in Gaza'. But there is a difficulty here, for the Sabbatian festival calendar marks the Seventeenth of Thammuz, the fourth month, as 'the first day of the illumination of the spirit and the light of AMIRAH'. Also, in two letters written in 1666, Sabbatai refers to the Seventeenth of Thammuz as 'the day of the regeneration of my spirit and my light'.

The significance of the latter date becomes clear from events that took place in the intervening month, during which Nathan announced that signs were evident that 'the exaltation of the rabbi

Sabbatai Sevi as the Anointed of the God of Jacob' was at hand. The Seventeenth of Thammuz was an ancient day of fasting, the beginning of a three-week period of austerity culminating on the Ninth of Ab, the day commemorating the destruction of the First and Second Temples. Sabbatai (or perhaps Nathan) startled the Jews of Palestine by announcing that the fast of Thammuz was abolished. The prohibition was obeyed in Gaza, where, instead of the usual liturgy on that day, 'the Great Hallel [the festival psalms, numbers 113–18] was recited, and there was rejoicing in the gardens'. A letter sent from Gaza to Aleppo in July 1665 reports on the extraordinary events surrounding the emergence of the new Messiah, ending with the news that 'the Seventeenth of Thammuz was made a festival day of feasting and rejoicing in honour of the Shekhinah, for thus it hath been revealed'.

After the public proclamation that he was the Messiah, Sabbatai was surrounded by devoted believers. Samuel Gandoor writes with awe as he describes Sabbatai at the time: 'Blessed is he who beheld the countenance of the rabbi Sabbatai Sevi, like unto the awesome appearance of an angel of God, [surpassing] all the rabbis in the Talmud and Kabbalah, in majesty, virtue and saintliness.'

It would seem that many of the Jews in Gaza and Jerusalem became followers of Sabbatai soon after he proclaimed that he was the Messiah. His followers were known simply as 'believers', rather than as 'Sabbatians', the latter being a term used by his opponents. But Sabbatai's believers did not include the majority of the rabbis in Jerusalem, whose opposition to him became particularly evident after he abolished the fast of Thammuz. They were outraged by his referring to himself using some of the names of God, such as 'Shadday', and by his once actually declaring that he was the one referred to in the prayer 'It is our duty to praise the Lord of all.'

A letter from Gaza notes that shortly after his messianic proclamation Sabbatai said to his followers, 'Let us arise and go to Jerusalem.' Another source, dated July 1665, says that he took 'about forty men with him to Jerusalem', after which the writer describes the 'wondrous journey' and the miraculous incidents en route.

Thus did Sabbatai depart for Jerusalem, leaving Nathan behind in Gaza to spread the word that the Messiah had finally appeared. The Messiah and his prophet had been together only a few weeks, but in that time they had given rise to a movement that would quickly spread throughout the Jewish world, affecting it profoundly in ways that had never before been seen, as if the apocalypse was nigh.

# 7. The Messiah has Come

Sabbatai set out from Gaza to Jerusalem early in June 1665, accompanied by many of the followers who had begun to gather around him. One of his most most devoted disciples, Samuel Gandoor, alludes to Sabbatai's mysterious behaviour after he arrived in the Holy City: 'Sabbatai Sevi, accompanied by many followers, proceded via Ramleh to Jerusalem; and in Jerusalem he did many things that were strange and incomprehensible to all who beheld him.'

According to Solomon Laniado, in Gaza Sabbatai had appointed twelve rabbis who were to accompany him to the site of the Temple, then occupied by the Mosque of 'Umar, where he intended to perform a sacrifice. He also appointed Rabbi Jacob Najara, who had been his host in Gaza, to the ancient post of high priest of the Temple, which he, Sabbatai, was symbolically rebuilding by virtue of his visit as Messiah. According to Solomon Laniado, when news of this reached the rabbis of Jerusalem they went into mourning over the blasphemy, and they were also terrified that the Muslims would come down on them if Jews dared to visit a sacred Islamic shrine. The Jerusalem rabbis sent a letter to Sabbatai, pleading with him not to go through with his plans: 'Why do you want to deliver Israel to death and why do you destroy the Lord's inheritance?' Laniado concludes his account by saying that Sabbatai abandoned his pilgrimage, whereupon he 'smote his hands and cried: "Woe! It was so near, and now it has been put far off."'

Letters from Egypt report that the rabbis of Jerusalem denounced Sabbatai to the Turkish cadi, or judge, claiming 'that he wanted to rule and that he had embezzled some of the money of his mission'. But the cadi exonerated Sabbatai, according to Sabbatian sources, who looked upon this as a great miracle. Then, according to the same sources, Sabbatai received permission from the cadi 'to ride on horseback through the city, although [Ottoman] custom strictly forbade a Jew to ride a horse'. It is said that Sabbatai rode around the city seven times 'on his horse, and clothed in a green mantle according to his mystical intentions'.

Sabbatai's actions infuriated the rabbis of Jerusalem, who were already outraged by his other blasphemies, which included not only his abolition of the fast of Thammuz but also the fact that he had led some of his disciples to break an ancient dietary law. According to Moses ben Habib, Sabbatai had encouraged ten of his followers to eat *heleb*, 'fat of the kidney', and while they were doing so he had 'recited a benediction over this ritually forbidden food: "Blessed art Thou, O Lord, who permittest that which is forbidden." I also heard from a very pious scholar that he had done likewise, but had then repented of it.'

Emanuel Frances attributed the reaction of the Jerusalem rabbis to their anger at Sabbatai's messianic claims, as well as to their fear that these would bring down upon them the wrath of the Turks. According to Frances, the rabbinate of Jerusalem had written to their brethren in Gaza, advising them to 'separate yourselves from the tents of these madmen, lest both we and you be found sinning against the King [i.e. the Sultan]'.

In January 1666 a Dutchman in Izmir wrote to his friends in Holland that the rabbis of Jerusalem were so angry at Sabbatai's blasphemies that they wanted to kill him. Other letters that were received in Holland from Palestine in 1666 reported that Sabbatai had been 'banished and expelled by the rabbis of Jerusalem because of unusual actions which they could not understand'. The names of four of the rabbis who signed the decree of banishment are known: Abraham Amigo, head of the Jerusalem rabbinate; Jacob Semah, the leading Kabbalist in the city; Samuel Garmizan; and Jacob Hagiz, Sabbatai's former teacher. Thomas Coenen heard in Izmir that the rabbis of Jerusalem not only had banished Sabbatai but had excommunicated him as well, reporting on their actions to the chief rabbi in Istanbul. The chief rabbinate responded by sending a circular letter to all the Jewish communities in the Empire, informing them of the excommunication. The letter to the community in Izmir, which was written by Yomtob ben Yaqar and addressed to Hayyim Benveniste, contained a postscript condemning Sabbatai: 'The man who spreads these innovations is a heretic, and whoever kills him will be accounted as one who has saved many souls, and the hand that strikes him down without delay will be blessed in the eyes of God and man.'

The Chevalier de La Croix reported that the Jerusalem rabbis gave 'Sabbatai, his wife and servants' three days to leave the city. This is the only reference to Sarah's presence in Palestine, other than unsubstantiated stories that she had been with Sabbatai in Gaza. There she is said to have incited Sabbatai to declare himself the Messiah and 'to set himself up as king over Israel'. There is no evidence that Sarah ever took a prominent role in the Sabbatian movement, for she was content just to follow her husband's lead. When she wrote to friends she signed her letters with the symbolic name that Nathan had given her as the Messiah's wife: 'the lady Queen Rebekah, the daughter of Moses'.

Although the rabbinic authorities in Jerusalem had banished Sabbatai, he still had enthusiastic supporters among the rabbis there. Among them was Samuel Primo, a distinguished rabbinic scholar who later became Sabbatai's secretary. Another was Moses Galanté, a disciple and prophet of the Messiah until the time of Sabbatai's apostasy, after which he rejected his former master, saying 'I am cursing him every day.'

Sabbatai left Jerusalem early in July 1665 on the first stage of a journey that would take him back to Izmir. His first stopping place was Safed, where the Sabbatian movement was gathering force – so much so that by mid-November reports reached Egypt that ten prophets and ten prophetesses had emerged there 'and prophesied great things'. When he passed through Safed, Sabbatai would almost certainly have met the renowned Lurianic Kabbalist Benjamin ha-Levi, who became his devoted disciple, and who would later write to friends in Italy 'on the subject of our redemption by our king Sabbatai Sevi'.

Safed, the last resting place of Isaac Luria, was already predisposed to join the messianic movement, as evidenced by the testimony of Laurent d'Arvieux, a French traveller who visited the town in 1660. He writes that the Jews there believed 'that the Messiah who will be born in Galilee, will make Safed the capital of his new kingdom on earth. Those who will be there at the time of his advent – both the quick and the dead – may expect from him special graces.'

After leaving Safed, Sabbatai went on to Damascus, where prophets had also heralded the imminent arrival of the Messiah. Letters from Damascus report that when Sabbatai passed through the city he was surrounded by enthusiastic supporters. There he would have met Samuel Vital, son of Hayyim Vital, who had become a follower of Sabbatai while staying in Cairo some months earlier as a guest of Raphael Joseph.

Sabbatai then went on to Aleppo, where he arrived on the Eighth of Ab, 20 July 1665. Samuel Laniado, the rabbi of the Aleppo community, was told by Sabbatai 'that there had been much strife between him [Sabbatai] and the people of Jerusalem'. Sabbatai went on to tell Laniado that he had 'left Jerusalem and cursed them. But on his way he saw a group of Jews going to Jerusalem, and he was seized with pity for them. So he sent them a pardon, and turned his curse into a blessing.'

Laniado reports on the welcome that Sabbatai was given in his city, noting that 'he came here, to Aleppo, and the land was resplendent with his glory'. Laniado and another rabbi, Nissim ben Mordecai Dayyan, report on Sabbatai's behaviour during his stay in Aleppo in a letter dated 22 February 1666. They write that Sabbatai in public asked to be treated like any other rabbi; also he made no messianic claims and 'did not reveal anything' about himself. But in private he showed no such restraint, for he convinced Laniado and the other rabbis of Aleppo that he was in fact the Messiah. They had already been prepared for this by letters from Nathan, who warned the people of Aleppo not to make the same mistake as their compatriots in Jerusalem, who had driven away the Messiah and brought down upon themselves his curse.

Sabbatai remained in Aleppo for twenty-two days, after which he departed for Izmir. His stay is described by La Croix, summarizing a letter from Aleppo that had been shown to him by a former Sabbatian: 'The Messiah dwelt among them, and thus they depended no longer on Nathan's letters, for they saw with their own eyes and heard with their own ears, and signs were wrought to them. They entreated him to stay with them for at least two months, but he refused as he was in a hurry to get to Smyrna before the appointed time was fulfilled.'

Sabbatai's disciples in Aleppo provided him with guides for the first part of his journey, and on their return they reported wondrous things.

Every night they were joined by a host of people who would accompany them, but disappear again at dawn. He always travelled with his *tallith* [prayer shawl] drawn over his head. When they remonstrated with him that he was endangering his life . . . by thus showing that he was a Jew, as they might be killed by brigands, he . . . assured them that it was not of his own will but by command from above that he acted thus.

At the end of their letter, according to La Croix, the believers in Aleppo added that since they had accepted the prophecy of Nathan they

had decided to cease all business, to put on sackcloth and ashes, and to devote themselves to penitence, charity and prayer as to be worthy to behold the fulfilment of the prophet. They also established a fund for the poor, to enable them to give all their time to prayer. Finally they called on their friends [in Istanbul] to follow their example and not that of the people in Jerusalem, who had driven out their king.

After Sabbatai's departure many of his followers in Aleppo began to utter prophecies, according to La Croix: 'Some of them had fallen to the ground at the sound of the *shofar* [a ram's horn trumpet] and remained lying there cold and without pulse or movement, and a wonderful voice came out of their open mouths, articulating Hebrew words which they themselves did not understand, and in the end they said "Sabbatai Sevi our redeemer and holy one."'

Another source, Sem Tob ben Kohen, wrote to a friend in Istanbul to say that on the Day of Atonement that year, 19 September 1665, twenty prophets and four prophetesses appeared in Aleppo. Three of the prophets were rabbis, most notably Solomon Laniado, who was believed to be a reincarnation of King Solomon. The letter went on to say that the prophet Elijah himself appeared in the Aleppo synagogue, 'dressed in white with a belt of black copper'.

Meanwhile the Sabbatian movement had taken wing in Gaza, where pilgrims from all over Palestine were coming to see Nathan, seeking a *tiqqun* from the Messiah's prophet. Abraham Cuenque writes that 'Everybody went to the prophet in Gaza, and when the turn of Hebron came, I went with the whole congregation.'

Cuenque found that Nathan was totally transformed by his prophetic mission: 'When I stood before Nathan the prophet all my bones shook, for his countenance was completely changed. The radiance of his face was like that of a burning torch, the colour of his beard was like gold, and his mouth which would not utter even the most ordinary things now spoke words that made the listener tremble.'

According to Cuenque, the pilgrims who had come to Gaza to see Nathan were so numerous that 'the people slept in the streets and bazaars because the houses and courtyards could not contain' all of them. He goes on to say that 'No business is transacted, and all – boys and old men, young men and virgins, pregnant women and such as have just given birth – are fasting from Sunday to Friday without suffering any harm.' A similar scene is described in a letter from Gaza written in late September 1665: 'at the afternoon prayer there were two hundred and twenty penitents who were fasting for two days and two nights, not to speak of those who fasted even longer, and the women and children who fasted single days only'.

Cuenque's account of his pilgrimage to Gaza, which he wrote years after the event, ends with an expression of his wonder at the extraordinary scene that he had witnessed there and which he later learned had been repeated throughout the Jewish world:

Let no one think that such a thing, or anything remotely like it, has ever happened before. It was like the revelation at Sinai [Yahweh's covenant with Moses – Exodus 19] . . . it was supernatural that Israel should do such things in their exile, in the midst of the nations . . . in the kingdom of Ismael [Turkey] and particularly in the kingdom of Barbary [Morocco] and none turning against them to cut off their name, [for] the fear of the Jews had fallen upon the nations.

The messianic movement had now gone so far that in the Sabbath service Sabbatai's name was substituted for that of the Ottoman sultan in the traditional prayer for the ruler of the land. The Sabbatians now offered a prayer for the 'king of Israel, the sultan Sabbatai Sevi'. Letters from Gaza and Jerusalem were now dated by reference to the year 'of the kingship of Our Lord and King' Sabbatai Sevi, as if humankind had entered upon a new era beginning with the appearance of AMIRAH, as the Messiah was generally called from this time on by his disciples.

The extraordinary apocalyptic spirit of the time is particularly evident in a number of legends that spread from Gaza. One of them, reported by Sasportas, described Nathan as being 'encompassed with a Fiery Cloud' from which the prophetic voice of a *maggid* was heard. Sasportas also quoted from letters reporting that at Nathan's command

great stones had fallen from heaven on the house of worship of the Gentiles. Some say it is collapsed completely, others say only partly. On the Twenty-fifth of Kislev there would be a great darkness among the Gentiles; there should fall great Hailstones, Fire and Brimstone . . . which should destroy many houses of Idolaters, but among the Jews there should be clear light, without any hurt or disturbance.

The Yemenite apocalyptic work *Gey Hizzayon* described the cataclysmic events that would occur with the appearance of the Messiah: 'The sky will be overcast with clouds, and the earth with a thick mist that will surround Mount Zion and the Messiah, together with Elijah and Michael . . . A blazing fire will surround Zion and Hebron lest any Gentile or uncircumcised enter . . . Askelon and Ekron will disappear by sinking into the earth.'

Meanwhile Nathan had been corresponding with Raphael Joseph Chelebi in Cairo. This is noted in one of the collections of letters written from Gaza, which says that 'every day the lord Raphael Joseph would write to the aforementioned Rabbi [Nathan] to enquire of him whatever he desired to know . . . and every day the posts went out and returned from one to the other'. According to Sasportas, the Chelebi was supporting Nathan and his disciples as well as all the pilgrims who were passing through Cairo on their way to see the prophet in Gaza. 'He would provide food to all the people in Gaza that were with Nathan, and everyone that came from afar would leave his moneybag with him and then proceed to Gaza.'

Then on 5 September 1665 Nathan had a mystical experience that he described in a letter to Raphael Joseph: he heard 'a voice in the Celestial Academy, proclaiming that the Messiah, the son of David, would become manifest to the world in a year and some months'. The letter, which was written soon after Nathan's experience, was copied and distributed throughout the Ottoman Empire and Europe by the following month, becoming one of the basic documents of the Sabbatian movement. (Gershom Scholem notes that 'Later Sabbatian writers confused Nathan's initial prophetic experience . . . (spring 1665) with the celestial proclamation of September 5.' Thus the two experiences melded in tradition into one messianic prophecy.)

Nathan's letter appears in an account written by Leyb ben Ozer. According to this the Holy Spirit had revealed to Nathan that Isaac Luria had originally been destined to be the Messiah, but Luria's generation had not proved worthy of redemption. Thus it had fallen to the present generation to follow Sabbatai Sevi as the Messiah: as Leyb ben Ozer quotes Nathan, 'Every Jew must believe that Sabbatai Sevi is the true redeemer, he and no other, without seeking any sign or wonder from him, even though he has the power to do signs and wonders in multitudes as he has already, but it is forbidden to doubt him.'

The letter goes on to say of Sabbatai that

By his merit has this generation earned the right to see the beginning of the Redemption, which we have looked forward to for one thousand six hundred years and which no generation has merited until ours, therefore shall there be no mercy for the non-believers and infidels in whatever comes upon them, neither for them nor their flesh and blood.

Leyb ben Ozer then quotes Nathan's revelation of the apocalyptic events that will occur with the appearance of the Messiah. After stating that the revelation came to him from the Holy Spirit, Nathan says:

In another year and some months Sabbatai Sevi will take the kingship from the ruler of Turkey, without war, only by way of songs and hymns and by praise and gratitude to God, may He be blessed, and the Turkish ruler will place himself in his hands and go along with him as his servant throughout his kingdom and pass everything on to Sabbatai Sevi.

Sabbatai will conquer all the nations of the earth in this fashion, but there will not be any bloodshed among the Christians – the nations will give themselves up by their own goodwill. But at the same time, though Israel's exile will not yet end, and the Temple will not yet be rebuilt, 'all the Jews will be considered to be lords, and whatever they order, the nations will be obliged to carry out, and every one of the uncircumcised will stand before a Jew like a slave before his master and tremble and be filled with fear and terror of what the Jew will command'.

Quoting Nathan, Leyb ben Ozer goes on to say that 'Sabbatai Sevi will come from across the Sambatyon river, riding the Great Lion bridled by a fiery seven-headed snake from whose mouth comes forth consuming flames.' The Sambatyon, a mythical river that stops flowing on the Sabbath, appears in the legend of the Ten Lost Tribes of Israel. The legend is based on the Jewish tribes who were exiled to Assyria, 'beyond the river Sambatyon', after the conquest of Palestine by the Assyrian king Tiglath-pileser III in 733–732 BC.

Leyb ben Ozer continues quoting Nathan:

After Sabbatai humbles all the kings of the earth the Temple will descend in Jerusalem, having been rebuilt in heaven. And then Sabbatai Sevi and Moses our teacher and the Jews from across the Sambatyon will come to Jerusalem in great glory, and there will be no more than seven thousand Jews left in the Land of Israel who have remained strong in their faith throughout the great and terrible decrees.

Then the 'resurrection of the dead will take place in the Land of Israel for the righteous buried there, and the evil will be cast out of the land and will not rise until the general resurrection, after forty years, when all the dead outside the Land of Israel will rise'.

Around this time Nathan also composed his first penitential tracts, which he sent to Raphael Joseph and other Sabbatians. A member of the Chelebi's circle wrote at the time that 'in recent letters sent by him [Nathan] he very much urges repentance, for events will be moving rapidly. And whoever has not put on the breastplate of repentance as behoves him will suffer tribulations. He also sent penitential lessons for the day and for the night, as well as devotions for the reparation of sins.' According to Raphael Supino, a distinguished rabbinic scholar from Livorno, as quoted by Sasportas, Samuel Vital took charge of the devotions recommended by Nathan to Raphael Joseph, 'and he supervised the penitential exercises, including ritual immersions, prolonged fasts and flagellations, right from the beginning'.

Nathan's penitential lessons were revised and elaborated in both Gaza and Cairo, and eventually circulated throughout the Jewish world in 1666, playing an important part in the Sabbatian movement.

Another innovation made by Nathan was his new version of the *Tefillah*, or *Amidah*, a daily prayer originally consisting of a series of eighteen benedictions, to which a nineteenth was subsequently added. Nathan's version includes additional 'devotions for the *Amidah*' from the Lurianic writings of Hayyim Vital, which he recommended as 'a prayer conveying special grace which one should say with great devotion'. One of these prayers is a plea that Sabbatai Sevi be spared the fate suffered by an earlier messiah: 'Grant us a redemption without the sadness and the sorrow of seeing the Messiah of the House of Joseph, who hath begun to comfort us and to raise our banner above the nation, slain in our sight. For then all the Gentiles will arise to cut off our name, and the name of Israel will be remembered no more.'

The long-awaited Messiah had finally appeared, and the dispersed Jewish world readied itself for the forthcoming redemption.

# 8. The Lost Tribes of Israel

Early in the autumn of 1665 fabulous tales began circulating about the new messianic movement, many of them originating in the legends of the Midrash and the *Zohar*. A number of these stories concerned the Ten Lost Tribes of Israel. Tales were told that the Lost Tribes were still living beyond the legendary river Sambatyon, mentioned by Nathan in his apocalyptic letter of early September 1665, where he implies that Sabbatai will lead them back to Israel and redemption.

A rumour from Salé in Morocco, which reached Europe in September 1665, said that some of the Lost Tribes had appeared there and were on their way to Arabia, where the rest of their people were besieging Mecca. The source for this report is the Walloon scholar Peter Serrarius, of Antwerp, who was prominent among those Protestants awaiting the millennium predicted by St John the Evangelist in the Book of Revelation. One of those to whom Serrarius gave this news was Johannes Duraeus, an English theologian exiled in Berne. Duraeus reports, in a letter dated 28 October 1665, that

Mr Serrarius tells marvellous news of the Ten Tribes of Israel . . . They have already made their appearance at the borders of Arabia, conquered Mecca, where the tomb of Mohammed is, and other cities, and put to death all the inhabitants except the Jews . . . If the reports should prove to be true, then manifestly the face of the earth will soon be renewed.

A pamphlet about the Lost Tribes was published in London in the autumn of 1665, entitled *The Restauration of the Jews, or True Relation of their Progress and Proceedings in order to the regaining of their ancient Kingdom, being the substance of several letters from Antwerp, Leghorn, Florence.* The pamphlet consisted of a number of letters, two of them paraphrasing reports from Tunis, Florence, Livorno and Amsterdam, another summarizing the writer's discussions with a Christian millenarian who may be Serrarius himself, according to Gershom Scholem. The pamphlet makes no mention of Sabbatai or Nathan, and so, as Scholem suggests, the legend of the Lost Tribes may have revived independently of the new messianic movement. Sasportas, who in 1665 was still living in London as rabbi of the Jewish community there, writes of the supposed appearance of the Lost Tribes of Israel without mentioning the Sabbatians: 'multitudes of Israel had come by way of the desert to Mecca, the burial place of the prophet of the Muslims, which they had despoiled. When the Grand Turk marched against them with a mighty army they wrought vengeance on him . . . These rumours were accepted even by Christians in England.'

The most detailed of the reports concerning the reappearance of the Lost Tribes is a letter from Salé early in August 1665, evidently written by a Christian. This report estimated that the multitude consisted 'of about eight thousand Companies of *Troops*, each of which containing from one hundred to a thousand Men. They who went thither to see and enquire who they were, found them to be Strangers, and an unknown People, whose Language they understood not, only few of their commanders speak Hebrew.' The multitude was armed with 'swords, Bows, Arrows, and Lances, each man being well armed therewith, but no Guns at all. They have for their Chief Leader, or Captain, a *Holy Man* who understandeth all Languages, and marcheth before them, doing miracles.' These people had already captured several cities, slaughtering all the inhabitants except the Jews. 'They are a People of a middle stature, their Bodies comely, their Complexions fair: This Party saw no Woman amongst them, nor any other Arms, besides those above-mentioned; their Horses are many, their Attire blue, and their *Tents* black.'

At about the same time letters from Egypt began telling a similar story about the Lost Tribes, who in this version had appeared in the Arabian desert, where they would be joined by a larger army of their brethren marching from the trackless sands of the Sahara. Reports circulating in Italy said that the Turks were helpless against the Jewish tribes, 'their own swords and muskets turning against themselves'. The numbers of the tribesmen increased in each retelling, a pamphlet published in Amsterdam claiming that the Lost Tribes were being reinforced by eighty ships that had sailed from India to Palestine, 'and some say that one million and one hundred thousand Jews were on their way, on sea and on land. The sultan is said to have offered Alexandria and Tunis to the Jewish . . . conquerors of Mecca on condition that they give up Mecca, but they have demanded the entire Holy Land.'

A letter from Serrarius to Duraeus adds other fabulous details to the rumours, including a report that the approach of the Lost Tribes would bring about world harmony with the Last Judgement: 'Hence there will take place a general foregathering and assembly of all the nations of the world in one pasture which shall be in Zion, and all contentions shall cease . . . All public worship shall cease until the year 1672 because of that consternation, but . . . afterward a universal worship shall be raised up among all the people in the world.'

Reports from Morocco, Egypt and Palestine were also circulated in England, where they found a fascinated audience among millenarians. Robert Boulter, who in 1666 or soon afterwards printed a number of pamphlets on the Sabbatian movement, gives news of the Lost Tribes in *A New Letter from Aberdeen in Scotland, sent to a Person of Quality, wherein is a more full Account of the Proceedings of the Jews than has hitherto been published*. The pamphlet reported that on 23 October 1665 a ship arrived in Aberdeen with passengers who spoke only in broken Hebrew, and who said

That there is Sixteen hundred thousand of them together in Arabia, and that there came into *Europe* Sixty Thousand more; as likewise, that they have had Encounters with the *Turks*, and slain great numbers of them; none are able to stand up against them: They give Liberty of Conscience to all, except the Turks, endeavouring the Ruine and Extirpation of them.

The pamphlet describes their remarkable ship, which was bound for Amsterdam, as was stated by a letter in 'high Dutch' that they presented to the authorities: 'As for their Ship, the sails thereof are white branched Sattin, and all their Ropes are Silk of the same colour; and in the Sails was this Inscription in fair Red Characters THESE ARE THE TEN TRIBES OF ISRAEL, which was to discover them to be *Jews* . . .' Their letter stated 'that they have sent to all remarkable places in the World to their Brethren, to give them notices of their proceedings, to the end they may come unto, and joyn with them'.

A report reaching Vienna in December 1665 said that the armies of the Lost Tribes were approaching from Persia. Early in 1666 a rumour reached Casale Monteferrato in Italy that the Israelite host that had conquered Mecca 'now intends to march against the Germans and the Poles that had so much persecuted the Jews, and that they would have no pity or compassion on them'. A letter from Vienna was printed in London in February 1666, giving information about the Lost Tribes that had supposedly come from Persia. According to the letter, the Lost Tribes had been living in the remote region of Tartary in central Asia, where God had sent a prophet to muster them and lead them back to Palestine.

Early in 1666 pamphlets began circulating among Christians in Germany about the new Messiah and the Lost Tribes of Israel. The writers based their accounts on a manuscript written in 1642 about a purely imaginary messiah named Josua Helcam, who in some pamphlets is called Joshavel Cam, while his prophet is known as Nathan Levi. One of the pamphlets has a portrait of the Messiah leading an army of his disciples, with the accompanying legend identifying him as 'Ioasua Helcam, whom Nathan Levi, their new prophet, has chosen as chief general over them that are called the the Ten Tribes of Israel'. The pamphlets give fabulous accounts of the adventures of the Messiah. In one version Joshavel Cam is crowned King of the Jews, after which he is arrested by the Turks, who cut his throat, disembowel him, and hang him upside down to the lamentation of the Jews of Constantinople. In another version he is at first imprisoned in Constantinople, after which he appears in a dream to the Sultan, who then frees Cam and treats him with great honour.

A number of the legends concerning the Lost Tribes were associated with Nathan of Gaza, the earliest being in a letter to

Raphael Joseph Chelebi from his brother Hayyim Joseph. Writing from Gaza, Hayyim Joseph reported that Nathan had made three attempts to sail from Haifa in order to join Sabbatai in Izmir, but each time a hurricane had prevented his departure. An angel then appeared to him in a pillar of fire and told him to stay in Gaza, since the time of redemption had come. Then, as Hayyim Joseph writes, 'And when the prophet [Nathan] passed through the mountains of the wilderness, there appeared unto him the prophet Jehu, the son of Hanani, who confirmed the message of the angel . . . and that part of their tribes would all of a sudden appear in Gaza.' Another version of this legend has it that Israel Benjamin, a prominent Jerusalem rabbi, accompanied the prophet Nathan into the wilderness, where the prophet Jehu appeared to them and announced that two envoys of the Sons of Moses – the Lost Tribes of Israel – would arrive from beyond the river Sambatyon in two months. Still another version, published by Emanuel Frances, said that Nathan 'had prophesied regarding the tribes of Gad and Reuben, that they would conquer Palestine this year, and that there would be three days of darkness in Constantinople for the Gentiles, but unto all the children of Israel will be light in their habitations'.

Meanwhile Nathan's father, Elisha Ashkenazi, who had been travelling extensively on behalf of the Jerusalem community, stopped off at Livorno on his way back to Egypt and Palestine. There, in the autumn of 1665, he received news of his son's prophecy that Sabbatai Sevi was the Messiah. While in Livorno he met Shalom ben Joseph, an old rabbinic teacher from Amsterdam, who was en route to spend his last years in Jerusalem. The two travelled together to Cairo, where Elisha was received royally as the father of the prophet. Shalom ben Joseph, bearing a letter of introduction from Elisha, continued on to Gaza, where he met Nathan and asked him 'to consent to answer certain questions that he wished to ask . . . The prophet replied that he was too busy at present, but that at some other time he would gladly fulfil his wish.' Shalom ben Joseph wrote from Jerusalem in December 1665 to tell a friend in Amsterdam that Nathan 'is possessed of exceeding wisdom, and all scholars are coming from afar to hear his wisdom, and all agree that he speaks by the Holy Spirit'. He noted that most of the rabbis in Cairo still had their doubts about the Messiah and his prophet, but 'in Gaza there is exceeding joy every day. Lights are kindled in the synagogue, and hymns are recited. All are confident that as the Messiah has gone to Constantinople, the Turkish king would set the royal crown upon his head, not by might nor by power.'

The hymns that Shalom ben Joseph mentions would have sung of messianic redemption, a theme that had been developed by the Kabbalist poet Israel Najara, who died in Gaza in 1605. Nathan's hymns were based on the mystical poems of Najara, whose works were much admired by Isaac Luria. Luria used to say that the soul of Najara was a 'spark' of the soul of King David, and that his hymns enchanted even the 'family on high'. One of the poems of Najara that Nathan revived as a hymn sings lyrically of the day of redemption and its joy:

Soon the day of redemption, the day of redemption for innocent blood comes. Enough languishing among enemies. Come, rest in my bosom. Let me drink thy breath of spices, thou beloved mine. Let me hear thy sweet voice, sing to me thy songs, my only beloved, desired one. Sing thy song of joy – I come quickly to thy help, to free thee from long exile. Faithful is my love to thee, with a crown will I adorn thy head. I will renew thy youth, and thou wilt bloom like the willow tree near the fresh spring.

Shalom ben Joseph evidently believed in Nathan's prophecy that Sabbatai was the Messiah, for he wrote urging his children to sell all they owned and come at once to Jerusalem, since 'we have a king and a prophet'.

Shalom ben Joseph, accompanied by Meir Rofe, went on to Hebron, where Nathan was active in spreading the Sabbatian movement during the winter of 1665–6. Shalom ben Joseph's letters from Hebron are lost, but Nathan's activities there are described by Abraham Cuenque. According to Cuenque, Nathan arrived in Hebron with more than 300 of his followers, his intention being 'to perform his devotions at the cave of Machpelah and to undergo immersion in snow'. It seems that 'there is no snow in

Gaza owing to its warm climate, whereas Hebron has snow most years, and the snow remains on the ground for a few days because of the cold air'. Cuenque writes that Nathan and about a hundred of his followers went out into the fields, where they stripped naked 'and performed the immersions by rolling in the snow according to custom. The Muslims beheld it every day.'

Cuenque goes on to say that the most renowned rabbi in Hebron did not believe Nathan's prophecy. 'Esteemed among us as the greatest of our generation, [our] father in learning, R. Hayyim Abulafia said with his holy mouth that he did not believe it, though he would act as all the others so as not to "separate himself from the congregation".' According to Cuenque, after Nathan's departure the other rabbis of Hebron asked Abulafia if he had changed his mind. He replied that he respected Nathan as a rabbinic scholar, 'yet I persist in my opinion. I do not believe that the Messiah will come in this way. According to our tradition, this is not the way. I shall not oppose them [the Sabbatians], but the convictions in my heart have not changed.' Abulafia's attitude was typical of prominent non-believers who for one reason or another could not bring themselves to oppose the Sabbatians in the rising tide of the messianic movement, coming out into the open only after it ebbed following Sabbatai's apostasy.

Nathan was also active in Jerusalem that winter, as evidenced by letters sent from there to Italy early in 1666. One of these was written by 'R. Israel Iserles, the son of the scholar R. Samson', to R. Solomon Hay Saraval in Venice. Iserles wrote that he was

ready to go forth with the army of prayer, praying for your peace and prosperity . . . to God who 'standeth behind our wall', the holy Wailing Wall, which is the Gate of Heaven for our prayers. May we soon merit speedily to behold the glory of our might and our sanctuary, the place where our fathers prayed. For we have beheld many good signs, which must not be committed to paper, and everything depends on perfect repentance.

The reluctance to write down the 'many good signs' is typical of the Sabbatians, who apparently feared that they would be ridi-

culed by the non-believers and that this would weaken their movement. This is stated explicitly in a latter sent from Palestine to
Egypt, in which the writer describes the reticence of the believers:
'They write of the many things wrought by R. Abraham Nathan
[i.e. Nathan of Gaza], but they must not be exposed because people
would not understand them at once and make a mockery [of them]
and thus would bring great evil upon themselves and upon Israel.
For this reason they do not want to write down everything.'

The most outspoken of the non-believing rabbis in Jerusalem
was Samuel Garmizan, who had been on the rabbinic court that
had excommunicated Sabbatai. Garmizan's wrath was aroused by
letters that had been sent to believers by their Messiah, who identified himself by writing that 'I am the Lord your God, Sabbatai
Sevi.' Garmizan writes that, before a 'great multitude' in Jerusalem,
he preached a sermon in which he 'explained that every man should
know his worth and not wax proud . . . let alone make himself
God'. According to Cuenque, Garmizan objected to the fact that
four rabbis from Hebron had accompanied Nathan when he
returned to Gaza, having been asked to do so by Sabbatai Sevi.
Garmizan pleaded with them, 'Do not go! and if you fear the king's
[i.e. Sabbatai's] anger, I shall defend you.'

According to Sasportas, both Shalom ben Joseph and Meir Rofe
stated in their letters to Amsterdam, writing of Nathan, 'that they
had asked him for a sign or miracle regarding his prophecy, but he
refused, saying he was not permitted to perform one. They should,
rather, wait until they saw the fulfilment of everything. And R.
Shalom greatly marvelled at his [Nathan's] courage and his trust in
the fulfilment of his prophecies.'

Shalom ben Joseph returned home from Gaza bearing a letter
from Nathan addressed to the 'holy congregation of Amsterdam,
their leaders and sages, their judges, elders and officers with all the
men of Israel, may God preserve them'. The letter closes with this
exhortation: 'Strengthen ye the weak hands and confirm the feeble
knees, for thus saith the Lord, behold thy saviour cometh, his name
is Sabbatai Sevi, he shall go forth as a mighty man; he shall prevail
against his enemies. I pray that your eyes may behold the king in
his beauty. From Nathan Benjamin.'

The prophet had signed with the name that Sabbatai had given him – Nathan Benjamin – which he would use thenceforth. Beginning in the autumn of 1665, his followers also referred to him as 'the holy lamp', just as Sabbatai was known as AMIRAH.

During the winter of 1665–6 Nathan sent word to the Jewish communities of the Diaspora that they should no longer send money to support the Jews of Palestine, who had been impoverished by the restrictions imposed on their doing business in the Holy Land. This attitude had already been expressed by Meir Rofe, who was head of the yeshiva, or school for talmudic study, in Hebron, and was supported by the Amsterdam philanthropist Abraham Pereira. Rofe wrote to Pereira in the autumn of 1665 'that thenceforth they no longer required his gifts, but that they wished he would come and join them to behold the beauty of the Lord'. Early in 1666 there were rumours in Amsterdam that Nathan had given similar instructions to the leading rabbi of Palestine: 'Let not one more penny from the Diaspora come here: there will be sufficient treasures to distribute among all the tribes.'

Sasportas maligned Nathan by saying that the prophet was trying to starve the non-believers into submission by cutting off the charity from abroad that supported them. He wrote that

many people had ceased to contribute their annual charity for the poor in Palestine . . . , saying that 'Since you have the Messiah with you, you do not need our assistance.' Moreover they knew these vanities and that they held the Messiah in no account. Wherefore the great mass, who were fanatic believers in this false faith, considered all Jerusalemites as infidels who denied the prophet and the Messiah.

Nathan's policy of rejecting alms was probably based on an influential book published ten years earlier by Nathan Shapira Yerushalmi, which condemned the Jews of the Diaspora who were 'concerned with their bodies and their money'. Shapira said that the Jews of Palestine could support themselves with the buried treasures that would be revealed to them by the Messiah when he appeared:

As for underground treasure, the earth will form subterranean passageways so that all the royal treasures can be moved to Palestine, as it is written [Deuteronomy 33:19] of the 'treasures hid in the sand'. Everything will be revealed in Palestine to the messianic king, and he will distribute them among the returning exiles, to each man his share, and they shall be filled with great riches.

This would have been what Nathan had in mind when he wrote that 'there will be sufficient treasures to distribute among the tribes'.

Nathan had also condemned money-changing, which was one of the principal occupations open to Jews, along with commerce. And the preoccupation of the Jews of Palestine and Egypt with the messianic movement also brought their commercial activities to a standstill. A letter to the East India Company from Livorno reports that 'the Jews of Alexandria write to their correspondents here, to send them no more business. They will have no further thoughts of it, but of higher matters.' The Sabbatians had faith in Nathan's prophecy that the Messiah would be crowned king by the Ottoman Sultan himself.

Meanwhile rumours of the Lost Tribes of Israel continued to surface, spreading around the shores of the Mediterranean and throughout Europe as far as England, from where ships carried the news across the Atlantic to the English colonies in North America. The Revd Increase Mather, the famous pastor of the Old North Church in Boston, spoke of the Lost Tribes in several of his sermons in late 1665. These sermons are mentioned by John Davenport of New Haven in his 'epistle to the reader' that appears as a preface to Increase Mather's work on *The Mystery of Israel's Salvation explained and applied*, published in London in 1669. The preface, dated 1667, says that the sermons were delivered 'in a time when constant reports from sundry places and lands gave out to the world, that the Israelites were upon their journey towards Jerusalem, from sundry foreign parts in great multitudes'. It goes on to say that this return of the Lost Tribes of Israel was 'carryed on with great signs and wonders . . . to the . . . astonishment of all that heard it, and that they had written to others in their Nation, in Europe and America, to encourage and invite them to hasten to them. This seemed to many godly and judicious to be a beginning of that Prophesie.'

The prophecy to which Davenport refers is given in Ezekiel 37:1–14, the vision of the valley of dry bones, a sign of Israel's restoration.

Although neither Davenport nor the Revd Mather mentions Sabbatai or Nathan, it is evident that the reports referred to arose from the Sabbatian movement. Abraham Cardozo wrote in a letter, referring to Sabbatai Sevi, that 'his name was known as far as the Spanish Indies'. This is a reference to the West Indies, where a number of former Marranos (Christianized Spanish Jews) from Holland had settled. These Marranos had remained in contact with their Jewish brethren in Holland, who had apparently invited the exiles to join them in travelling to the Holy Land now that the Messiah had appeared.

Thus even in the New World the Jews of the Diaspora were readying themselves to travel to Jerusalem, following the lead of the Lost Tribes of Israel.

# 9. Sabbatai Returns to Izmir

Sabbatai Sevi returned to his native Izmir late in the summer of 1665, after an absence of three years. Letters from believers in Egypt later in 1665 reported that 'he had safely arrived in Smyrna . . . and the whole congregation, and his family in particular, were rejoicing greatly'.

But it is doubtful that Sabbatai's return was really greeted with general rejoicing by the Jewish community of Izmir, although he had a growing number of believers there by that time. The local rabbis would have been informed by the chief rabbinate in Istanbul that Sabbatai had been excommunicated by the rabbinic court in Jerusalem, and would have received the rabbinate's recommendation that he be eliminated. This may have been the reason why Sabbatai 'kept himself in private' for two to three months after his return, according to Thomas Coenen, whose sources included a large number of both Jews and Gentiles in Izmir. Another reason might be that Sabbatai was undergoing one of his periods of depression, and that he did not act until he once again experienced a 'great illumination'.

Coenen reports that Sabbatai slept little after his return to Izmir, rising at midnight for his customary ritual sea-bath, then being among the first to enter the synagogue for prayer in the morning. Samson Bacchi, a rabbi from Casale Monferrato, reports that Sabbatai arrived in Izmir in September 1665, 'and there he remained silent until December. He would go to the synagogue early in the morning and recite the devotional prayers according to the Sephardi rite, with an agreeable voice that greatly pleased those who heard him. He also gave alms to the poor very liberally, fed them, and performed similar acts [of piety and charity].'

Sabbatai appears to have entered one of his periods of 'illumination' early in December 1665. Solomon Joseph Carpi, a rabbi in Mantua in the first half of the eighteenth century, writes that on one of the first days of the Hanukkah festival Sabbatai came to the synagogue clad 'in royal apparel, and intoned prayers and hymns, making a great rejoicing on that day'. Baruch of Arezzo, reporting on the same incident, says that Sabbatai 'began to intone melodiously the morning psalms, so that all the congregation marvelled at his melodious singing'. Baruch goes on to report that, during the first week of Hanukkah, Sabbatai 'began to do things that appeared strange: he pronounced the Ineffable Name, ate fats, and did other things against the Lord and His Law, even pressing others to do likewise'.

During that first week of Hanukkah a delegation of two rabbis and two laymen from Aleppo arrived in Izmir. The four had probably left Aleppo soon after Sabbatai, but they had first gone to Gaza to see Nathan before they moved on to Izmir. The two rabbis were Daniel Pinto and Moses Galanté of Jerusalem, both of whom were believed by the Sabbatians to be prophets. According to Samson Bacchi, when the delegates from Aleppo arrived in Izmir, Galanté 'truly testified that he [Sabbatai] surely was the Messiah'.

Galanté's announcement, together with Sabbatai's return to a state of 'illumination', created a great deal of excitement among the Jewish community of Izmir, many of whom came to pay homage to the Messiah. The earliest mention of this appears in a letter to England from a Christian in Izmir, dated 7 December 1665:

Here is a Jew in Town, who came about two months since from *Jerusalem*; and gives out publickly, That the Messiah is come, and had got to his Party a great many of the Jews. And not only in this place, but at *Constantinople*, and many other places through which he hath passed. And God alone knows whether he may be a means of the conversion of that stiff-necked Generation.

According to Coenen, wherever Sabbatai walked in Izmir he was surrounded by a rabble 'bodyguard' made up of the poorest Jews in the city, including 'fishermen, vendors of eggs and poultry, oarsmen in the port, and servants, and more of this sort of noblemen, even the richest of whom had nothing to lose'. Sasportas writes, quoting correspondents in Turkey, that Sabbatai's followers in

Izmir were 'the frenzied rabble . . . the miserable beggars . . . the poorest of the land'. Samson Bacchi writes of Sabbatai's disciples that 'everyone who is in distress and trouble, and all vain and light persons followed him'. But Coenen and other sources report that Sabbatai also had followers among both eminent rabbis and leading laymen of the Jewish community – the former including two of his early supporters, Isaac Silveira and Abraham Barzillay.

At the time, the office of chief rabbi of Izmir was shared between Hayyim Benveniste and Aaron Lapapa. During Hanukkah week Benveniste presided over several meetings of the rabbinate, at the first of which he read the letter from the chief rabbi of Istanbul on Sabbatai's excommunication and condemnation. No action was taken concerning Sabbatai, but rumours concerning the hostility of the rabbis towards him enraged his disciples. Leyb ben Ozer writes that 'The believers greatly hated the non-believers.' He goes on to say that, although the Sabbatians were afraid to speak up, they resented the fact that the non-believers would not go with them and visit Sabbatai Sevi, and thus 'hated them with a greater hatred than that of Midian and Moab [referring to the struggles between the ancient Israelites and the people of Midian and Moab], and they would fain have drunk their blood'.

The dispute reached a head on Friday, 11 December 1665, when a group of Sabbatians had a heated argument with Hayyim Pena, a wealthy merchant who supported Hayyim Benveniste in his condemnation of Sabbatai. Pena was forced to flee to his home, which was stoned by the Sabbatians, and bloodshed was averted only when the mob dispersed with the beginning of the Sabbath at sunset.

The subsequent events are described by a number of observers, most notably Samson Bacchi and Thomas Coenen. According to these accounts, on the Sabbath morning Hayyim Pena went as usual to the Portuguese Synagogue, while Sabbatai and his disciples went to another synagogue. Sabbatai had been offended by the remarks that Pena had made to the Sabbatians the previous day, and he sent word to the elders of the Portuguese Synagogue that the 'unbeliever' should be removed from the congregation. The elders refused, whereupon Sabbatai led 500 of his disciples to the Portuguese Synagogue, where, finding the door locked, he took an axe and forced his way in, while Pena escaped through a window. While Sabbatai's supporters took over the synagogue, which thereafter became the centre of Sabbatian activities in Izmir, he himself presided over the services, changing the liturgy in unprecedented ways.

According to Bacchi, Sabbatai interrupted the hymn that the congregation was singing and began to preach a blasphemous sermon, 'continuing with more hymns and prayers until the time for the statutory morning prayer had elapsed. Then he announced, "Today you are exempt from the duty of prayer", after which he took a printed copy of the Pentateuch from his bag, declaring that it was holier than the Torah scroll.' Sabbatai read the Pentateuchal lesson, calling his elder brother Elijah first to continue the reading as if he were a priest and making him king of Turkey, while his second brother Joseph he appointed emperor of Rome. Bacchi goes on to say that Sabbatai 'called none of the many priests and Levites present in the synagogue to the reading of the Torah, but he called many [other] men and even women to whom he distributed kingdoms, and he forced all of them to pronounce the Ineffable Name'.

At the conclusion of the prayers Sabbatai cupped his hands and blew into them to trumpet as if he held a shofar, the ram's horn traditionally blown for the New Year's Festival – doing this, according to Gershom Scholem, 'to confound Satan and to weaken the power of the qelippoth'. He explained his unorthodox behaviour to the congregation, saying that 'It is time to work for the Lord, [therefore] the Law may be transgressed', and telling them that by the breaking down of the doors of the synagogue 'many qelippoth of the evil power had been broken, and this was a profound mystery'. He attacked the chief rabbi and three others who were his principal opponents, likening them to the unclean animals mentioned in the Bible. He said that each of the four non-believers should 'eat his own flesh', meaning that of the animal the sceptic was compared to, likening Benveniste to a camel and the other three in turn to a hare, a pig and a rabbit. Then, according to Coenen, he attacked those in the rabbinate who had in times past opposed Christ, saying, 'What has Jesus done that you ill-treated him thus? I shall see to it that he will be counted among the prophets.' Next he spoke of a certain R. Abraham Zalman, who had been killed in the Chmielnicki massacres

*Harbour at Izmir*, by Thomas Allom, 1838

*Izmir Street Scene*, by Thomas Allom, 1838

Penitential exercises of Sabbatians in Salonika

Athens, 1678

The main shopping street in Corfu, seventeenth century

Ottoman Rhodes

Sabbatai Sevi preaching to his followers

*Rabbi Jacob Sasportas*, by Isaak Luttichuijs, Amsterdam, *c.* 1680-90

*Bazaar of the Coppersmiths in Cairo*, by David Roberts, 1842

*The Port at Constantinople (Istanbul)*, by William Bartlett, 1839

Sultan Mehmet IV (reigned 1648–87)

*Mourners in Jewish Cemetery in Hasköy, Istanbul*, by Preveziozi

A caravan leaving the Damascus Gate, Jerusalem

*Istanbul Synagogue in Jerusalem*, by David Roberts, 1842

Ware afbeeldinge van den genaemde propheet
**Nathan Levi** van *Gaza.*
Vray portraict du dit prophete
**Nathan Levi** de *Gaza.*

Nathan of Gaza, sketched by an anonymous artist in Izmir, 1667

of 1648, and whom Sabbatai said was the Messiah ben Joseph, who had been destined to die in the messianic wars. Sabbatai 'paid him a great honour as he recited for him the prayer for the defunct, and all the people marvelled thereat'.

(Gershom Scholem refers to a 'doubling of the figure of the Messiah, its split into a Messiah of the House of David and one of the House of Joseph'. He goes on to say that 'The Messiah ben Joseph is the dying Messiah who perishes in the messianic catastrophe', while the Messiah ben David is the one 'who once and for all defeats the Antichrist'.)

When Sabbatai finished speaking he went to the Ark and took a Torah scroll in his arms 'like a bridegroom coming out of his chamber, the husband of the beloved Torah'. The Torah was the divine Shekhinah herself, the bride of the Messiah, to whom Sabbatai sang his favourite song, the Castilian romanza 'Meliselda':

> To the mountain I ascended
> To the river I descended
> Meliselda I met there,
> The king's daughter bright and fair.
> There I saw the shining lass
> As she came up from the bath.
> Her arched brow dark as the night
> Her face a gleaming sword of light
> Her lips like corals red and bright,
> Her flesh as milk, so fair and bright.

Sabbatai went on to explain the mystical significance of his song, after which he proclaimed to the congregation that he was the Messiah, the redeemer of Israel, telling them of the course of events that would follow until the ingathering of the Jews in the Holy Land and the resurrection of the dead. Here, in beginning his apocalyptic sermon, Sabbatai followed Nathan's prophecy of the sequence of events – at least according to the report of Sasportas:

In a few days he would take away the kingdom from the Turk [the Sultan], who would become a servant unto tribute, and more such strange things as never came to pass. But the rabble listened to his words as if they were the voice of God, and never considered whether he conformed to the criteria laid down by Isaiah, that is, whether he 'smelled with the fear of the Lord'.

When Sabbatai finished his sermon, Hayyim Benveniste asked him if he could give them a sign to demonstrate his messianic mission. This infuriated Sabbatai, who said that he would excommunicate Benveniste until he begged to be forgiven, threatening once more to feed him on the flesh of his fellow camels. He then called on several in the congregation to demonstrate their faith in him by speaking the Ineffable Name.

This led Benveniste to have a sudden change of heart, and the following day he became a disciple of Sabbatai, proclaiming, 'Brethren, he is the true Messiah; he and no other!' According to Leyb ben Ozer, Benveniste, probably motivated by fear of Sabbatai's new power, said to his friends, 'Know ye that I have long been mistaken, but now I confess that I have sinned.' Sabbatai immediately accepted Benveniste into the fold and praised his virtues, explaining his own change of attitude by saying that 'he bestoweth loving kindness upon a man in accordance with his works'.

Sabbatai's power was such that he was able to force the council of rabbis to make a new arrangement for the office of chief rabbi, which had been shared by Hayyim Benveniste and Aaron Lapapa since the death of Joseph Eskapha. Dominated by Sabbatai, the council dismissed Lapapa and gave Benveniste undivided authority. An anonymous responsum from Izmir describes how Sabbatai, acting as if he were a king, issued

a royal proclamation that everybody should repair to the Portuguese Synagogue to kiss the hands of the chief rabbi . . . They that thirsted for the salvation of the Lord sped thither with haste, but even the unbelievers went . . . and kissed Rabbi Benveniste's hand, for fear of the punishment which the rabble would wreak on those who rebelled against the Lord's anointed.

According to the responsum, Lapapa was ostracized and forced to hide in terror in his house. 'And from this day on R. Aaron Lapapa, may the Lord preserve him, lived ostracized and retired in a corner of his house and dared not go out, not even to the synagogue, because people would insult, revile, and abuse him for being an infidel. But he heard his reproach and made no answer.'

Samson Bacchi's version of the story tells how Sabbatai celebrated his triumph on the following Monday, when 'there was a great rejoicing as the Scroll of the Law was taken from the Ark, and he sang all kinds of songs – also Christian songs in the vernacular – saying there was a mystery in these impure songs. He also declared that "This day is my Sabbath day."' That night Sabbatai held a banquet at which all his followers lined up to kiss his feet as he distributed money and candles; Jews and Gentiles alike were all forced to utter the Ineffable Name. 'Even the Turks were talking about the affair, though no miracle was ever seen, not even a natural sign. But many unlettered men and women experienced all manner of convulsion and prophesied – though none of their prophecies ever came true – and exclaimed, "Sabbatai Sevi is the king of Israel!" and the like.'

According to Baruch of Arezzo, the first to prophesy in Izmir were the two emissaries from Jerusalem and Aleppo, Moses Galanté and Daniel Pinto. He also says that one of the first prophetesses to emerge in the city was Sarah Sevi, whose 'divinely inspired' declaration that her husband was the Messiah-king led other women to make similar prophecies.

Leyb ben Ozer writes of how the daughters of the unfortunate Hayyim Pena emerged as prophetesses. It seems that the two girls were wearing black clothes in mourning for their deceased mother. When Sabbatai noticed this he told Pena that his daughters should remove their mourning costume and dress in their best clothes. Pena, who 'made peace with Sabbatai Sevi and believed in him because of his fear', told his daughters to obey the command of the Messiah. As soon as they did so they began prophesying, as Pena discovered one day when he came home and found a crowd gathered around his house. He asked the crowd why they were there, and was told that it was because his daughters were uttering prophecies. When Pena went inside, 'he saw that his daughters were shaking and having convulsions and speaking great things. They said that they saw the sage, Sabbatai Sevi, seated upon a throne in Heaven and the crown of kingship upon his head, and many other things. And when they had finished their words, they called out several times in succession: "Crown, crown."'

Sabbatai's unprecedented act of calling women to read the Torah may have been due to the influence of his wife, Sarah, as some have suggested, but it was more likely a result of his general revolutionary desire to overthrow all the established laws of religion and human behaviour as part of the new and final order resulting from his emergence as the Messiah. Coenen suggested that Sabbatai's calling of women to read the Torah was due to his desire to win them over to his cause. One of Sabbatai's addresses quoted by Coenen is nothing less than a promise that, as the Messiah, he had come to liberate women from their ancient bondage: 'Woe unto you, miserable women, who for Eve's sin must bring forth your children in sorrow, and are subject to your husbands, and all that you do depends on their consent. Blessed are you, for I have come to make you free and happy like your husbands; for I have come to take away Adam's sin.'

After his return to Izmir, Sabbatai deliberately flouted the traditional patterns of social relations between the sexes. While visiting the homes of old friends he met both of the wives he had divorced and sat with them in familiar conversation. Sources in Italy report that he hosted a banquet in which men and women among his followers danced together, while he himself took his first wife into another room and remained there alone with her. This incident led Emanuel Frances to write one of his satirical anti-Sabbatian poems:

> Is he the Lord's anointed or a traitor,
> A wicked sinner and a fornicator?
> In public he the Sabbath desecrates
> And of the synagogue he breaks the gates.
> To pronounce the Name Ineffable he dares,
> And with profanity he impiously swears.
> Forbidden women he embraces;
> At first the one, and then the other he caresses.
> The foolish people, gaping as spellbound,
> Affirm: This is a mystery profound.

Sabbatai's wife, Sarah, also gave occasion for scandal at this time, when she seduced, or tried to seduce, a doctor's son. According to Moses ben Habib, a rabid anti-Sabbatian, Sabbatai himself persuaded the doctor's son to enter Sarah's room, but the youth apparently fled when she approached him. This led Sabbatai to complain of the doctor's son that, 'if he had done her will, he would have performed a great *tiqqun*'.

Other stories of Sabbatai's deliberate violation of sexual taboos probably refer to incidents later in his career, extrapolated back in time to his stay in Izmir at the end of 1665. One such story that may actually date from late 1665 is told by Sasportas, who says that while Sabbatai was in Izmir 'three virgins were delivered into his hands. He kept them for several days and then returned them, without having touched them.'

On the Tuesday after his seizure of the Portuguese Synagogue, which was the Seventh of Tebet, Sabbatai startled all his disciples by the announcement of a revelation that had come simultaneously to him and to his wife. He said that his marriage with Sarah had not yet been consummated, and that their sexual union was required in order to fulfil the messianic prophecy. Sabbatai and Sarah duly consummated their marriage that night – or so they said – and on the following morning he exhibited their blood-stained bedsheets to his cheering supporters. This bizarre episode is reported by Leyb ben Ozer. Apparently Sabbatai announced that the Holy Spirit had revealed that he should have intercourse with Sarah, whom he had not touched till then, as had been the case with his first two wives. Sarah also said that it had been revealed to her that 'she must cleave to her husband, and so that is what they did on the Seventh of Tebet, in the five thousand and four hundred and twenty-sixth year of creation [1665]. And on the next day she showed the evidence of her virginity as is the bride's custom, which stirred great rejoicing among the Jews of Izmir who believed in him.'

Leyb ben Ozer goes on to describe Sabbatai's subsequent triumphal procession to one of the synagogues in Izmir. The procession was led by an acolyte carrying a great silver bowl filled with fragrant spices, followed by two others, each holding a vase of roses and other flowers in water, and behind them a 'sage carrying a comb in its sheath'. Then

Sabbatai Sevi was seen, striding between two sages, carrying the large fan plated with silver which he had with him always and with which he would on occasion touch the head of whomever he wished to honour. And thus he walked to the synagogue and hundreds of people walked in his train to honour him, and more came out singing psalms that were only sung on the holy Sabbath day.

After leading prayers in the synagogue, Sabbatai ordered that the Ineffable Name be spoken, which disturbed many of those present though they did not dare to object. At the conclusion of the prayers Sabbatai led the congregation in making donations to the poor, as Leyb ben Ozer writes at the conclusion of his account. 'A great sum of money was collected for no one wished to hold back, on account of the honour of Sabbatai Sevi, even though there were those who gave against their will. And when he came forth from the synagogue hundreds ran after him and kissed his hands – young and old, boys and elders, women and men – to pay him honour.'

That same day, according to Coenen, Sabbatai also announced in the synagogue that Sarah had conceived a son, whose life was fated to be short. It has been suggested the whole incident was staged to disguise both Sabbatai's impotence and Sarah's harlotry, but in point of fact she did bear a son early in October 1666, and the boy died in adolescence, fulfilling the prophecy.

Events were now happening so rapidly that the chronology of contemporary sources is somewhat confused. One dramatic event that probably occurred within a week of Sabbatai's dramatic takeover of the Portuguese Synagogue was his visit to the cadi, the chief judge of Izmir. Sabbatai had probably been called before the court because of complaints that the cadi had received from non-believers. According to Coenen, the cadi believed that Sabbatai was a fool or a madman, and so he let him go, having in any event been bribed by both believers and non-believers. Sabbatai had been accompanied to the court by a large crowd of his followers, to whom he repeatedly sang Psalm 118:16 – 'The right hand of the

Lord is exalted; the Right Hand of the Lord doeth valiantly' – repeating it triumphantly when he emerged free after his appearance before the cadi.

This appearance before the cadi gave rise to a number of legends, one of which was reported by Coenen. Apparently, when Sabbatai entered the court and began to speak, a jet of flame emerged from his mouth and singed the cadi's beard. A pillar of fire then sprang up between Sabbatai and the cadi, who cried out in terror, 'Take him away from here, for fear and trembling have fallen upon me. This is no flesh and blood, but an angel of God.'

Rycaut tells how Sabbatai attracted more and more disciples after he took control of the Jewish community in Izmir:

No invitation was now made in *Smyrna* by the Jews, nor Marriage, or Circumcision held, where *Sabatai* was not present, accompanied to the solemnities with multitudes of his Followers, and the streets covered with Carpets or fine Cloth for him to tread on; but the humility of this Pharisee appeared such, that he would stoop and turn them aside, and so pass.

Rycaut goes on to describe how Sabbatai, 'having thus fixed himself in the opinion and admiration of the people', and taking 'on himself the Title of Messiah and the Son of God', rewarded his leading disciples with royal titles: '*Sabatai Sevi* growing more presumptuous, that he might correspond with the Prophecies of Greatness and Dominion of the Messiah, proceeded to Election of those Princes which were to govern the Israelites in their March towards the Holy Land, and to dispense Judgment and Justice after their Restauration.'

Sabbatai rewarded some of his disciples by appointing them to rule the present kingdoms of the earth, while others he recognized as reincarnations of the ancient kings of Israel and Judah. Sabbatai had already ennobled his brothers, as has been noted, having appointed Elijah king of Turkey and Joseph emperor of Rome. Now he gave them the most important biblical titles as well, appointing Elijah to rule over all the kings of Israel, and Joseph over the kings of Judah. Some of the newly appointed kings asked for and received letters from Sabbatai confirming their titles; these were so highly valued that one of the Sabbatian royalty, a pious beggar who thenceforth was known as 'King Rubio', refused to sell his kingdom even when offered a large sum of money. According to Coenen, the titles were taken seriously by the believers in Izmir, and the new rulers were addressed with their royal titles, so that, for example, Isaac Silveira was thenceforth known as 'King David' and Abraham Yakhini as 'King Solomon'. According to Sasportas, who writes that Sabbatai also made Yakhini ruler of Constantinople as well as giving him prophetic powers, 'It is said that the Master laid his hand on him and thereby put upon him his spirit of prophecy. Thereupon something resembling a brilliant star grew on his forehead – and it seems to me it was the planet Saturn – and it is said that he too then prophesied concerning the new kingdom, and confirmed it.'

Several other sources record that a prominent Jewish physician was made king of Portugal, though he cannot be identified by name. A French source notes that this king was a Portuguese Marrano who had long been a resident of Bordeaux, going on to say that 'Many of his relatives are still there, attempting to conceal their Jewish religion; and he firmly believed that he would soon be ruling over Portugal, because the Messiah promised it to him when he made him king, shortly before leaving Smyrna.'

Sabbatai's next act of messianic drama was staged on Friday 18 December 1665, the Tenth of Tebet, one of the fast days commemorating the destruction of the Temple. Sasportas reports that Sabbatai abolished this fast too, proclaiming that all such mournful occasions were to be discontinued, and 'the sorrow of the fast turned into the rejoicing of gladness'. This outraged the few non-believers who still held out against the rising Sabbatian tide in Izmir, most notably the rabbi Solomon Algazi, who, along with several of his associates, refused to break the fast. Sabbatai's followers attacked the 'infidels' and almost lynched them, forcing Algazi and two other rabbis to flee from Izmir, while the others saved themselves by breaking the fast and joining the Sabbatians.

On Saturday 19 December Sabbatai publicly apologized for his behaviour in the Portuguese Synagogue a week earlier, proclaiming a general fast to atone for 'the desecration of the last Sabbath'. But then early in the afternoon, according to Emanuel Frances, he changed his mind and bade all his followers to break the fast, since God had forgiven them.

Coenen reports that on that Sabbath some of the synagogues in Izmir were decorated with a flower-bedecked coronet identified as 'The Crown of Sabbatai Sevi'. He also notes that a revolutionary change was made in the customary prayer for the ruler of the land, in which the name of the Ottoman sultan was replaced by that of Sabbatai Sevi, referred to as 'Our Messiah, the Anointed of the God of Joseph, the Celestial Lion and Celestial Stag, the Messiah of Righteousness, the King of kings, the sultan Sabbatai Sevi. May the supreme King of kings exalt his star and his kingdom, and inspire the hearts of rulers and princes with goodwill toward him and us and all Israel, and let us say, Amen.'

The period of illumination that Sabbatai experienced after his return to Izmir lasted for only about two weeks, through the middle of December 1665, after which his manic pace slowed down as he lapsed into the lethargy and depression that came upon him in his dark state. It was time to move on to Istanbul, the Ottoman capital, and so Sabbatai booked passage on a small caique with three or four rabbis who bore the title of King, including Moses Galanté, Daniel Pinto and a rabbi from Poland named Elijah, leaving Sarah to make the trip overland at a later date with his other followers. Sabbatai's sudden departure may have been precipitated by the Turkish authorities in Izmir, who, according to a Dutch source, had given him three days to leave the city.

Sabbatai set sail from Izmir with his companions on 30 December 1665, and was fated never to return to his native city. Twice he had left as an obscure exile, while now he departed in triumph as the Messiah, about to come into his kingdom.

Baruch of Arezzo reports that on the Fourth of Sebat, January 1666, while Sabbatai was en route to Istanbul, Abraham ben Jacob Jessurun, an otherwise unknown Sabbatian, issued a lengthy prophecy in Izmir, beginning with a statement that the Messiah-king had at last appeared:

Lord I have heard thy speech. The Lord reigneth, the Lord has reigned, the Lord shall reign for ever more. Hear, O Israel, the Lord our God, the Lord is one. Blessed be his name, whose glorious kingdom is for evermore. Our king Sabbatai Sevi has been crowned with the crown . . . The king Sabbatai Sevi sitteth on the throne of his kingdom.

# 10. Apocalypse Nigh

By the time that Sabbatai Sevi left Izmir, in the last days of 1665, his movement had already taken wing, as letters and rumours spread throughout the dispersed Jewish world that the long-awaited Messiah had finally arrived to lead the Jews back to the Land of Israel and their redemption.

Leyb ben Ozer writes of how this news led Sabbatai's followers to prepare themselves for salvation through repentance: 'The prophet Nathan prophesied and Sabbatai Sevi preached that whoever did not mend his ways would not behold the comforting of Zion and Jerusalem, and that they would be condemned to shame and to everlasting contempt. And there was a repentance, the like of which has never been since the world was created and unto this day.'

According to Leyb ben Ozer, Sabbatai's followers fasted throughout the week, rising after a few hours' sleep to recite the midnight devotions and then at dawn immersing themselves in a ritual bath while they confessed their sins. During the winter some of them would do their ritual immersions by rolling naked in the snow, after which they scourged themselves with thorns and nettles.

Leyb ben Ozer writes that many of the Sabbatians divested themselves of their worldly goods in preparation for the coming journey to the Holy Land and eternal salvation. 'They sold their houses or property for almost nothing, for they firmly believed that they would soon go to Palestine and therefore sold everything at half price, so as to leave nothing behind.' He notes that 'There were wealthy youths who married poor orphan girls without dowry for the sake of heaven. No young man wanted to remain a bachelor, and each one married the first and best woman he could find.'

Differences of wealth no longer mattered, says ben Ozer: 'There was no distinction between rich and poor . . . and nobody was really poor because people wanted nothing but their immediate needs, and those who had nothing received their wants from those who had.'

He also notes that all business and trade came to a halt among the Sabbatians:

No Jew attended to business. The shops were closed, and the artisans plied penance and fasts instead of their trade. People tried to sell their goods and belongings at any price they could get, and kept themselves in readiness for the moment when the Messiah and the prophet Elijah would appear and announce the end, so as to proceed without delay.

Leyb ben Ozer concludes by remarking that this mass repentance was far more pronounced in Ottoman lands than in Christendom: 'But in Turkey they did ten times more, because they were especially exhorted to repent and they beheld miracles with their own eyes, where in these countries we received this news by letters only.'

Reports from all over the Ottoman Empire tell much the same story: that the followers of Sabbatai Sevi had stopped all their customary activities to devote themselves to prayer and penance. A letter from Egypt written late in 1665, undoubtedly reporting on conditions in Gaza, said that the King – i.e. Sabbatai – was about to depart for Istanbul, where he would be crowned by the Sultan himself, according to the prophet Nathan. The writer said that the Ottoman pashas of Jerusalem had kissed the hands of the prophet Nathan, 'and the Confluence of People from all sides (both Jews, Turks, and Christians) is so great, and the Vertues which are seen among them are so eminent, that all Neighbouring Nations do tremble at it'. He goes on to say that all those assembling were

plying nothing but Devotion, Penitence and Almsgiving; abstaining not only from all Vanity, but from Merchandizing and Trading; and especially from Exchange (which Nathan terms to be meer Usury) yea, such largeness of heart there is among them at Jerusalem: that for One penny, may now be bought what was wont to cost Tenpence.

A letter from Alexandria, written on 24 September 1665 by Joseph Azobib to his friend Moses Tardiola, reports that Nathan of

Gaza has proclaimed that Sabbatai Sevi is the Messiah and will rebuild the Temple in Jerusalem 'in five years' time'. Azobib remarks that 'even if I wrote to you for two weeks, day and night, I could not report a thousandth part of the new things continually revealed by the prophet, all uttering speech concerning our redemption'. In Alexandria there is 'a great repentance such has never been before, for over a third of the community have put on sackcloth'. Azobib goes on to urge his friend to spread the Sabbatian message in Tripolitania, where Tardiola was then travelling on behalf of the community in Jerusalem.

One of those who heard the message in Tripolitania at the time was Abraham Miguel Cardozo, who would become one of the great prophets and theologians of the Sabbatian movement, rivalling and eventually succeeding Nathan of Gaza as its leading spirit.

Cardozo was born in 1627 of a Portuguese Marrano family and grew up in Madrid under the care of his much older brother Isaac, going on to the medical school at the University of Salamanca, where he also studied Christian theology for two years. At the age of twenty-one he set out with his brother Isaac, first to Venice and then to Livorno, where both of them returned to the Jewish faith of their ancestors. Abraham Cardozo resumed his medical studies, probably at Padua, and continued to practise medicine for the rest of his long life. At the same time he studied the Hebrew language and literature with great diligence, 'sitting in the tent of the Torah', as he put it, also immersing himself in the 'hidden wisdom' of Lurianic Kabbalah. His studies took him so deeply into the Kabbalah that he began to have visions, in the first of which, in 1658, Isaac Luria actually appeared to him, he claimed. He also began to utter prophesies that the end of the world was approaching and that the Messiah would soon appear.

Cardozo spent five years in Cairo, where he may have met Sabbatai in the circle of Raphael Joseph Chelebi. He then went on to Tripolitania, where in 1664 he became personal physician to Osman Pasha, the bey of Tripoli. His first letters from Tripoli state that he had a vision there in which it was revealed to him that the Messiah would appear the following year. When news came that Nathan of Gaza had announced that Sabbatai Sevi was the Messiah,

Cardozo became an enthusiastic supporter of the Sabbatian movement. As he wrote to his brother Isaac at the time, 'I believe with perfect faith, without any hesitation or doubt, that the true Messiah is Sabbatai Sevi, may his majesty be exalted.' Cardozo declared that Sabbatai was the Messiah of the House of David, while he himself was the Messiah of the House of Joseph. Thus he was the revealer of the true faith and the object of persecution by the rabbis, who must precede the final appearance of Sabbatai (at least according to Cardozo's interpretation of ancient prophecies). Writing to his brother, Cardozo said that it was good that there was opposition to the Sabbatian movement from rabbinic leaders, because if doubt was cast upon Sabbatai's claim to be the Messiah then those who believed in him would do so as an act of pure faith.

A letter received in Amsterdam early in 1666 by the teacher Jacob Taussig notes that 'Our brethren from Safed wrote . . . that we should prepare ourselves to offer the statutory sacrifices [in the rebuilt Temple] still in this year.' Other letters from Safed talk of a new Sabbatian prayer book composed by Nathan of Gaza, in one edition of which the Amsterdam rabbi Solomon Oliveira added this sentence in the introduction: 'And now behold a new thing has come to us from Safed, and I gave myself no rest until I laid it before you.'

The disciples in Safed included the eminent Kabbalist Benjamin ha-Levi, who had been one of the first editors of Hayyim Vital. According to Baruch of Arezzo, Benjamin and his son Solomon wrote in 1666 to their friends in Mantua 'at great length concerning our redemption by our king Sabbatai Sevi'.

Baruch also writes of the prophets who emerged among the believers, and the manner in which they gave their prophecies. He says that at first they went into a deep sleep, after which they fell to the ground as if dead. After about half an hour, although their lips did not move, a voice would sound from their mouth uttering verses of praise and consolation, and all would say 'Sabbatai Sevi, the anointed of the God of Jacob'. When it was over 'they would arise without remembering what they had done or said. In Smyrna more than a hundred and fifty prophets prophesied.'

The enthusiasm among the believers in Istanbul on the eve of

Sabbatai's arrival is described in a work entitled *Relation de la veritable Imposture du faux Messie des Juifs, nommé Sabbatay Sevi*, written in 1667 by a Catholic clergyman who may have been Jacob Becherand. The author of this work reports that the believers, who expected the Messiah to overthrow the Sultan, awaited Sabbatai's arrival with 'transports of joy such as one can never understand unless one has seen it . . . All their conversation turned on the war and the imminent establishment of the kingdom of Israel, on the fall of the Crescent and of all the royal crowns in Christendom.' The war referred to here is the conflict between Venice and the Turks over Crete, which was now approaching its climax – a struggle that many interpreted as the prelude to the apocalyptic emergence of the messianic kingdom.

The Sabbatian movement had taken root in Italy by the end of 1665, as evidenced by the fact that newborn Jewish boys in Siena were given the name 'Sabbatai' as early as December of that year, 'for in all the provinces of Israel reports were heard regarding imminent redemption by the rabbi Sabbatai Sevi', as noted a mohel, or circumciser, in a northern Italian town. The mohel made this note in a copybook listing the boys whom he had circumcised at this time, beginning 'in the first year of the coming of our Messiah'.

By then the movement had also reached Venice, where a Jewish traveller from the Veneto notes that his fellow Sabbatians were active, so that 'the sinners and many illiterates who could not even read the *Shema* prayer [a passage from Deuteronomy 6:4–9] . . . and the bastards are diligently studying with three rabbis who teach them without payment'.

This same traveller wrote to his family from Casale Monferrato on 16 February 1666, telling them, among other tidings of the Sabbatian movement, that believers from as far away as Frankfurt were making preparations to go to the Holy Land:

I pray you to announce to the whole holy congregation that they should settle all their affairs as soon as possible. Let this hint suffice that they should cease from all trade, since there is hope that our redemption may come sooner than we expected. Four hundred families are waiting in

Frankfurt, all ready for the journey, and many others of the same neighbourhood have already left.

The writer goes on to say that the good news had arrived only the night before, and 'caused such a great excitement that many wept for excess of joy. Immediately all copies of the roles of the comedy which they intended to perform were torn up, since this is not a time for vanities but for the study of the Law and good works. New devotions will be introduced today, and I shall send you a copy of it for the Sabbath.' He concludes by saying that further reports were expected, and that he would pass them on before he departed, though he was sorry to leave at such a time. 'I regret that I have to leave here, because I believe that great things will happen in this congregation. Everyone must seek the welfare of his fellow man if we want to share in this blessedness. Nobody here enters any claims against anyone, but the most important thing is to restore all dishonest gain.'

The admonition to restore all dishonest gain does not appear to have been heeded, at least by the believers in Italy. Baruch of Arezzo notes that 'throughout Italy not one case has been reported of a man saying to his fellow: here are a hundred *scudi* which I dishonestly took from you'.

A number of prominent rabbis held back from the general conversion to Sabbatianism. Joseph ha-Levi, the leading rabbi of Livorno, preached to his congregation that true penance did not require mortification of the flesh, and tried to prevent them from being led astray by the prophet of the new Messiah. As he wrote in a letter to Sasportas, 'As many were led astray in these parts and commanded me to preach about the ways of repentance, I spoke out in public . . . and exhorted them to perfect repentance.' He told them that they were 'wrong in thinking that repentance was a matter of fasting and penitential devotions, when it really meant giving back that which they had dishonestly taken from their fellow men, to do away with all hatred among themselves, to abstain from Gentile wine and from shaving off the sidelocks and from associating with strange and pagan women and the like'. This displeased most of the people – especially the matter of returning ill-gotten gains, for there was a widespread belief that those who simply believed were assured of salvation. As ha-Levi remarked to Sasportas, it was said that the prophet Nathan 'had written that an unbeliever, though he had the Torah and good works, could not be saved . . . This heresy was believed by everybody as if it were the Law of Moses. And I openly preached against it and said that lack of faith did not matter, and that the main thing was the Torah and good works.'

By the end of 1665 news of the Sabbatian movement had reached London, where it particularly attracted the attention of Henry Oldenburg, a native of Bremen who had become secretary of the Royal Society. Early in December 1665 Oldenburg wrote to his friend Baruch Spinoza about the new messianic movement. He remarked that 'there is a rumour everywhere concerning the return of the Jews, who have been dispersed for more than two thousand years, to their native country. Only a few here believe in this, yet there are many hoping for it.' He asked Spinoza whether he too had heard news of this movement, which he himself could not credit unless it was confirmed by reliable sources in Istanbul. 'May it please you to communicate to a friend what you have heard regarding this matter, and what you think of it. As for me, I cannot believe this report until it is confirmed by reliable people from the city of Constantinople, which it touches most of all. If the tidings prove to be true, it is sure to bring about an upheaval of everything in the world.'

Spinoza's reply to Oldenburg is lost, but his opinion concerning the restoration of the Jews in Israel is recorded in one of his letters: 'I am inclined to believe that, with the opportunity afforded, since human affairs are notoriously changeable, they may again recover their kingdom, and God elect them to Himself anew.'

Oldenburg's letters to friends show that he kept himself informed about the new messianic movement. His correspondents in this matter included some of the leading figures in the seventeenth-century scientific movement, most notably Robert Boyle and Johannes Hevelius. Oldenburg also corresponded with Isaac Newton, but their published letters deal only with scientific matters. Newton had a deep interest in religion, but most of his voluminous writings in that area have not been published, though one suspects that he would have had something interesting to say about a new Messiah who was being talked about with such excitement even in London.

The modern Jewish community of London had come into existence only in 1656, after Oliver Cromwell had called a conference to establish that there was no legal bar to their return. The spokesman for the Jews who hoped to enter England had been Menasseh ben Israel, a rabbi from Amsterdam, who in 1655 had sent a '*Humble Address*' to Cromwell. Aside from explaining the advantages to England of allowing entry to the Jews, Menasseh ben Israel pointed out why it was necessary for the Jewish people themselves: 'our nation at the present is spread all about . . . in the most flourishing parts of all the kingdoms, and countries of the world . . . except only in this considerable and mighty island. And therefore this remains only in my judgement, before the Messiah come and restore our nation, that first we must have our seat here likewise.'

The lord mayor and Corporation of the City of London tried to have the Jews expelled in 1664, and twice again in the next two decades. The Jewish community asked for and received protection from Charles II, who agreed to be 'their advocate and assist them with all his power'. Jacob Sasportas, rabbi of the Sephardic community in London, looked upon this as 'a time when God has seen fit greatly to ameliorate the condition of His people, bringing them forth from the general condition of serfdom into freedom . . . in that we are now free to practise our own true religion'.

Sasportas was born in Morocco in about 1610 and was ordained a rabbi there, serving in turn the communities in Salé and Tlemcen. He was forced to leave North Africa in 1647 and took refuge in Amsterdam, where he lived for seventeen years. During that time he taught in the local yeshiva and wrote a Kabbalistic commentary on a prayer book by Moses Albaz, a Moroccan scholar. Then in 1664 he left Amsterdam to accept an offer from the Sephardic community in London to be their rabbi. He remained in London for only a year, fleeing to Hamburg with his family in the autumn of 1665 to avoid the Great Plague. He arrived in Hamburg on 7 November, but had to remain in quarantine for six weeks, during which time the first letters arrived in the city with news of the

Sabbatian movement. The elders of the community were convinced that the Messiah had appeared, and on 9 December they recorded a resolution to that effect. They praised God 'for the news that came from the East, and from Italy, and from other countries, to the effect that He in His grace has given us a prophet in the Holy Land, the rabbi Nathan Ashkenazi, and a messianic king, the rabbi Sabbatai Sevi, whom the Lord has chosen to deliver His people from the nations and to exalt His Name that is profaned among the Gentiles'. Their resolution noted that they believed the messianic reports 'on account of the many signs and miracles performed, according to the letters, by the Prophet and the King', and that they had 'sung today the Festival Psalms as on the Festival of the Rejoicing of the Law. May it be the will of the God of Israel that this news be confirmed and that we will be granted the inheritance of our land. May it be the divine will that our eyes shall behold this great salvation.'

Sasportas read that Nathan had proclaimed that Sabbatai was the Messiah, and he immediately tried to verify the authenticity of the prophet. When his friends in Amsterdam questioned his doubts as being inconsistent for a Kabbalist, he wrote back to explain his hesitation: 'I never claimed it [i.e. Nathan's prophecy that Sabbatai was the Messiah] to be impossible as such, for it is indeed possible that the rabbi Sabbatai Sevi will be our king and saviour. If the prophecy is duly authenticated, I shall accept as true whatever a duly confirmed prophet says.'

Early in 1666 further news of the new Messiah came to Hamburg, and the growing number of believers there rejoiced as even the Gentiles came to the synagogue to watch the Sabbatians playing music and dancing with the Torah in their arms. According to Sasportas, those who did not believe were insulted 'and called infidels, so that my hand waxed feeble and I could not speak out, for so few followed me that a child might write them. Even they dared not speak loudly, but only in secret . . . and many a time they [the Sabbatians] wanted to excommunicate the unbelievers.'

Sasportas was forced to give a sermon on redemption, in which he was so cautious and ambiguous that the Sabbatians complained that he seemed to doubt that the Messiah had appeared, while others wrote to Amsterdam to say that he had spoken in praise of Sabbatai and Nathan.

The excitement of the believers in Hamburg reached such a peak that on 25 February 1666 they resolved to send a delegation to Istanbul 'to prostrate themselves, as is fitting, before our king Sabbatai Sevi'. But the elders had second thoughts and decided to delay the pilgrimage 'on account of the harm that might result for our envoys on the way, from the letters they were carrying, and that might result therefrom for the other congregations of our brethren in Germany; and also because it was estimated that the journey from here to Constantinople will take about three months'. As they conclude, 'Now we hope and hold it for certain that Our King will be in Palestine before the end of that period, and to follow him and then bring us his reply, this would take more than a year. Therefore we consider this voyage and the expenses connected with it superfluous.'

The elders also resolved to offer up for sale all the real estate owned by the congregation, in order to pay all their debts 'and to prepare ourselves for the journey which we soon hope to make with God's help'.

Early in February 1666 the Ashkenazi rabbi of Altona, near Hamburg, had received a letter from Gaza which quoted the testimonies of Abraham Gedaliah and other respected rabbis of Gaza confirming the authenticity of Nathan as the prophet of the Messiah. This so impressed Sasportas that for a time he became a believer. He wrote to his friend Isaac Nahar in Amsterdam on 9 February to confess that he had changed his mind and to apologize for his hesitation in believing that Sabbatai was the Messiah. However, subsequent letters from Izmir revealed that some of the rabbis there were doubtful about the messianic claims of Nathan and Sabbatai, and this quickly led Sasportas to revert to his original position, so that by mid-March he had become an outspoken opponent of the Sabbatian movement. This caused him to edit the records of his earlier correspondence concerning the messianic movement – for example, the record of his letter of 9 February to Isaac Nahar was changed to make it appear as if Sasportas was denouncing Sabbatai as an impostor.

Meanwhile the Sabbatians had taken control of the Hamburg synagogue, and in March the name of Sabbatai Sevi was substituted for that of the monarch in the traditional prayer for the well-being of the ruler of the land. Sasportas was too careful to object to this publicly as yet, but in his writings he describes how the aged David Kohen de Lara, the former rabbi of the congregation, showed his contempt for the Sabbatians by walking out of the synagogue whenever the prayer for King Sabbatai was read. This led the believers to stop Kohen from leaving the synagogue, and one of them, an eminent physician, insulted the old rabbi and had to be restrained from assaulting him.

And so for the time being Sasportas remained quiet, in fear of being abused by the believers as an infidel. Late in May he wrote to his friend Raphael Supino repudiating Nathan and Sabbatai, but his fear of the Sabbatians made him delay posting the letter for more than three months, explaining that 'they believe so firmly that I postponed dispatching the letter, lest [its contents be known] and the mob lay their hands upon me'.

Meanwhile the Sabbatian movement was spreading throughout Europe. Its progress in eastern Europe is described by a Greek Catholic priest, the archimandrite Johannes Galatowski: 'Not long ago, in 1666, the Jewish heresy raised its head in Volhynia, Podolia [Podilska, in Ukraine], in all the provinces of Little Russia, in the Duchy of Lithuania, in the kingdom of Poland and the neighbouring countries . . . At that time an impostor called Sabbatai Sevi appeared in Smyrna, who called himself the Messiah of the Jews and drew them to his side by false miracles.'

Galatowski goes on to describe the fervour and penitential excesses of the Sabbatians, who by his testimony also included some Christians:

At that time they fasted several days in the week because of the Messiah, and some fasted the whole week. They gave no food even to their little children, and they immersed themselves in winter under the ice while reciting recently invented prayers. Many Jews died during the winter because of their immersions in the severe cold . . . Even some fools among the Christians acted and thought like them.

The excitement of the eastern-European believers led them to carry pictures of Nathan and Sabbatai Sevi in public processions, as well as to distribute pamphlets about their messianic movement. The Catholic bishop of Przemysl, Stanislaw Sarnicky, wrote in a pastoral letter on 22 June 1666 that the Jews were 'carrying in public processions in the streets some printed pamphlets that offend against [the Christian] religion, as well as pictures of their vanities'. This public display had so enraged the Christians that mobs of them attacked the Jews in Pinsk, Vilna and Lublin early in the spring of 1666. This violence led the King of Poland, John II Casimer, to issue an edict on 6 May, forbidding the Jews to carry pictures of their supposed Messiah. The edict notes that

villainous persons who are contriving schemes and plotting to destroy the Jews in this state have – with the intention to plunder – launched rumours alleging that the high courts of the kingdom have given permission to all to harry the Jews and to destroy them. As a result there have been riots, oppressions, plundering and bloodshed in several places, as is known to all.

It goes on to say that the Jews 'have also waxed insolent' and are spreading a false report about a supposed Messiah through printed pamphlets and pictures. 'In some places where Jews are dwelling . . . the results of this folly are already visible, and even greater trouble is approaching, which threatens to bring affliction and distress upon those Jews, since under the pretext of these forgeries there will be occasion to plunder the belongings and the property of the Jews.'

An unknown prophet arose in Sana'a, the capital of the Yemen, where the anonymous manuscript entitled *Gey Hizzayon* appeared in 1666. The first lines of this work tell of the new messianic spirit: 'Verily there is a spirit in Israel, and the breath of the Almighty awakens them, the sparks of prophecy are beginning in the children who prophesied regarding the messianic king . . . It is an acceptable time to pray for divine mercy.'

The Sabbatian movement in the Yemen found its poet in Shalom Shabbazi, whose lyrical verses sing of how word of the Messiah's emergence had 'winged its way like an eagle' from Egypt to the Yemen. Like other Yemeni poets, Shabbazi wrote in both Hebrew and Arabic, often moving from one language to the other in alternate lines. He writes thus in addressing his Muse, who at the same time is the congregation of Israel and the Torah:

Strengthen and arouse my spirit when I write and create poems. Satisfy and refresh the flower of my garden. Accept, thou lovely-eyed, the poor and helpless one with grace and love. Let the end, the redemption, arrive speedily. Let us hear the glorious tidings. Come is the Messiah, accompanied by Elijah! Let the cry resound. Ascend to Zion with a song of joy!

The Yemenite Jews sold all their goods and land and stopped whatever work they were doing, so as to prepare for their journey to the Holy Land. This alarmed the Arabs and led their religious leader, the imam Ismail al-Mutawakkil, to publish a decree punishing the Jews for their unlawful behaviour. The imam forced the men to go about in public without their turbans, so as to shame them, and restricted their celebration of the coming Passover festival, in which he

forbade all meat but that which was roasted and wine even on the nights of the festival. He ordered the women to shave their heads and the men to cease from sexual intercourse; required all to eat their food humbly, without salt and upon the earth . . . , not to wear their customary garments of black wool, and to go and pray, to cover their faces and other things.

Nevertheless the Yemenite Jews continued their preparations to leave for the Land of Israel, following their leader, the rabbi Süleyman al-Aqt'a. But Süleyman was executed by the local Arab ruler, Prince Ali, who hung the rabbi's body from one of the watchtowers outside the main gate of the city, allowing the Jews to remove the corpse for burial only after its stench became unbearable. The incident is recorded in the *Chronicle* of Ahmad ibn Nasr al-Zayidi, who conveys the power of this messianic movement in the story's last lines: 'The Jews were filled with great joy and gathered en masse to bring him down and bury him. Every Jew who managed to touch the man and take part in carrying him was filled with unparalleled happiness; the Jews buried him in their own cemetery.'

A colophon in a Yemenite prayer book for 1670 notes 'the year of glad tidings 5427' and regrets 'the delay of the coming of our Messiah because of our sins', which has 'brought upon us heavy persecutions'.

Thus did the messianic movement and its apocalyptic message spread all over the dispersed Jewish world. Meanwhile Sabbatai himself approached the imperial city of Istanbul, where all the believers in the capital awaited him, along with the Sultan's men.

# 11. The Messiah Imprisoned

Voyages from Izmir to Istanbul normally took about two weeks, depending on the wind, but Sabbatai's caique was so storm-tossed that it was at sea for thirty-nine days. According to several reports, the caique at one point was on the verge of being sunk by huge waves when Sabbatai ordered his companions to recite with him Psalm 107, and the sea became calm while they were chanting verses 28 to 30: 'Then they cry unto the Lord in their trouble, and He bringeth them out of their distresses. He maketh the storm a calm, so that the waves thereof are still. Then are they glad because they are quiet; so He bringeth them unto their desired haven.'

Paul Rycaut, in his account of the voyage, says sarcastically that Sabbatai exercised little power over the elements. 'But though *Sabatai* took few into the Vessel with him, yet multitudes of Jews travelled over land to meet him again at *Constantinople* . . . The Wind proving Northerly, as commonly as it is in the *Hellespont* and *Propontis*, *Sabatai* was thirty-nine days in his Voyage, and yet the Vessel not arrived: So little power had this Messiah over the Sea and Winds.'

Meanwhile Sabbatai's disciples in Istanbul had been waiting anxiously for his arrival. A letter from Izmir to Amsterdam, written shortly after his departure, gives a picture of the excited mood among the Sabbatians in the Ottoman capital at that time. 'Two days after his departure, two emissaries arrived from the congregation in Constantinople, carrying letters of credence . . . by which all Jews acknowledge him as their king, placing their lives and strength in his hand, and entreating him to speed his journey because the Grand Turk was eager to see him.'

The letter goes on to tell of what was happening in Istanbul, where the believers were spending all their time in prayer and penance. They said that the prophet Elijah had appeared to the chief rabbi and led him out of the city, where he saw a vast army and was told that 'These are the hosts of Israel!' Thereupon the chief rabbi saw Sabbatai descending from heaven, seated on a golden throne set with sapphires and diamonds. Elijah then said to the chief rabbi, 'Go and tell the Jews that redemption has come, and that they should celebrate a festival.'

Jacob Becherand, if he is in fact the author of the French *Relation*, notes that the believers in Istanbul were so convinced that the Messiah was coming that they warned the Gentiles that they too should show subservience to the messianic king: 'They threatened us with dire disaster if we failed to join them as soon as possible, and of our own good and free will walked in front of the king who would rule over them, acknowledging his kingdom and submitting to the religion and the laws which he would establish in the world.'

According to Abraham Galanté, the long delay in Sabbatai's arrival made the believers in Istanbul very anxious, and when they passed in the street they repeatedly asked one another '*Geldime?*' ('Has he come?') The Turkish street urchins picked this up, and whenever they encountered a Jew they mocked him by chanting '*Geldime?*'

There are several variant accounts of Sabbatai's arrival in Istanbul, on 7 February 1666. The most probable version says that his caique was intercepted in the Sea of Marmara by two ships carrying Turkish officers, who arrested him and escorted him to the port of Istanbul. Sabbatai was brought ashore in chains, while one of his Turkish guards struck him with a truncheon to move him along. Crowds of believers had come out to meet Sabbatai's caique, and when he was led away they tried to crowd around him, but his guards beat them away. The guards then locked Sabbatai up in a dungeon, after which his disciples fled to their homes, where they remained for three days in terror that they would be massacred. During that time they fasted and prayed, waiting for their Messiah to show a sign or perform a miracle.

Some sources suggest that Sabbatai was arrested because non-believers among the Jews in Istanbul had denounced him to the Turkish authorities. According to Samson Bacchi, the elders of the Jewish community 'secretly went after him to the Vizier, and at their request he was imprisoned'. But the truth is that Sabbatai's arrest was instigated by the Grand Vizier, Fazıl Ahmet Pasha, as Paul Rycaut reports in his version of the episode:

The Grand Vizier . . . having heard some rumours of this Man, and the disorder and madness he had raised amongst the Jews, sent two Boats . . . with Commands to bring him up Prisoner to the Port, where accordingly *Sabatai* being come, was committed to the most loathsome and darkest Dungeon in the Town, there to remain in farther expectation of the Veziers Sentence.

Rycaut reports that Sabbatai's disciples came to visit him in prison, coming before him

with the same Ceremony and Respect in the Dungeon, as they would have done, had he then sate exalted on the Sublime Throne of *Judah* . . . with their Eyes cast down, their bodies bending forward, and hands crossed before them . . . the undecency of the place, and present subjection not having in the least abated their high thoughts and reverence towards his person.

The dungeon where Sabbatai was imprisoned was almost certainly the infamous Bagno, a Byzantine tower on the Golden Horn just upstream from the present Galata Bridge that for centuries had been used to incarcerate galley slaves. But not long afterwards he was transferred to 'fairly comfortable quarters', according to Giambattista Ballarino, the Venetian *bailo*, or ambassador. Ballarino's report to Doge Domenico Contrarini, dated 18 March 1666, describes the conditions of Sabbatai's imprisonment. He says that Sabbatai was under the supervision of the *kasem bashi*, or jailer, 'who permitted him to speak freely with the Jews who wanted to visit him'. Ballarino also notes that Sabbatai 'confirmed the fasts and the severe penitential exercises. He himself kept regular fasts of three days, at the end of which he caused torches of light to appear by his conjuration in the whole prison. After a time he was allowed, albeit under strong guard, to go to the sea for his ritual immersions.'

According to Ballarino, 'The Jews dared not walk the streets, because of the abuse with which the Gentiles, and the Turks in particular, reviled them.' He goes on to say that the heads of the Jewish community went to the Grand Vizier to obtain passes that would allow them to walk in the streets without being molested. They finally obtained the passes at a cost of 60,000 reales plus another 40,000 reales for permission to visit Sabbatai at any time, the money being raised by a levy in the Jewish community, in which each paid according to his capacity. The Grand Vizier even offered to release Sabbatai for another 40,000 reales. Ballarino writes that 'They all consented in their hearts to this new offering, and they went away to announce it to the prisoner.'

But, according to Ballarino, Sabbatai forbade his disciples to pay anything for his release. There was no need for this, he told them, 'since in a few days great things would happen. And the masses of the Jews were greatly elated by the hopes which were thus aroused.'

Three days after his arrest Sabbatai was brought before the Divan, the imperial council, which met in a hall (also called the Divan) in the Second Court of Topkapı Sarayı, the great palace of the sultans on the First Hill of the city. The council, which was presided over by the Grand Vizier, also included the pashas who commanded the Ottoman armed forces and the principal departments of the government, as well as the chief black and white eunuchs and the aga of the Janissaries, the elite corps of the army. Everyone except Sabbatai's disciples thought that he would be executed, but instead he was spared and taken to the 'fairly comfortable quarters' referred to by Ballarino, perhaps in the Grand Vizier's headquarters. According to Ballarino, Sabbatai was spared because Fazıl Ahmet Pasha took a liking to him, but it may also have been because the Grand Vizier did not consider the supposed Messiah to be a threat and did not want to alienate a large part of the Jewish community by executing him.

According to Rycaut, Sabbatai's imprisonment led his believers to halt all their commercial activities. Some of the Sabbatians stopped paying the money they owed to the English merchants of the Levant Company in Galata, who asked Sabbatai to intercede for them. Sabbatai agreed to help, and wrote a letter telling his disciples to pay their debts – a message quoted by Rycaut:

To you of the Nation of the Jews, who expect the appearance of the Messiah, and the Salvation of Israel, Peace without end. Whereas we are informed, that you are indebted to several of the English Nation, It seemeth right to us to enorder you to make satisfaction to these your just debts: which if you refuse to do, and not obey us herein; know you that you are not to enter with us into our Joys and Dominions.

The letters sent from Istanbul's Jewish community to western Europe at this time reflect the schism between believers and non-believers, each group seeing Sabbatai's imprisonment through a different lens. The report by Jacob Sasportas is undoubtedly based on letters he received from non-believers, giving a somewhat distorted view of the chain of events; nevertheless it does provide some idea of the state of mind of the believers early in 1666. He begins by describing the situation immediately after Sabbatai's arrest: 'the believers continued to go to him in large crowds, openly rejoicing and praying with him. They wrote letters telling of the great miracles which he wrought in prison, such as curing a dying person by giving him something to eat, the appearance of pillars of fire and clouds, and the greatness which the viziers accorded to him.'

Sasportas then corrects the Sabbatian version of what happened, based on the information he had received from non-believers. He says that the Sabbatians did not tell the truth: seven days after Sabbatai's arrest he was put in chains and brought to an even worse dungeon, 'so that he himself begged of the Jews to intercede for him with the Vizier's *chelebi* to plead for him and obtain his transfer to any other place, for he could no longer suffer. After they had bribed the Vizier, they suggested to him that it would be advisable to remove Sabbatai from the city, where he would not stir up people with his follies.'

Sasportas concludes his report by describing Sabbatai's transfer to a new place of imprisonment, at Gallipoli. According to Sasportas, some of the leading members of the Jewish community in Istanbul realized that if Sabbatai could not save himself he certainly could not save others, and so 'they repented of their faith and held him for a fool. But the majority of the crowd were not disturbed by his imprisonment; indeed, their faith increased because they said that the Messiah had predicted that he would suffer much on behalf of Israel, in order to lighten the messianic woes.'

The 'Vizier's *chelebi*' referred to by Sasportas is probably Judah ben Mordecai ha-Kohen, Fazıl Ahmet Pasha's Jewish banker and financial adviser, who seems to have been a disciple of Sabbatai.

The Grand Vizier was at the time preparing for a great campaign against the Venetian fortress at Candia, the capital of Crete. This was the only part of Crete that had not fallen to the Turks, who had first invaded the island twenty years before. Sabbatai's presence in Istanbul was proving to be a considerable distraction, for the cessation of business by his believers was seriously hampering commerce in the capital, and it was this that made Fazıl Ahmet Pasha decide to have Sabbatai transferred to Gallipoli. Sabbatai arrived there on 19 April 1666 and was imprisoned in the Byzantine fortress whose ruins still stand on the shore of the old port. It was the eve of the Passover festival, which Sabbatai celebrated in his usual contrary way, violating biblical prohibitions by sacrificing a lamb and roasting it with its fat. According to Moses ben Habib, as Sabbatai was doing so he said, as a benediction, 'Blessed art Thou, O God, who permittest that which is forbidden.'

The appearance of Gallipoli at that time is described by Jean de Thevenot, who stopped there on the first stage of his travels in the Levant, which began in 1655. He writes that 'Several Greeks live there, who, for the most part, sell Raki, or Brandy . . . In this town there is a square Castle with a Tower, joined to it by a Pomel of a Wall; but for what I can judge of its Antiquity, I believe it hath been built by the Christians.' This castle was to be the place of Sabbatai's imprisonment, famous in Sabbatian literature as the Tower of Strength.

The circumstances of Sabbatai's imprisonment are described in a letter to Amsterdam written by one of his disciples in Izmir – one of those who had accompanied him to Istanbul. The original letter is lost, its contents surviving only in an English summary which may have further distorted the disciple's already highly coloured account. The writer says that Sabbatai – whom he refers to as 'the King' – was sent to Gallipoli because of the tumult his presence was causing in Istanbul. He notes that 'The King since his Arivall had assured the Jews that the Redemption of Israel is at hand, and that as soone as the Prophet Nathan shall be arrived, who is expected every houre that the same shall by great wonders and miracles be proclaimed and made known to all the world.' He goes on to say that Sabbatai had with him several rabbis and scholars, 'and the free exercise of all their Ceremonies that any Jew might freely come to visit him, and that the Great Turke had sent him word that he might goe abroad in Publick wheresoever it pleased him, whose Answer was he would not do so until he was assured from God that the tyme was come in which he should publickly manifest himselfe'.

The letter concludes with a description of several miracles associated with Sabbatai: 'that a piller of fire surrounded with severall Starres was seen hovering over the place where he was, of his appearing in the Turkes Bed Chamber, and in short sayth the letter a confirmation of what we had last Post, and over and above this that Severall who were sent from the Visier to strangle him fell down dead in his presence.'

These events are described somewhat differently by Rycaut, who says that the transfer of Sabbatai from Istanbul to the Dardanelles convinced his followers that he was indeed the Messiah, for otherwise the Turks would never have spared his life. 'This removal of *Sabatai* from a worse Prison, to one of a better Air, convinced the Jews with greater confidence of his being the Messiah, supposing that had it been in the power of the Vezier, or other officers of the Turks, to have destroyed his Person, they never would have permitted him to live unto that time.' Rycaut goes on to say that the leniency of the Turks was all the more remarkable, since Sabbatai 'had not only declared himself the King of *Israel*, but also by Prophecies published fatal things to the Grand Signior and his Kingdoms'.

Leyb ben Ozer says that Sabbatai was imprisoned in the fortress on the Dardanelles for 'over five months at the expense of the Turkish ruler, which greatly rejoiced the hearts of Jews everywhere who thought this a great matter . . . People came to speak with him in this fortress from all quarters of the world and brought him fine gifts and paid him honour with large donations.'

According to Leyb ben Ozer, 'The guard who kept watch over him made a great deal of money from what he was paid to let people in to see Sabbatai Sevi. Everyone who came to see him left his presence requited and completely faithful to the belief that Sabbatai Sevi would gain great things from the Turkish ruler.' He writes that Sabbatai was 'dressed in red clothes and the scroll of the Torah that he had with him was clothed in red and set by his right side always, in a red cover with gold decorations. The room he sat in was a king's chamber. The walls were covered in golden Turkish textiles of fine quality and great worth.' He goes on to say that 'On the floor lay the most precious carpets and before him stood a pure silver table inset with precious stones and all the vessels that stood upon the table were made of silver or gold inset with special stones. To his right was a bed of gold and at its head a silver scarf and on his left he had a fan with a handle of gilded silver.'

And so, Leyb ben Ozer continues, Sabbatai 'dwelt in the fortress like a king in his court. And there were many rooms and a beautiful garden with a little house for his entertainment and it was all for his use. The courtyard was enclosed from outside and Turkish guards kept watch over it.'

Leyb ben Ozer spoke with people who visited Sabbatai, 'who ate and drank and were near him in the fortress when he was imprisoned and who were not his proponents and they told me there was none like him in stature and in the way his face looked, like that of one of God's angels'. As Leyb ben Ozer's sources describe Sabbatai's appearance at that time, 'His cheeks were always ruddy. And they testify that when he sang Sabbath hymns to God, may He be blessed, which he did several times a day, it was not possible to look into his face, for one who looked at it, it was as if he looked into fire.'

By April 1666 the Sephardic Jews in London had received news of Sabbatai's initial arrest and imprisonment. There was already considerable interest in London about Sabbatai – even more so among Christians than in the small Jewish community. People in London at the time are known to have wagered on whether Sabbatai would in fact take control of the Ottoman Empire and other kingdoms. Samuel Pepys notes in his diary that he had been told 'of a Jew in town, that in the name of the rest do offer to give any man £10 to be paid £100, if a certain person [Sabbatai] now at Smyrna be within these two years owned by all the Princes of the East, and particularly the Grand Signor, as the King of the World . . . and . . . the True Messiah.' The Jews in Hamburg were giving the same odds until the elders of the community prohibited the practice.

News of Sabbatai's activities was sent abroad by his disciples in Istanbul. One such newsletter, which survives only in a summary by a Christian correspondent, was sent by a group of six Sabbatian rabbis from Istanbul on 1 June 1666, arriving in Amsterdam on 23 July. The correspondent – who refers to Sabbatai as 'the king' and to Nathan as 'the prophet' – first reports on the mood of the believers in Istanbul and the situation in Gallipoli: 'Everything seems to be going as well as can be, and they have no doubts but their deliverance will take place very soon. The king is in Gallipoli, enjoying great freedom, the doors of the palace are open to all, and the king publicly celebrated the Passover and holds divine service there in the presence of four hundred people.'

He reports that he was told, 'on the authority of the king and the prophet, that the gathering of Israel to their land' would take place in the year beginning in September 1666. 'All this greatly encourages the Jews here [in Amsterdam] in a wondrous manner and causes them to persevere in their penances, all the more as the counsels came to them from their chiefest rabbis in Constantinople who had written in answer to the questions which the rabbis of Venice had asked them as to what they thought of the matter.'

The letter from the rabbis of Istanbul to those of Venice had been written on 25 May 1666. Phrased as if in answer to a query as to whether merchandise belonging to a certain R. Israel (who is actually Sabbatai) will be worth the price, the Istanbul rabbis say that it will be profitable 'but it will be necessary to wait until the time of the Great Fair next year when, with God's help, it will be sold at a high price, under the benevolent Providence of the Cause of all Causes and the Origin of all Origins'. The letter to the Venetian rabbis, who are referred to as 'priests', concludes by saying that 'All this we carefully investigated and the truth is with the aforementioned R. Israel, as we assured ourselves beyond peradventure. And it is incumbent upon you the priests to act accordingly. And God grant peace to the quarrelling parties that they mind their deeds and no longer doubt this matter, for R. Israel is established before God.'

This letter was later the subject of controversy, for some of the six signatories claimed that they had never seen it and that their signatures were forgeries. But this was after Sabbatai's apostasy, and those who protested may have been trying to hide the fact that they had been believers.

By the summer of 1666 believers in the Jewish communities in the Ottoman Empire, Persia, Italy, Poland, Germany, Holland and France had sent delegations or letters of homage to Sabbatai at his prison in Gallipoli. A letter from the believers in Amsterdam, the original of which still survives, is addressed to the 'Light of Israel . . . the beauty of the pride of Jacob . . . the King whom our eyes may behold in his beauty . . . Our Lord and Our King . . . the rabbi Sabbatai Sevi, may his seed live for ever before the Rock who dwelleth on high'. The fourteen signatories ask Sabbatai to guide them in 'the way we must walk and the work we must do . . . and we know not what to do . . . and are waiting for the reply and commandment of Our Lord'. The letter is dated 24 September 1666 – eight or nine days after Sabbatai's apostasy.

The believers in Holland faced a serious problem in their plans to move en masse to the Holy Land, for the maritime war then being waged between England and Holland put them at risk of being captured at sea. This led Jean d'Illan, a Jew of Amsterdam, to write on 5 February 1666 to Charles II of England, informing him that he and other members of his community were going to rent a vessel so that they could go to Jerusalem. 'Since I behold that God in his mercy has begun to gather in his scattered people and has raised up a prophet for us, therefore I and several of my Jewish brethren, together with fifty poor families desire to hire a ship to bring us to Jerusalem.' He was petitioning Charles for a pass that would allow their ship to go unmolested by the King's warships: 'And in order that this may be accomplished without being captured and molested on the high sea, we humbly petition Your Majesty to grant us a pass for one Dutch ship which is to sail from here . . . without let, search, or molestation by vessels of his Majesty's fleet, and after arriving in Jerusalem we shall pray for his Majesty's success.'

Meanwhile Samuel Primo had taken upon himself the task of serving as Sabbatai's secretary in Gallipoli. One of his letters, written 'at the behest of the messianic king', orders the Jewish community in Venice to punish with severity any non-believer, 'slaying him even on the Sabbath'. Primo concluded his message with an exhortation to the faithful:

Rejoice in our King, your Saviour and the Redeemer of your souls and your bodies in heaven and on earth, who will resurrect your dead and save you from subjugation to the kingdoms and from the punishment of hell. These things are beyond the power of the mouth to utter, for none can fathom the Shin Daleth Yod [i.e. Shadday, one of the names of God], which is Our Lord [i.e. Sabbatai Sevi].

Sabbatai added a few lines in his own hand to Primo's letter – a statement that he had established a new order which transcended the power of temporal rulers, despite the fact that he was in prison.

The castle in Gallipoli soon came to be known among the Sabbatians as *Migdal 'Oz*, the Tower of Strength, taking its name from Proverbs 18:10, which Sabbatai refers to in a circular letter that he sent to believers soon after his imprisonment. Here he hints at the deep depression from which he had recently emerged into the full glow of his transcendent illuminated state: 'For my soul, which was sorely troubled and afflicted has now been filled with a great splendour and exults with joy . . . And in my solitude Scripture will be fulfilled and confirmed: "The name of the Lord is a tower of strength; the righteous runneth into it and is safe."'

Sabbatai concludes his message with these instructions to his followers: 'Behold now is the time of love, therefore be strong and of good courage in the faith, in prayer, in penitence, in fasts, and in many and frequently repeated ritual immersions, for the redemption of Israel is at hand with the help of God. [signed] Sabbatai Sevi.'

# 12. The Tower of Strength

During the early months of 1666 thousands of Jews converged on Istanbul to join Sabbatai while he was still imprisoned in the city. Then, after he was transferred to the castle in Gallipoli, the 'Tower of Strength', the Sabbatian pilgrims hired all the boatmen in the capital to take them across the Sea of Marmara to the Dardanelles. As Jacob Becherand reported, 'Regular pilgrimages were organized from the capital to the Dardanelles . . . and never did the business of the boatmen flourish more. Day and night long rows of boats plied in both directions. The governor of the fortress collected immense sums from the sale of permits for visiting his prisoner.'

Paul Rycaut describes the scene in even greater detail, writing that

the Jews flocked in great numbers to the Castle, not only from the Neighbouring Parts, but also from *Poland, Germany, Ligorn* [*Livorno*], *Venice, Amsterdam* and other places . . . on all whom, as a reward for the expence and labours of their Pilgrimage, *Sabatai* bestowed . . . his Benedictions, promising encrease of their Store and enlargement of possessions in the Holy Land.

Rycaut says that the guards in the fortress charged admission to all those who came to see Sabbatai, as well as setting exorbitant prices on their food and lodging, 'by which gain and advantage to the Turks, no Complaints or Advices were carried to *Adrianople,* either of the Concourse or Arguments amongst the Jews in that place, but rather all Civilities and Liberties indulged unto them'. Rycaut's reference to Adrianople – Turkish Edirne – was occasioned by the fact that the Sultan, Mehmet IV, was in residence there at the time, having moved his court from Istanbul a few years earlier.

Several sources report that the chief of the naval police at Istanbul on one occasion stopped seven or eight large boats that were carrying believers to Gallipoli. He and his men stripped the pilgrims of their possessions and beat them, and then, when the victims returned to Istanbul and complained to the *Kaymakam*, or provincial governor, he had them beaten again and then thrown into prison.

An Armenian source in Istanbul reported that, the Grand Vizier having left for Crete, on 12 April 1666, 'The Jews, men, women and children, in fact everybody, betook themselves to the Straits [i.e. the Dardanelles]. Our city is full of pilgrims from Poland, the Crimea, Persia, and Jerusalem, as well as from Turkey and the Frankish lands.'

Stories abounded of miracles performed by Sabbatai and of prophets and prophetesses raving with legends of the Messiah, with even infants mouthing oracular pronouncements. According to Sasportas, letters from Egypt reported that some 500 prophets and prophetesses arose in Istanbul during the summer of 1666, the most notable being 'a very celebrated and old rabbi . . . R. Mordecai the Pious', who was probably from Poland. Sasportas, quoting from one of the letters, says that Rabbi Mordecai went to see Sabbatai at the Tower of Strength, but could hardly look at him because his face was shining with a supernatural light so that Mordecai was almost blinded, yet he saw a crown of fire rising from Sabbatai's head. 'Thereupon Mordecai fell on his face, and he went through the streets, crying with all his might, "He is Our Lord, and there is none other. In truth he is our King and there is none beside him." Then the Holy Spirit descended upon him and he became a celebrated prophet.'

After Sabbatai was imprisoned at Gallipoli he wrote letters to his disciples far and wide urging them to be diligent in their penance and prayers, for the time of redemption would soon be at hand. (Although these letters were signed by Sabbatai, they may have been written by his secretary, Samuel Primo.) According to Leyb ben Ozer, Sabbatai told his disciples that, 'although it was now the time for the end, there might be a delay of some months or years. He urgently begged that none should spare himself, but everyone should better his works and pray for the Messiah that God in His great mercy prosper his way, and that His kingdom should be made manifest soon and the *qelippoth* be made to pass away.'

According to Sasportas, the wealthy Jews of Istanbul sent Sabbatai garments, fabrics and other sumptuous gifts, so that he was dressed like a king and surrounded by all the trappings of royalty when he received the crowds of pilgrims who came to pay homage to him: 'all the Jews coming from the ends of the earth and beholding his splendour and his apparel, and the many gifts arriving all the time, were easily misled into believing that he was the messianic king'.

While Sabbatai was imprisoned at Gallipoli he instituted a number of new festivals that became part of the Sabbatian liturgy. He and his disciples celebrated the Seventeenth of Thammuz as the 'day of the revival of his spirit and his light'. Two days after the celebration of this feast in Gallipoli, Sabbatai issued a proclamation that the following Monday, the Twenty-third of Thammuz (26 July 1666), would be celebrated as a 'festival of lights', in which every house should be illuminated by seventeen candles of fat and one of wax. Leyb ben Ozer describes the festival as it took place in Gallipoli, based on the account of two envoys from the chief rabbi of Lvov, R. David ha-Levi, namely his son R. Isaiah Mokhiah and his stepson R. Aryeh Leyb ben Samuel Sevi Hirsch. According to the envoys, 'There was an incredible rejoicing in the synagogue. They took all the Torah scrolls out [of the Holy Ark], dancing and singing hymns in honour of Sabbatai Sevi. In the *Amidah* prayer they said: "this day of the festival of lights, the season of our tidings".'

The envoys from Lvov report that Sabbatai 'also sent word to the Jews of the Straits [the Dardanelles] that the following day, Wednesday, the Twenty-fifth of Thammuz, was to be the Great Sabbath', to be strictly observed on pain of death by stoning.

The envoys had an audience with Sabbatai, an account of which is preserved by Leyb ben Ozer and two other sources. According to Leyb ben Ozer, when they came to see Sabbatai he had open on his table a chronicle of the Chmielnicki massacres of 1648–9, a work by R. Moses of Shrbreshin entitled *Suq ha-'Ittim* (*The Troubled Times*). He told them that he always kept this book open, 'because the day of vengeance is in my heart'. He then revealed to them many Kabbalistic mysteries, after which 'he began to sing hymns and songs according to the alphabet'. Sabbatai then took a scarf from the neck of one of the rabbis present, and told each of them to hold one end of it. 'When they had done so, Sabbatai stood facing them and began to dance, singing melodiously verse 20 of Psalm 118, "This is the gate of the Lord, The righteous shall enter into it", and after every repetition he repeated ten times, with his eyes raised heavenward, verse 17: "I shall not die, but live . . ."'

Sabbatai continued to sing and dance for about half an hour, and the envoys could hardly contain their joy. Then Sabbatai ordered everyone else to leave the room, and when he was alone with the two envoys he said, 'I adjure you not to divulge to anyone, not even to your aged father R. David ha-Levi, that which I am now going to reveal to you', whereupon he revealed to them the secrets of great Kabbalistic mysteries. They asked Sabbatai if they could stay in Gallipoli and serve him, but he bade them 'Go in peace and bring glad tidings to your brethren.' Before leaving, they asked him for a written message to their fellow Jews in Poland, and he wrote a letter to their father and signed it 'on the tenth day of the revival of my spirit and my light'.

The two envoys left Gallipoli for Istanbul at the beginning of August, and in the latter half of September they were back in Lvov. There, according to Sasportas, they reported on what they had seen at Sabbatai's court in the Tower of Strength — 'the glory which they had beheld, and the abundance of gold, silver, precious cloth and ornaments, and the royal apparel which he was wearing every day, and the multitudes that were attending on him, and the honour shown him by the Gentiles who would not touch any of the Jews that came to visit him'. They also brought Sabbatai's letter to their aged father, the rabbi David, 'and the whole of Poland was in agitation and the fame thereof was heard in all those parts, and their fame was greatly strengthened'.

Towards the end of August Sabbatai sent a circular letter commanding all his followers to abolish the fast of the Ninth of Ab, which thenceforth would be celebrated as a great festival commemorating the day of his birth:

And ye shall make it a day of great banqueting and great rejoicing, with choice food and delicious drinks, with many candles and lights, and with

many melodies and songs, for it is the birthday of your king Sabbatai Sevi,
highest among the kings of the earth. And concerning work, observe it
like a full holiday, with your best clothes and the festival liturgy.

Detailed instructions for the liturgy of the new feast were distributed to all Sabbatai's disciples. This included a new kiddush, the
festive blessing over the cup, which was adapted from the traditional
benediction: 'And thou hast given us in love, O Lord Our God,
appointed times for gladness, festivals and seasons for joy, this day
of the Feast of Consolation, the season of the birth of our anointed
king, Sabbatai Sevi.'

The various Sabbatian communities celebrated the new festival
with great rejoicing, although Sasportas reports that there were a
few non-believers who stubbornly refused to follow the 'new
religion'. Only in Istanbul, however, did the non-believers attempt
anything like organized resistance to this and other innovations
introduced by the Sabbatians. An Armenian source reports that
eighty prominent members of the Jewish community in Istanbul
publicly protested against the abolition of the fast of the Ninth of Ab,
deriding Sabbatai as an epileptic with mad delusions of messianic
grandeur. The Sabbatians were enraged by this and stoned the
non-believers, according to the Armenian source, who writes that
'the mass of the poor adhered to him [Sabbatai] with great love,
and even the notables were full of hope and sent to do homage to
him. Many who went thither disguised themselves as Armenians
to escape the jeers and insults of the Turks.'

Around this time the non-believing rabbis in Istanbul wrote a
letter to the chief rabbi of Jerusalem, Abraham Amigo, who headed
the rabbinic court that had excommunicated Sabbatai and banned
him from the city. The signatories reported on the dangers that the
messianic movement had created for the Istanbul community,
'particularly in such close proximity to the seat of government';
they had counselled the believers to be patient and prudent, but
the enthusiastic masses of Sabbatians had paid them no heed. They
reported to Amigo that 'So far we have not beheld a single miracle
or sign, only the noise of rumours and testimonies at second-hand
. . . Hence we cannot examine the matter properly, wherefore

there is no unanimity on the subject but diversity of opinions . . . This has given rise to contention on both sides . . . and no peace coming out of strife.'

The Istanbul rabbis went on to suggest that a delegation of rabbis headed by Amigo be sent to see Nathan of Gaza, 'and if they agree that they have seen the signs and miracles . . . according to the principles of our holy Torah and the holy Talmud, let them write to us. But if the matter remain doubtful and uncertain in their eyes, they should notify us in their wisdom . . . in order that we may at least warn the people.' But Amigo never answered this letter, and the dissident rabbis of Istanbul were unable to stem the rising tide of the messianic movement in their city.

The Sabbatian movement was particularly strong in Salonika, which at that time was perhaps the largest Jewish community in the world, numbering some 60,000. According to Thomas Coenen, the believers in Salonika surpassed all other Sabbatians in the fervour of their faith and in the extremes of their penitential activities. Coenen reports that the believers would present themselves before a court of rabbis to confess their sins and receive their penances. Many of the penitents buried themselves up to their necks and remained that way for three hours, during which time they recited litanies of Sabbatian penitential prayers. The Sabbatians in Salonika believed in the tradition that the Messiah would not appear until all souls had entered the bodies destined for them. They therefore married off all their young children so that the girls would conceive as soon as possible, so hurrying along the final redemption. Coenen reports that 700 to 800 marriages involving children took place in Salonika at the height of the Sabbatian movement, further disrupting the community, where many believers were reduced to poverty when their shops and places of business were closed in anticipation of the Messiah's arrival.

The Sabbatian movement was also strong in Edirne, where Sultan Mehmet IV spent most of his time. Christian sources there report that the entire Jewish population of the city had joined the messianic movement, but in fact there were at least two prominent rabbis, Jacob Danon and Abraham Magreso, who opposed the Sabbatians.

The movement had also taken root in the Balkans and central Europe, and the believers in Belgrade sent two envoys to Sabbatai in Gallipoli. The apocalyptic atmosphere in this region is described in the memoirs of Hirsh ben Jacob, who was born in Budapest in 1658, studied in Salonika, and served for years as rabbi of Sarajevo. As he recalled, 'At that time there were women who said, "Let us go and slay demons." They dressed themselves in white linen garments and made strange motions in the air with their hands . . . as if they were slaughtering demons.' He goes on to say that 'There was one woman who would say, "Who wants me to give him the smell of Paradise?" and then she would raise her hands heavenward, catch something in the air, and offer an exceedingly fragrant odour to anyone who wanted it.'

Sabbatai's wife, Sarah, joined him in Gallipoli before the Ninth of Ab, after permission had been obtained from the sirdar, the commander of the fortress. She had been treated royally by the believers in the capital, where she took an active role in the preparations for celebrating Sabbatai's birthday and even in the planning for his eventual coronation as the messianic king. According to Coenen, the believers in Istanbul referred to Sarah as the 'Queen of Palestine', a title that would have been given to her by Sabbatai.

Another visitor from Lvov arrived in Gallipoli on 3 or 4 September. This was Nehemiah Kohen, an enigmatic figure who suddenly and dramatically transformed the course of the Sabbatian movement in an unexpected manner. Contemporary sources and modern scholars are equally divided on the background and details of the dispute that arose between Sabbatai and Nehemiah during their meeting in Gallipoli, which lasted two or three days. Gershom Scholem remarks that 'The historian . . . who tries to investigate the details of this strange incident is faced with insoluble riddles.'

One version of the story's beginning is given by Sasportas, who based his account on rumours from Poland. Sasportas writes that 'Sabbatai learned of the existence [in Lvov]. . . of a man who had been prophesying and who was generally regarded as mad. He now sent for him . . . in order to lead people astray by putting into his mouth prophecies concerning his messiahship.'

According to Leyb ben Ozer, several Jewish communities in Poland had contributed money to send Nehemiah to Gallipoli, apparently because he had a local reputation as a Kabbalist and prophet. Nehemiah seems to have relied for his apocalyptic knowledge not on the *Zohar* but on a work known as *Othoth Mashiah, The Signs of the Messiah*, which he interpreted in strictly literal fashion. He had examined Sabbatai's career to date, and he found that it was not in keeping with the predictions in *The Signs of the Messiah*. Leyb ben Ozer tells the story of the rancorous debate between Sabbatai and Nehemiah:

one Kabbalist book after the other was brought in all day long, and they angrily disputed until midnight when they ceased and slept for a few hours. Thereafter they began to argue anew, but none would yield and all proofs adduced by Sabbatai Sevi were dismissed by R. Nehemiah, who said that they were all vanity and that Sabbatai did not understand the meaning of the Kabbalistic books.

Paul Rycaut tells the story quite differently, apparently relying on Jewish sources in Izmir and Istanbul. According to Rycaut, Nehemiah's Kabbalistic studies had convinced him that there were to be two messiahs, one called Ephraim and the other David. 'The first was to be a Preacher of the Law, poor and despised, and a Servant to the second, and his Fore-runner; the second was to be great and rich, to restore the Jews to *Jerusalem*, to sit upon the Throne of *David*, and to perform and act all those Triumphs and Conquests, which were expected from *Sabatai*.' Nehemiah was content to be Ephraim, according to Rycaut, and Sabbatai was perfectly agreeable to this. But Nehemiah accused Sabbatai of being too forward in proclaiming himself as the Messiah, before his forerunner Ephraim had first become known to the world. Sabbatai took offence at this, and suspected that Nehemiah was trying to usurp his position as Messiah. 'Thereupon', as Rycaut writes,

the Dispute grew so hot, and the Controversie so irreconcilable, as was taken notice of by the Jews, and controverted amongst them as every one fancied; but *Sabatai* being of greater Authority, his Sentence prevailed, and *Nehemiah* was rejected as Schismatical, and an Enemy to the Messiah, which afterwards proved the ruine and downfall of this Imposture.

Rycaut goes on to tell how Nehemiah, frustrated after his visit to the fortress at Gallipoli, acted together with a number of anti-Sabbatian rabbis to take his revenge. Together they went to Edirne to see the *kaymakam*, who in the absence of Fazıl Ahmet Pasha in Crete was serving as deputy grand vizier. According to Rycaut, the Ottoman authorities in Edirne knew nothing of the activities of Sabbatai and his court at Gallipoli, nor had they heard the prophecies that the Messiah would overthrow the Sultan. Nehemiah informed the *kaymakam* 'that the Jew Prisoner at the Castle called *Sabatai Sevi* was a lewd person, and one who endeavoured to debauch the minds of the Jews, and divert them from their honest course of livelihood, and obedience to the Grand Signior, and that therefore it was necessary to clear the world of so factious and dangerous a Spirit'. The *kaymakam* then informed the Sultan, who immediately sent a *chavush*, or messenger, with orders to bring Sabbatai to Edirne. Rycaut ends his account of this incident by telling how the *chavush* 'executed his Commission after the Turkish fashion in haste, bringing *Sabatai* in a few days to *Adrianople*, without further excuse or ceremony, not affording him an hours space to take a solemn farewel of his Followers and Adorers, who were now come to the vertical point of their hopes and expectations'.

Rycaut is not correct in his statement that the Turks knew nothing of Sabbatai's revolutionary ambitions before Nehemiah Kohen denounced him to the authorities. The Armenian source mentioned earlier notes that Sabbatai's circular converting the fast on the Ninth of Ab into a feast celebrating the 'Nativity of Our King and Messiah' had been translated immediately by the Sultan's chief scribe, who would have sent it to the court of Mehmet IV in Edirne. The Armenian source does corroborate Rycaut's statement that the *kaymakam*, who at the time was Kuru Mustafa Pasha, had been informed of Nehemiah's complaints against Sabbatai, and he would have passed these on to the Sultan as well. Another unnamed source reports a complaint by the Turkish notables of Gallipoli against the sirdar, who had, for his own enrichment, allowed Sabbatai to establish his messianic court there, greatly inconveniencing and offending the Muslim population of the town.

Rycaut's quote of Nehemiah's complaint that Sabbatai was 'a lewd person' is supported by two Armenian sources. One of these – a poem – says that Sabbatai 'was found to have relations with women', while the other – a prose account – records accusations of his 'lewdness and debauches with women and with favourites'. In his reverential description of the Messiah-king's court in the Tower of Strength, Abraham Cuenque writes that Sabbatai had in attendance 'seventy beautiful virgins, the daughters of the most illustrious rabbis. Sarah was like unto a queen.' In referring to the complaints to the Turkish authorities, Cuenque also mentions accusations of 'unbearable . . . abominations committed at the king's [i.e. Sabbatai's] court'.

The Turkish authorities acted quickly as soon as Nehemiah's complaints reached the Sultan's court at Edirne, which seems to have been on 5 or 6 September. A week later four armed messengers arrived in Gallipoli from Edirne to take away Sabbatai, who was put into a carriage and driven off under a strong escort of soldiers. An Armenian source gives a slightly different version, saying that the *kaymakam* had first sent an officer with orders to hang Sabbatai on the spot, but that this had been countermanded by a second messenger who was to bring the prisoner to Edirne 'lest they spread the rumour that he [Sabbatai] had ascended to heaven and someone else had been hanged'. The sparing of Sabbatai's life is mentioned in a report by Count Gautier de Leslie, ambassador of the Habsburg emperor to the Sublime Porte (the Ottoman government in Istanbul), who advised the Grand Vizier, now returned from Crete, not to make a martyr out of Sabbatai Sevi. The same position was taken by the ulema, the Muslim religious leaders, who advised the imperial council against taking Sabbatai's life 'lest they [the believers] make a new religion'.

And so Sabbatai was removed from the fortress in Gallipoli, which had served him as a Tower of Strength during the weeks of his imprisonment. He had lived there more like a debauched sultan than a messianic king, if the accusations made against him were true – which they may very well have been, given Sabbatai's statement that God 'permittest that which is forbidden'.

# 13. Apostasy

Sabbatai and his escort arrived in Edirne on 15 September, having spent only three days on the road from Gallipoli. This was less than half the time that travellers ordinarily took for this journey, a distance of about 120 miles, so the Sultan's messengers must have been under orders to bring their captive as quickly as possible.

Edirne had been the capital of the Ottoman Empire for nearly a century before the capture of Constantinople in 1453 by Mehmet II, the Conqueror, and the sultans had adorned the town with a number of mosques and other imperial foundations. Mehmet's father, Murat II, had erected a sumptuous palace called Edirne Sarayı, building it for seclusion on an island in the Tunja, the Greek Hebrus, the river that flows around the western side of Edirne. Mehmet, who succeeded his father in 1451, when he was nineteen, enlarged and adorned Edirne Sarayı, adding a number of new buildings and gardens.

The Greek historian Kritovoulos of Imbros describes this pleasure dome in his *History of Mehmed the Conqueror*, writing of the first year of the Sultan's reign:

During that same period he also built a splendid palace near Adrianople, on the banks of the Hebrus river, beyond the city. It was adorned with splendid stones and transparent marbles, and was resplendent with much gold and silver within and without and embellished with sculptures and paintings and with many other costly things carefully designed and wrought. Around it he planted gardens and all sorts of shrubs and domestic trees bearing beautiful fruit. In these gardens he put various kinds of domestic and wild animals and flocks of birds, and made the place attractive with many other beautiful things which he knew would bring enjoyment and beauty and pleasure. And in his zeal he constructed a royal courtyard very near this, and made ample barracks for the new cavalry and infantry troops, in it and around it, guarding the place on all sides.

Most of the Conqueror's successors tried to spend the summer months at Edirne Sarayı when they were not on campaign, escaping from the crowded confines of Topkapı Sarayı in Istanbul. Mehmet IV spent virtually all his time in Edirne Sarayı, for he had an almost pathological hatred of Topkapı. There, in 1648, he had witnessed the execution of his father, the mad Sultan Ibrahim, whom he succeeded when he was only six years old. Three years later he had seen the murder of his grandmother Kösem, who had been assassinated on orders from his mother, Turhan Hatije. Hatije then ruled as regent for Mehmet until 1656, when the Sultan was considered to have come of age, though he was only fourteen. Soon afterwards he abandoned Topkapı and took up residence in Edirne Sarayı. He set up his harem there, his favourite being Rabia Gülnüs Ummetüllah, a Greek girl from Rethymnon on Crete, captured when she was a child at the beginning of the Turkish invasion of the island in 1645. Gülnüs bore Mehmet a son, the future Mustafa II, born on 5 June 1664. Mustafa was the first male in the imperial Ottoman line to be born in twenty years, and his birth was the occasion of week-long celebrations in both Istanbul and Edirne.

At the end of Hatije's regency she secured the appointment of Mehmet Köprülü as grand vizier, a post he held with great distinction until his death in 1661, when he was succeeded by his son Fazıl Ahmet Pasha. Fazıl Ahmet Pasha proved to be every bit as capable as his father, relieving the young Sultan of virtually all his state responsibilities. This allowed Mehmet to spend most of his time hunting in the countryside around Edirne, exhausting his court and creating an insupportable burden for the people thereabouts.

Evliya Chelebi describes Mehmet IV as he was at about the time that Sabbatai was brought to Edirne – every inch a king except in his disinclination to rule other than as a figurehead:

Though very weak when he mounted the throne, he acquired strength when, at the age of twenty, he took to field sports. He had broad shoulders, stout limbs, a tall figure, like his father Ibrahim; a powerful fist, like his uncle Murat [IV], open forehead, grey eyes, a ruddy countenance, and an agreeable voice, and his carriage was princely, in short, that of an emperor. He had a small beard, large mustaches, and was much devoted to hunting.

Mehmet rarely interrupted his hunting to deal with affairs of state. And so Fazıl Ahmet Pasha, just returned from the Cretan campaign, had to persuade him that it was vitally important to have Sabbatai Sevi brought to Edirne Sarayı and interviewed there. The Grand Vizier had been receiving reports about the supposed Messiah who had so excited the peacable Jews of the Ottoman Empire, and when Nehemiah Kohen denounced Sabbatai he had decided to act at once.

Fazıl Ahmet Pasha's actions concerning Sabbatai were strongly influenced by his personal religious adviser, Vani Mehmet Efendi, a preacher from the eastern Anatolian city of Van. Vani Efendi had become a leader in the religious movement known as the Kadızadeli, named for the reformer Kadızade Mehmet Efendi, who had been active in Istanbul in the 1630s. The Kadızadeli were a puritanical Islamic group that had arisen in opposition to the mystical Sufi sects of the various dervish brotherhoods such as the Halveti, who had come to monopolize the position of imam, or preacher, at the imperial mosques in Istanbul and the other cities of the Ottoman Empire. The Kadızadeli advocated a return to the practices of Islam as they were in seventh-century Medina, and their rejection of all subsequent innovations made them opposed to the Halveti and other dervish brotherhoods. They demanded the destruction of all dervish *tekkes*, or lodges, as well as the banning of pilgrimages to the tombs of Sufi saints. The Kadızadeli were also violently opposed to the use of alcohol, coffee and tobacco, not to mention the opium that fuelled the pipe dreams of so many mystic poets of the Sufi orders. They were also totally opposed to the traditional Ottoman policy of tolerance to non-Muslims.

The Kadızadeli came to the fore when their leader Vani Efendi became the personal imam of Fazıl Ahmet Pasha, who in turn had the complete confidence of Sultan Mehmet IV. In his diary, Dr John Covel, chaplain of the Levant Company in Pera, the European quarter of Istanbul, described Vani Efendi as 'the great preacher among the Turks': 'He is an old huncht-back man, very grey, a crabb'd countenance, yet his shrivl'd flesh is clear, not black or swarthy, but pale; and Nature hath marked him in the face, for his right eye is lesse than his left, as it were shrunk.'

Covel goes on to tell of the power that Vani held through his association with the Grand Vizier. 'He is of such authority among the Turkes, as about 6 year since he preach'd down all publick Tavernes and ale-houses and the Dervises' publick meetings; yet I believe there is as much wine drunk (or more) and as many tavernes by connivance and bribery as ever there was. The fame of this old cox comb is more than a Pope among them.'

According to Rycaut, Vani persuaded the Grand Vizier 'that the terrible Fires in Constantinople and Galata in the year 1660, and the last years unparalleled Pestilence, and the inconsiderable advance of the Turks on the Christians for some years, were so many parts of Divine Judgments thrown on the Musselman . . . in vengeance of their too much licence given to the Christian religion'.

Vani Efendi saw the Sabbatian movement as an opportunity to convert a major segment of the non-Muslim population of the Ottoman Empire to Islam, particularly after Sabbatai's followers began converging on Istanbul and Gallipoli after his imprisonment. When Nehemiah Kohen came to Edirne to denounce Sabbatai, castigating him as an immoral revolutionary, Vani Efendi convinced Fazıl Ahmet Pasha that the supposed Messiah should be interviewed with a view to having him persuade his followers to embrace Islam – or so it would seem.

Sabbatai spent his first night in Edirne under close guard somewhere in the town, from where he would be brought out to Edirne Sarayı the following morning. According to a Jewish source, he had been accompanied from Gallipoli by three rabbis, who were to remain with him through the events that followed. According to Robert de Dreux, chaplain at the French Embassy in Istanbul, who was present in Edirne at the time, the local Jews were in a fever of excitement when they learned that Sabbatai had arrived, believing that he had come to dethrone the Sultan and take over the rule of the Ottoman Empire and the other kingdoms of the earth. De Dreux was awakened in the middle of the night by the sound of excited voices outside, and he looked out to see crowds of Jews spreading carpets along the street. He was told by his Jewish inn-keeper that the Sabbatians were doing this to prepare the way for Sabbatai's interview with the sultan at Edirn Sarayi in the morning. When de Dreux made a sarcastic comment about this he was repri-manded by the innkeeper's son, who said, 'There is nothing to scoff at, for before long you will be our slaves by the power of the Messiah.'

Leyb ben Ozer describes Sabbatai's procession through the streets of Edirne the following morning, when he was joined by many of his supporters, who prayed for him as he was led by his captors to Edirne Sarayı. 'On the way he told them: "Behold what I have done; I am going to the King [girt] with a green and miserable belt and I am much distressed about this." When they heard him thus they were afraid and their spirit melted away, and they said: "First he said that he was about to take the crown from the Sultan's head, and now he is afraid of appearing before him in a green belt."'

Among those who were present during Sabbatai's interrogation at the palace was Hayatizade Mustafa Fevzi Efendi, one of the Sultan's physicians, who was a Jewish convert to Islam, the former Moshe ben Raphael Abravanel. Three years later Hayatizade became the Sultan's *hekimbashı*, or chief physician, a position he held along with the honorary rank of chief justice of Anatolia until 1691. His family converted to Islam with him; one of his sons became a professor in a *medrese*, or Islamic theological school, and two of his grandsons followed him as chief physician to the Sultan, one of them rising to the position of *sheyhülislam*, head of the Islamic religious hierarchy in the Ottoman Empire. Hayatizade served as Sabbatai's interpreter during the interrogation at Edirne Sarayı, as Paul Rycaut notes in his account of this historic occasion, referring to him as 'a Doctor of Physick'.

According to Rycaut,

*Sabatai* appeared much dejected, and failing of that courage which he shewed in the Synagogue. And being demanded several questions in Turkish by the Grand Signior, he would not trust himself so far to the vertue of his Messiahship, as to deliver himself in the Turkish Language, but desired a Doctor of Physick (who had from a Jew turned Turk) to be his Interpreter, which was granted to him.

Sabbatai's failure to speak Turkish was noted by those present at the interrogation, who felt that if he was in fact the Messiah 'his Tongue would have been loosed into Eloquence and perfection of Languages', as Rycaut puts it. Rycaut goes on to tell how the Sultan demanded a miracle from his prisoner:

But the Grand Signior would not be put off without a Miracle, and it must be one of his own chusing; which was that *Sabatai* should be stripped naked, and set as a mark to his dextrous Archers; if the arrows passed not his body, but that his flesh and skin was proof, like Armour, then he would believe him to be the Messiah, and the person whom God had designed to those Dominions and Greatness he pretended.

Sabbatai, 'not having faith enough to stand so sharp a tryal', responded to this challenge by renouncing 'all his Title to Kingdoms and Governments, alledging that he was an ordinary Cocham [rabbi] and Jew, as others were, and had nothing of priviledge above the rest'. The Sultan, not wholly satisfied with this confession, declared

That having given publick scandals to the Professors of the Mahometan Religion, and done dishonour to his Sovereign Authority, by pretending to withdraw from him so considerable a portion of the Land of *Palestine*, his Treason and Crime could not be expiated without becoming a Mahometan Convert: which if he refused to do, the Stake was ready at the Gate of the Seraglio to impale him.

Rycaut ends his account by telling how Sabbatai, having now been cornered, had no doubt as to what he should do,

for to dye for what he was assured was false was against Nature, and the death of a mad man: [so he] replied with much chearfulness, that he was contented to turn Turk, and that it was not of force, but of choice, having been a long time desirous of so glorious a profession, he esteemed himself much honoured, that he had an opportunity to owne it first in the presence of the Grand Signior.

Contemporary Turkish sources tell much the same story as Rycaut, differing only in a few details. These sources – including the Turkish chroniclers Nishanji Abdi Pasha, Fındıklılı Silahtar Mehmet Efendi and Rashid Efendi – say that the Sultan did not meet Sabbatai face to face, but was in an adjoining chamber separated from the council chamber by a *kafes*, or latticed screen, through which he could see and hear what was happening without being seen himself. The actual interrogation of Sabbatai was carried out by the Sultan's Privy Council, which in this case consisted of the Grand Vizier, Fazıl Ahmet Pasha, the *kaymakam* of Edirne, Kuru Mustafa Pasha, the *sheyhülislam*, Minkarizade Yahya Efendi, the Sultan's imam, Vani Mehmet Efendi, and the Sultan's physician, Hayatizade Mustafa Fevzi Efendi, who acted as interpreter.

Nishanji Abdi Pasha notes that when Sabbatai was offered the chance of saving his life by embracing Islam he hesitated at first and whispered to his interpreter in Ladino, saying that if he apostatized he would disgrace himself in the eyes of his followers. Hayatizade told Sabbatai not to be concerned, for after his conversion he could justify his actions to his followers and persuade them to convert too. Thus reassured, Sabbatai agreed to become a Muslim. Under Vani Efendi's direction, Hayatizade then had Sabbatai memorize a few Arabic phrases which he recited in formally making his conversion to Islam, after which he took the Turkish name of 'Aziz Mehmet Efendi'. The Sultan expressed his pleasure by sending word that the new convert was appointed *kapıcıbaşı*, or head gatekeeper at the palace, with the generous salary of 150 akcha a day. This ended the meeting, with all present pleased with the outcome – or so say the Turkish sources.

Sabbatai was then taken to the Ichoglan Hamamı, the Bath of the Janissary Recruits, where after being bathed he was dressed in the costume of a *kapıcıbaşı*. He was also given a fur coat as a token of the Sultan's pleasure at his conversion to Islam, along with two or three purses of silver coins.

The *kapıcıbaşı* was one of the senior members of the Sultan's household staff, supervising all the gatekeepers who guarded the entrances to the palace. He also acted as master of ceremonies at imperial audiences, and escorted important guests, such as ambassadors, to the Sultan's presence. Originally there was only a single *kapıcıbashı*, but later sultans often had several, as in the case of Mehmet IV, who would already have had at least one chief gatekeeper before he appointed Sabbatai. Sabbatai's position as *kapıcıbashı* would have been merely honorary, and he would not have been expected to perform the usual duties of a chief gate-keeper. Nevertheless he would have worn the colourful outfit appropriate to his position, dressed in a kaftan, or long gown, with a fur-lined sleeveless robe over it, and wearing a *mücevveze*, a tall cylindrical headdress widening upward from the brim.

Sabbatai's wife, Sarah, was brought to Edirne soon afterwards and also converted to Islam, taking the name 'Fatma Kadın', or 'Lady Fatma'. She did so under the patronage of the Sultan's mother, Turhan Hatije, the *valide Sultan*, or Queen Mother – an indication of how important Sabbatai's conversion was considered by the Ottoman court. According to Jacob Becherand, Sabbatai was asked to take a second wife from among the *Valide*'s slave girls, since as a Muslim he was allowed to have four wives, but there is no record of his having availed himself of the opportunity.

The news of Sabbatai's apostasy was announced first by the Ottoman authorities, and was confirmed a few days later by reports from the Jewish community in Edirne. Most Jews at first did not credit the reports – particularly the Sabbatians, for his disciples felt that Sabbatai would have died a martyr's death rather than embrace Islam. But when the news was confirmed the Sabbatians were mortified, and they and other Jews in Turkey were made fun of by their neighbours. According to Becherand, 'Wherever the Jews showed themselves, Christians and Turks would pursue them with ridicule until most of them hid in their houses for several days.' Leyb ben Ozer writes of the shame felt by all Jews at Sabbatai's apostasy: 'He brought ignominy upon the whole of Jewry by denying his faith and apostatizing, which nobody would ever have expected of him . . . that a holy man, scholar and Kabbalist like him should suddenly become a renegade from the God of Israel.'

Nevertheless, many of the Sabbatians kept the faith, adopting the view that Sabbatai's apostasy was part of an apocalyptic drama known for the moment only to him, and which he would explain at the proper time. As Becherand wrote, 'Some of the believers pretended that the new Muslim still was their true Messiah, but that he had to disguise himself for a while for the better success of his great design.' Sasportas reported that in Hamburg 'a considerable majority still adheres to their faith', and that Sabbatai's disciples believed that he had not converted to Islam but had ascended to heaven, and only his 'shape appeared to them in the likeness of an apostate'.

All observers were impressed by the calm attitude taken by the Ottoman authorities throughout the rapid rise of the Sabbatian movement and its apparent collapse with Sabbatai's apostasy. The relief at the peaceful resolution of the crisis is apparent in a letter written on 2 December 1666 by the rabbis of Istanbul to Isaac Jessurun, a wealthy and scholarly leader of the community in Izmir:

As for Sabbatai Sevi, you have received a full report, wherefore we do not wish to expatiate at present on the details of the affair. Let it suffice to say that we and our children should render infinite praise and thanks to God who has saved us from the sword to which our lives would have been forfeited, had it not been for a mediator who interceded for us.

The sensational news of Sabbatai's apostasy spread throughout the world in a variety of versions, nearly all of them distorted by the prejudices or religious beliefs of the sources, with the Sabbatians interpreting his conversion to Islam in a manner favourable to their Messiah and the non-believers condemning him.

Sasportas, writing from Hamburg in 1667, says that news of what had happened in Turkey had been delayed by the war between the Ottomans and Venice, and that four different interpretations had arisen among Sabbatai's followers concerning the meaning of their Messiah's apostasy.

The first interpretation, according to Sasportas, was 'that Sabbatai Sevi did not change his religion and has been libelled'. Sasportas then describes the scenario according to this theory: 'Sabbatai Sevi went to the King singing hymns and without a sword, as was prophesied. When the King beheld him, he embraced him and kissed him. He set the crown of the kingdom upon his head, as was prophesied, and wound a green scarf about it. One who caught a glimpse of this thought he had converted to Islam.'

Sasportas then presents the next theory: 'A second school holds that if he converted there is a deep purpose in it; that he wished to explore all the treasuries of the King of Turkey and his ancestors, so that when his kingdom came to be, he would be expert in all the ways of kingship.'

According to Sasportas, 'A third school has it that there are numberless secrets [involved] in his conversion. God has ordered it. Sabbatai Sevi must go into the world of the shards [the *qelippah*] to subdue them. Therefore he has dressed himself in them.'

The final theory presented by Sasportas turned out to be the one that eventually became the official Sabbatian dogma for the Messiah's apparent apostasy: 'A fourth school says simply that if he converted, it was not he himself, but a shadow. He himself rose into the sky and disappeared.'

Sasportas also writes of the rumour, which otherwise seems unfounded, that Sabbatai had asked the Sultan for a small grant of territory where he could rule over those of his disciples who followed him into Islam: 'it has been reported to us from Constantinople that this villain asked the Sultan to grant him dominion over some part of his territories and he promised the Sultan that the Jews would follow him and that he could then convert them to Islam'. Sasportas goes on to say that when this became known to the rabbinic authorities they forbade, on pain of excommunication, any Jew to visit Sabbatai or talk to him, 'Because there were many who even after his apostasy were seduced by his explanation that for mystical reasons it had to be thus that the Messiah enter for a certain period the realm of the *qelippah*, even as David did with Achish, the king of Gath [1 Samuel 21:10–15].'

The account written by Baruch of Arezzo is typical of those that tried to explain away Sabbatai's apostasy to his disciples. According to this fable, Mehmet IV had decided to exterminate all the Jews in Istanbul, but when Sabbatai embraced Islam the Sultan was so pleased that he relented. As Baruch writes at the close of his account, referring to Sabbatai as 'Our Lord', 'Our Lord made request before the Sultan for the Jews to reverse the letters of wrath and anger which he wrote to destroy all the Jews in Constantinople . . . and no Jews suffered any harm because of this.'

Meanwhile many rumours had been spreading about Nathan of Gaza, particularly after Sabbatai's apostasy. Contrary to most of the rumours, Nathan had remained in Gaza throughout the summer of 1666. According to a Sabbatian source, Nathan left Gaza only after learning that Sabbatai had 'set the fair mitre upon his head', as the believers referred to their Messiah's apostasy, and travelled 'in the company of more than twenty rabbis from Palestine to behold the face of Our Lord'.

Nathan's first known stop was at Damascus, where on 20 November 1666 he sent a letter to Sabbatai. In this, as quoted by Rycaut, Nathan made a veiled reference to Sabbatai's apostasy, followed by assurances that he and all other Sabbatians retained their faith undiminished: 'And though we have heard of many strange things, and our heart is as the heart of a Lyon, nor ought we to inquire a reason of your doings, for your works are marvellous and past finding out, and we are confirmed in our fidelity without all exception, resigning up our very Souls for the Holiness of your Name.'

Nathan went on to tell Sabbatai that he and his companions had come as far as Damascus, from where they were soon going on to Scanderone (Iskenderun), according to his command, 'that so we may ascend and see the . . . face of the King of life: and we servants of your servants shall cleanse the dust from your feet, beseeching the Majesty of your excellence and Glory, to vouchsafe from your habitation to have a care of us, and help us with the force of your right hand of strength, and shorten our way which is before us'.

Rycaut goes on to quote from a letter that Nathan wrote in Damascus to the Sabbatians of Aleppo. After extending his greetings to the believers in Aleppo, Nathan wrote that 'According as he [Sabbatai] has commanded us and the Twelve Tribes to elect unto him twelve men, so have we done: and we now go to *Scanderone* by his command to shew our faces together with part of the principal of those particular friends to whom he hath given licence to assemble in that said place.'

Nathan then told the disciples to hold fast to their belief in

Sabbatai: 'though you have heard strange things of our Lord, yet not let your hearts faint or fear, but rather fortify yourselves in your faith, because all his actions are miraculous and secret, which human understanding cannot comprehend; and who can penetrate into the depths of them?'

He then ended his letter by reassuring the believers that Sabbatai himself would soon dispel all the doubts that now troubled them: 'In a short time all these things shall be manifested clearly unto you in their purity, and you shall know and consider, and be instructed by the Inventor himself, and blessed is he who can expect and arrive to the Salvation of the true Messiah, who will speedily publish his Authority and Empire over us now and for ever.'

Nathan's letter was passed on by the Jews of Aleppo to the chief rabbinate in Istanbul. Nathan's words alarmed the non-believing rabbis in Istanbul, leading ten of them to write a circular letter to the major Jewish communities in the Ottoman Empire about the activities of the believers 'who hold fast to their folly', and at the same time informing their colleagues that the chief rabbinate had excommunicated all Sabbatians. According to Coenen, the anti-Sabbatian rabbis in Istanbul admitted that 'there were many who did not mind the ban and have strengthened themselves in their faith, more especially since rumours have spread that Nathan Ashkenazi of Gaza is on his way to these parts. It was to forestall these rumours and to thwart his [Nathan's] plans that the rabbis wrote to several places.'

Rycaut also quotes the circular letter from the anti-Sabbatian rabbis of Istanbul, which was written between 5 and 9 December 1666. According to Rycaut, the rabbis warned that Nathan's prophecies concerning the new Messiah would bring great trouble for the Jews, and that Nathan should be stopped before he went any further on his journey:

For we would have you know, That at his Coming he will begin again to move those tumults, which have been caused through Dreams of a new Kingdom, And that miracles are not wrought every day. God forbid, that by his Coming, the People of God should be destroyed in all places where they are, of which he will be the first, whose bloud be upon his own head.

The ten rabbis who signed this appeal sent out another circular letter on 30 January 1667, reiterating their warnings about the Sabbatian movement. This warning is mentioned by Rycaut in his account of how the news of Sabbatai's apostasy was received in Turkey: 'the Cochams of Constantinople . . . condemned the belief of *Sabatai* being Messiah as damnable, and injoyned them to return to the ancient Method and Service of God, upon pain of Excommunication'.

According to Rycaut, after Sabbatai's apostasy many of those who had believed in him were ashamed of their gullibility: 'The News of *Sabatai* turning Turk, and of the Messiah to a Mahometan, quickly filled all parts of *Turkie*; the Jews were strangely surprised at it, and ashamed of their easiness of belief, of the arguments with which they had perswaded others, and of the Proselytes they had made in their own Families.'

Rycaut, like Becherand, also notes that the Sabbatians were subjected to public ridicule after their Messiah had turned Turk:

Abroad they became the common derision of the Towns where they inhabited, the Boys shouted after them, coining a new word at *Smyrna* (*Poustai*) [Greek slang for a male homosexual] which everyone seeing a Jew, with a finger pointed out, would pronounce with scorn and contempt; so that this deceived people for a long time remained with confusion, silence, and dejection of spirit.

Nevertheless, according to Rycaut, most of the Sabbatians continued to keep faith in their Lord, believing that Sabbatai had not turned Turk,

but his shadow only remains on Earth, and walks . . . in the habit of a Mahometan; but that his soul and body are taken into Heaven, there to reside until the time appointed for accomplishment of these Wonders; and this opinion began so commonly to take place, as if this people resolved never to be undeceived, using the Forms and Rules for Devotion prescribed them by their Mahometan Messiah.

The opposition of the anti-Sabbatian rabbis in the major Jewish centres changed Nathan's plan to sail from Iskenderun to Izmir, and instead he travelled overland across Anatolia, beginning the missionary journeys that would continue for the rest of his days.

Meanwhile Sabbatai was beginning his new life as a Muslim honorary gatekeeper at the Sultan's palace at Edirne. The earliest extant statement by Sabbatai after his apostasy is a letter which he wrote to his brother Elijah Sevi in Izmir, dated 24 September 1666, 'the ninth day since my renewal according to His will'. The letter is very brief, ending in a note of melancholy resignation: 'And now let me alone, for God has made me a Turk. Your brother Mehmet, the honorary head gatekeeper.'

# 14. Redemption Delayed

After Sabbatai's apostasy the anti-Sabbatian rabbis concentrated their efforts on discrediting Nathan of Gaza, dogging his footsteps wherever he went, for they realized that, as the prophet, he was the one who had given the spark to the messianic movement, which would not die out as long as he remained its spokesman.

During the summer of 1667 the rabbis of Istanbul and Izmir demanded that their communities strictly observe the traditional fast of the Ninth of Ab, which had been transformed by Sabbatai into a feast, and they threatened to excommunicate those who violated their directive. According to Sasportas, those among the rabbis who had formerly followed Sabbatai now ruefully admitted their error, saying that 'We went astray like sheep . . . by relying on the staff of broken reed, Nathan of Gaza . . . whom we took to be a true prophet . . . but now we know all was lies and deceit.'

Nevertheless, many of Sabbatai's followers continued to keep the faith, and the attitude of the rabbinic authorities, particularly in Izmir, was to leave the Sabbatians alone so long as they did not create a stir that would lead the Turkish authorities to come down upon the Jewish community. As Joseph ha-Levi wrote in a letter from Livorno in April 1667, there were rabbis in the city who

to this day acquiesce in the words of the fools, in order to find favour in the eyes of the community, or at least keep silent. And I have been told by trustworthy informants that the rabbis in Smyrna and similarly in other cities have now issued a proclamation enjoining the avoidance of strife and quarrels, and permitting everyone who wants to do so, to believe [in Sabbatai].

Nathan's itinerary on his journey northward across Asia Minor from Iskenderun is not clear, for the excommunication pronounced upon the Sabbatians by the rabbinate in Istanbul made him avoid the larger towns. His entourage is known to have included thirty-six companions, including his father-in-law, Samuel Lissabona, other members of his family, his constant companion Samuel Gandoor, and several representatives of the Twelve Tribes of Israel.

Nathan's first known stop was Bursa, the first capital of the Ottoman Empire, at the foot of Mount Olympus of Bithynia, where he arrived towards the end of January 1667. The Sabbatians there received him with great rejoicing, their faith apparently unshaken by the apostasy, and their enthusiasm undiminished by the warnings from the rabbinate in Istanbul. According to Coenen, the believers held banquets in honour of Nathan and sang hymns to Sabbatai, crying out 'Long live Rabbi Sabbatai Sevi, our King and Messiah!' But this led the non-believers to complain to the Istanbul rabbinate, who warned the community in Bursa to get rid of Nathan. The rabbis in Bursa complied by excommunicating Nathan, who was told to leave the city immediately.

Nathan thereupon fled towards Izmir. Only six members of his original party stayed with him, including Samuel Lissabona and Samuel Gandoor. Some of his other companions remained in Bursa, others went to Istanbul, while the representatives of the Twelve Tribes of Israel went on to Edirne, where they planned to reunite with Nathan after they met with Sabbatai.

Nathan's next stop was at Bornova, a village on the outskirts of Izmir, where he arrived on the evening of 3 March 1667, a Friday. On Sunday he was met there by a group of Sabbatians who had come out from Izmir as soon as they heard of his arrival. But at the same time he received a message from the rabbis of Izmir warning him not to organize any public meetings. According to Coenen, the messenger was Abraham Leon, one of those to whom Sabbatai had given royal titles, in his case 'King Ahaz', another of the rulers of the ancient tribes of Israel.

Nathan thus entered Izmir very quietly, staying at the house of the Dr Barut mentioned by Coenen, a former Portuguese Marrano whom Sabbatai had appointed 'King of Portugal'. While in Izmir, Nathan made a pilgrimage to the grave of Sabbatai's mother, fulfilling an earlier promise he had made. He also took a ritual bath in the sea opposite the island of Khios, at the place where Sabbatai had nearly drowned in a whirlpool, only to be saved miraculously. Nathan then made an excursion to Khios before returning to Izmir, where he now stayed in the house of Elijah Sevi, Sabbatai's brother.

Gershom Scholem is doubtful that Nathan actually travelled across to Khios, on the grounds that 'it is incompatible with what we know of Nathan's itinerary'. But a voyage to Khios from the point where Nathan took his ritual sea-bath would have taken only a few hours in good weather, and there seems no reason why Nathan could not have gone across to the island and back while he was in Izmir and its vicinity. There is known to have been a group of believers on the island, and Nathan may very well have wanted to visit them. This community of Sabbatians on Khios continued in existence until the end of the Ottoman period, when it finally disappeared in the population exchange following the Greek–Turkish war of 1919–21.

According to Abraham Epstein, writing in 1893, Nathan wrote from Khios to Sabbatai's two brothers in Izmir, although Scholem says that the letter was written in Bursa. Nathan had to admit that 'the Word is not with me at present to reveal anything . . . It is sufficient that the servant be like unto his master', by which he meant that, like the imprisoned Sabbatai, he was not in a state of illumination and was unable to produce prophecies. Nevertheless Nathan was confident in the truth of his previous prophecies, proclaiming that 'I lift up mine hand unto the Lord . . . nor alter that which is gone out of my lips; that without doubt this is the year of our redemption and our salvation is at hand.' But he advanced the date of redemption to the spring of 1667, adding 'and I trust in God that thus it will be'.

Shortly before Nathan's arrival in Izmir two emissaries had come from the believers in Casale Monferrato. The envoys, Samson Bacchi and Hayyim Segré, brought a letter of homage to Sabbatai from their community. The letter, written before the news of Sabbatai's apostasy had reached Italy, told of 'the poor sheep of the congregation of Casale Monferrato in Italy, who are far away from the Holy Land and upon whom the splendour of the glory of your exalted and excellent Majesty has not shone directly, but only indirectly, as through the eye of a needle, by various reports . . .

which all agree that God has visited the people'. It went on to say that since 'the voice was heard for the first time and your fame went through all the provinces, we have not transgressed the commandments of the prophet of Gaza regarding penitential exercises and liturgies, and we have been mindful to praise your exalted and holy Majesty every day'.

The letter also said that the members of the community apologized for not coming themselves, for 'we feared for our lives from the government – and this hint will suffice', and that they had instead sent two envoys who would return with the Messiah's commandments.

The envoys also brought a letter of introduction to Nathan of Gaza, 'the man of God, who beholds visions of the Almighty as in a bright glass, and the light is with him, he that bringeth good tidings and announceth peace, and giving us a true prophet whose inspiration is true, and we confess and believe that his word is faithful and his promise steadfast'. The letter continued, 'Wherefore we of the congregation of Casale have bestirred ourselves to dispatch, on behalf of the whole community, two envoys. May they be graciously received by His Majesty and also benefit from the light of the Holy Spirit that is in you, so that they may instruct us in exoteric as well as esoteric teaching . . . to lead us to perfection.'

When Bacchi and Segré landed in Izmir, they learned from two Jews in the custom house that Sabbatai had apostatized. Despite their shock and dismay, they decided to remain for a while in Izmir, to see if the report of the apostasy was true and to learn more about the current state of the Sabbatian movement. They visited Elijah Sevi, who told them that the apostasy was an illusion and that his brother Sabbatai had actually ascended to heaven. This apparently reassured them, particularly since Elijah informed them of the imminent arrival of Nathan, who would personally enlighten them. While waiting, they met at Elijah Sevi's house with Thomas Coenen, whose book on Sabbatai preserves records of his conversations with the two envoys, from which it would seem that they were beginning to lose hope in their Messiah.

When the envoys finally met Nathan, after he had tried to evade them, they found him in a despondent mood. According to

Coenen, Nathan told the envoys that his life was in danger from the Turks and that he dared not speak to them. When they presented the letters from the community at Casale he refused to accept them personally, asking the envoys to give them to Hayyim Abulafia on his behalf. Nathan appeared unwilling to talk with the envoys about Sabbatai and the messianic movement, putting them off by saying that he would discuss these matters with them at a later time. He then abruptly left them, and the envoys never saw him again, although they were able to speak to several of his companions, including Samuel Gandoor. The envoys finally returned to Italy, telling Coenen before they left that they now considered Nathan to be a false prophet who spread dangerous ideas, saying in conclusion 'may God save us . . . and send us relief from another place'.

After Nathan left Izmir he headed for Edirne, probably taking a ship to Gallipoli and travelling overland through Thrace along the same route that Sabbatai had taken on his way to the Sultan's palace. Halfway between Gallipoli and Edirne he stopped at Ipsala, an ancient crossing point of the Maritza river, where there was a small Jewish community. Most of the community in Ipsala apparently still believed in Sabbatai, for Sasportas notes that the rabbis in Edirne were aware that the masses of Jews in the surrounding region 'still persevered in their deceitful faith'. Thus Nathan decided to take refuge among these believers, while he awaited word from Sabbatai as to whether it was safe for him to come to Edirne.

Rumours abounded about the conditions of Sabbatai's life at Edirne Sarayı in the days immediately after his apostasy, with his detractors mocking and vilifying him, while his faithful disciples invented legends to explain his conversion. Samson Bacchi, one of the disillusioned envoys from Casale Monferrato, wrote that Sabbatai was 'despised by the Turks and trying to ingratiate himself with them by spending most of his day in the mosque, where, however, according to the credulous believers, he devoted himself to the Torah and Kabbalistic meditations'. Bacchi also noted that the Jews of Edirne were strictly forbidden to visit Sabbatai or to communicate with him in any way, which would explain why Nathan interrupted his journey in Ipsala.

But other sources say that Sabbatai continued to communicate with his followers while he was at Edirne Sarayı. Some of his disciples followed him in his conversion to Islam, though, according to Israel Hazzan, Sabbatai commanded his followers to become Muslims only when he was in one of his states of illumination. Even then he urged only certain individuals to convert, and never advised that his followers should apostatize on their own initiative. Vani Efendi's plan of a mass conversion of the Jews to Islam would have made him encourage Sabbatai to continue his contacts with his disciples. But Sabbatai was playing his own game in this regard, though eventually he lost.

There was great excitement among the Jewish community in Istanbul when they learned that Nathan was in Ipsala. Several members of the rabbinate and lay leaders of the Istanbul community were in Edirne at the time, for the presence of the Sultan's court had brought many business people there from the capital. This group, who are referred to in the sources as the 'noble Lords of Constantinople', sent a delegation of three rabbis to meet Nathan at Ipsala and interrogate him as if they were a rabbinic court. Their report, signed on 31 May 1667, was published under the title of *A Memorial unto the Children of Israel*. The rabbis reported that Nathan had denied that he was a prophet or that he had the ability to perform miracles. He testified that he had made only a single prophecy, which was that Sabbatai was the Messiah, and that the day of redemption would come within a period of a year and several months. This prophecy would be falsified if the Messiah did not manifest himself before the Twenty-fifth of Elul – that is, within the period noted in Nathan's prophecy. When the rabbis asked Nathan to give them a prophetic sign, he told them 'to wait until the feast of the Pentecost . . . for he had been told by the Holy Spirit that [on that day] the man in Adrianople [Sabbatai Sevi] would have a great illumination and that by virtue of that man he would be able to perform a miracle. They waited . . . but nothing happened, and instead of an illumination a great darkness fell upon him.'

The report of the rabbis states that Nathan signed a pledge in which he agreed to four conditions. These were that he would not come closer to Edirne than twelve days' journey (Ipsala was only about two days distant); that he would not communicate in any way with Sabbatai; that he would not make any public appearances or even talk with anyone other than Samuel Lissabona and Samuel Gandoor; and that he would admit that all he said was false if the Messiah did not appear before the Twenty-fifth of Elul.

Nathan subsequently repudiated his pledge, saying that the rabbis, whom he cursed and compared to three unclean animals – the hare, the rabbit and the locust – had obtained it under pressure and had distorted his statements to them. As he wrote in his repudiation:

All those who hold steadfastly to faith in him [Sabbatai] are the fruit of the King Messiah's tree, and those who inveigh against him belong to the 'mixed multitude'. And those who keep quiet and do not vilify him are not from the same root as the souls of the 'generation of the Messiah', but their wisdom will be judged according to the measure of their generation.

Nathan in any event broke his agreement by remaining in the vicinity of Edirne for some weeks, moving from Ipsala further west to the town of Komotini, now in the Greek province of Thrace. During this time, according to Sasportas, he 'added to his wickedness by trying to convert others to his faith'. He also tried to revive the waning messianic movement by re-establishing its new rituals, proclaiming once more the transformation of the fast of the Seventeenth of Thammuz to a feast day.

The 'noble Lords of Constantinople' were considerably embarrassed by Nathan's activities, particularly by his renewal of the Sabbatian innovation of changing the fast day to a festival. This led them, secretly, to send an envoy to Sabbatai asking him to exert influence on his followers to observe the fast of the Seventeenth of Thammuz. The envoy was Joseph Karillo of Bursa, who had been ennobled in Izmir by Sabbatai as 'King Abiah' and had followed him to Edirne. According to Sasportas, Sabbatai wrote a letter to his followers directing them to ignore Nathan's proclamation and to observe the fast, entrusting this message to Karillo. Karillo communicated this message to the 'noble Lords of Constantinople', but he refused to show them the actual letter, probably because it vilified the rabbis. The rabbis responded by denouncing Karillo to the Turkish authorities, who fined and imprisoned him.

The rabbis then stepped up their anti-Sabbatian campaign, reporting that Sabbatai had appeared before them the day after Karillo's arrest, panic-stricken, and had produced a most extraordinary letter in which he 'confessed' that the entire messianic movement had been a fraud concocted by Nathan.

According to this letter, the affair had begun when Nathan 'discovered' the *Vision of R. Abraham*, which he altered by erasing the name of the real redeemer and inserting that of Sabbatai Sevi. Sabbatai claimed that 'He [Nathan] thus seduced me and led me astray with lies and deceits, and made me stray from the ways of the Lord until I myself began to lead astray the people who still believe in me to this day.' The 'confession' – which concluded, 'Thus speaketh the man that hath seen affliction without measure, your very young brother Sabbatai Sevi' – was dated 'in the week of the Pentateuchal lesson', which would have been in early December 1668. The confession itself was addressed to the rabbis of Edirne, who passed it on to the 'noble Lords of Constantinople'.

After addressing 'Our brethren of the House of Israel', the writer begins by saying that 'the bearer of this letter, may God's mercy be with him, is now with me', after which he makes his confession:

I announce to you that having come to think better of it I now realize with utter certainty THAT THERE IS NOTHING WHATEVER ABOUT ME and that whatever has befallen me in this matter, whether through myself or through those who prophesied about me, was nothing but a spirit of utter folly or a spirit of some other kind, and that the world will continue as usual until the true Redeemer arises.

He goes on to tell everyone to return quietly to their normal affairs: 'Wherefore let everyone be quiet at home and pursue his usual business, and let them not regard vain words but wait for the true salvation, which has not yet come, until heaven have mercy on us.' He concludes the letter with a blessing: 'And God Almighty give you mercy and protect you and all that is yours, and spread the tabernacle of peace upon you, and grant you to behold His salvation and your eyes may see the true king in His beauty. Amen.'

The 'bearer of this letter' was supposedly Aaron ben Hananiah, one of a group of envoys from the believers in Persia and Kurdistan who had come to see Sabbatai but, having arrived in Istanbul, were told that he had converted to Islam. Presumably, however, Sabbatai had changed his mind and decided to deliver the letter in person. In fact the letter was obviously a forgery, as was evident to anyone familiar with Sabbatai, who even after his apostasy continued to conclude his messages by writing 'thus speaketh the man who was raised up on high'. Throughout 1667 he continued to receive homage from visitors as if he were king. Israel Hazzan notes that when he and his friends from Kastoria visited Sabbatai in Edirne they would address him as if he were a Jewish king 'who has imparted of his glory to them that fear him'. Sabbatai responded by showing them gematria, written in his own hand, which were taken from the Bible and showed that he was in fact the Messiah.

The rabbis of Edirne announced that they had excommunicated Nathan, for he had broken his pledge to remain more than twelve days' journey from Sabbatai. They also asked their colleagues in Istanbul 'to wreak vengeance on these evil-doers', evidently meaning Nathan and all others who continued to be active in the Sabbatian heresy.

Around that time a new apocalyptic work made its appearance, written by Nathan or one of his disciples, its purpose being to explain Sabbatai's apostasy in Kabbalistic terms. Nathan's later writings continually refer to this work and quote it as proof of his own message: 'Behold all this has befallen AMIRAH and not one thing has remained unfulfilled.' The new apocalyptic work gives a dramatic description of the fateful events of 1666, when the Messiah was imprisoned and the believers lost faith, as a result of which the date of redemption would now be delayed by seven years.

The delayed redemption also brought forth a circular letter from a Sabbatian in Istanbul, probably after the messianic date set by Nathan for the spring of 1667 had passed. The writer exhorted all his fellow believers to keep the faith and be patient, 'for the word of the Lord shall not return void, and, though it tarry, wait for it, and the prudent shall keep silence until this word cometh to pass, for there are many mysteries and secret and hidden things have not been revealed, and that which has been revealed . . . the heart must not divulge to the mouth'.

The writer goes on to say that he 'who has *seen with his eyes and heard with his ears* even a small part of them will realize the depth of these things and not doubt the ways of God'. He expresses his hope 'that the sins of this generation prevent not the messianic fulfilment', and bids the faithful to pay no heed to the calculations of messianic dates and times, 'nor to voices nor rumours nor spirits, and be not disturbed by changes or contrarieties, for His thoughts are not our thoughts and the Lord looketh on the heart'. Meanwhile, he concludes, all that the faithful can do is to repent, to fast and pray, to bear witness to the truth, 'and to assist the Shekhinah . . . and not to do like unto them that say *if it is true and the Messiah comes, then we shall return* [to believe in him] *but not otherwise,* for they do not know, neither do they understand. They walk in darkness, and by their sins they cause the delay of redemption, for all Israel are responsible for one another.'

The day of redemption had been delayed, and all those who still believed in Sabbatai waited for a sign from him or his prophet, Nathan of Gaza, who had by then embarked on a strange mission to Rome.

# 15. The Prophet's Strange Mission

While Nathan was in Komotini he finally managed to arrange a clandestine meeting with Sabbatai in Edirne, although the exact date and circumstances of their brief reunion are unknown. All that is known – and this is only by inference – is that at this meeting Sabbatai sent Nathan on a mysterious Kabbalistic mission to Rome, which he embarked upon soon after his return to Komotini, accompanied by his father-in-law, Samuel Lissabona, and his faithful companion Samuel Gandoor.

The first stages of Nathan's journey took him across northern Greece, stopping in the various Jewish communities along the way. Here and on the later stages of the mission Nathan claimed that his itinerary was dictated by a *maggid*: this celestial presence always accompanied him, and 'at its command he journeyed and at its command he pitched', according to Sasportas. As Gershom Scholem writes of Nathan's tactics in explaining the reasons for his journey, 'To those who were not of his party he pretended that he intended to do public penance in Venice for his errors, whereas to the believers he confided he was going to Rome, where the ruin of the Gentiles would commence.'

Nathan's first stop after leaving Komotini was Salonika, where the Sabbatian movement had its strongest support. But even there the anti-Sabbatian rabbis had taken control of the Jewish community and prevented Nathan from speaking publicly with the believers. Then, after Samuel Lissabona took ill and died, Nathan was forced to leave the city, accompanied only by Samuel Gandoor.

Nathan headed across the Pindus Mountains of northern Greece to Ioannina, the hauntingly beautiful lakeside town in Epirus, in north-westernmost Greece. According to Evliya Chelebi, who visited the town in 1670, there were then about 160 Jewish families in Ioannina, principally employed in the manufacture and sale of silk. There were two Jewish quarters at this time, both of them

outside the walled inner city, where only Muslims were allowed to
live. Later the Jews were allowed to live within the city walls,
where they were safe from Albanian brigands.

There is no record of how long Nathan stayed in Ioannina, nor
of his activities there. Nor is there any record of a community of
believers in the town other than the tombstone of a Dönme from
Ioannina that I recently discovered in Istanbul. There were believers
at the time in Arta, some fifty miles to the south. This is attested in
an account of the Sabbatian movement by Meletios, the Greek
Orthodox bishop in Athens, who writes of how the believers in
Greece took to looking at the clouds and saying that these would
carry them to Jerusalem. He goes on to say that one night a follower
of Sabbatai in Arta thought to soar up to the clouds and jumped off
his roof, only to be dashed to death on the ground.

After Nathan left Ioannina he crossed the western ramparts of
the Pindus Mountains and made his way down to the Adriatic coast
at Igoumenitsa. There he took a ship across the strait separating the
mainland from Corfu, the northernmost of the Ionian Isles, where
he arrived early in 1668. This took him out of Ottoman territory
for the first time, for Corfu and the other Ionian islands were then
part of the maritime empire of La Serenissima, the Serene Republic
of Venice. Nathan's voyage would have involved subterfuge and
considerable risk, for at the time the Venetians and Turks were
locked in the last and most violent stage of their war over Crete,
which had begun in 1645 and lasted for nearly a quarter of a century.

Nathan would have stayed in Corfu town, which was guarded
by the great Venetian fortress that the Turks had twice besieged
and failed to take in the sixteenth century. There was a large
community of believers in the town, who apparently were in the
majority of the 500 Jewish families on the island, according to
the contemporary Corfiote historian Andrea Marmora. Marmora
writes of a prophetess who arose there in 1666, a daughter of the
merchant Hayyim ben Aaron, a Venetian Jew who had settled in
Corfu. When the girl began prophesying, which she did in a manic
convulsive state, the rabbis had her confined to her father's house
so as not to provoke the Christians into attacking the Jewish
community. While she was confined, 'everyone was running to

the house to revere her and bringing her presents', according to Marmora.

Early in his stay in Corfu, Nathan wrote to a fervent believer on Zante, the southernmost of the Ionian Isles; this was Joseph Hamis, a renowned physician who was also noted for his book on Kabbalism, *Belil Hamis*, published in Venice in 1624. (The Venetian Jewish scholar Leon Modena, who supervised the publication of this book, accused Hamis of encouraging fornication by providing advice to Gentiles on the use of love charms and amulets in this work.) Hamis had written to Nathan asking about 'the Lord whom we seek and for whom we wait every day and every hour . . . the Great Sabbath [i.e. Sabbatai] which is the Holy Sabbath'.

Nathan's answering letter emphasizes the necessity of Sabbatai's apostasy, the reasons for which are shrouded in Kabbalistic mystery, and bids Hamis to be of good faith while he waits for the delayed redemption. Nathan tells him that the believers have learned that Sabbatai has not been profaned because of his donning the turban, but has had to act thus because of the sins of Israel. 'Wherefore, my brethren and all faithful believers in Israel who stand and wait and tremble at these words, be strong and be of good courage, be not affrighted nor dismayed, turn unto the Lord your God with all your heart and soul and give thanks unto his great name, for verily we will behold what our ancestors have not seen.' Nathan concludes by saying that he himself will persist in his mission, comforting the believers who still wait for redemption.

And although people may say that these words of comfort are mere vanity because I am unable, at present, to work a miracle, yet I shall not desist from comforting the downcast who tremble at this word, that ask of me righteous ordinances and desire to draw near unto God, the poor and the needy who are in trouble and distress for the holiness of God's name.

Hamis was convinced by Nathan, and he remained a believer for the rest of his days, composing in his latter years a book of Sabbatian homilies. As Isaiah Tishby writes of him, 'the apostasy was but a minor accident, a kind of temporary fall of the Messiah and a test for Israel . . . Since he firmly believed that redemption was imminent, his main problem was whether Israel, having forsaken the Messiah, still merited salvation.' Hamis interpreted contemporary historical events in apocalyptic terms, seeing the conflict between Venice and the Ottoman Empire as the war between Gog and Magog that represented, according to *The Signs of the Messiah*, the birth pangs of the emerging messianic age. When the war on Crete ended with the final surrender of the Venetians, followed by a peace treaty in September 1669, Hamis was bitterly disappointed, for it meant that the final act in the drama of the messianic redemption had not yet begun.

Nathan's residence in Corfu is the subject of legends that grew out of the enthusiasm of his followers. His disciples reported that Nathan's death was sought by the local 'princes' – either the Corfiote nobility or the lay leaders of the Jewish community – but that these 'princes' were all miraculously struck dumb and eventually treated him with great honours. Another report from Corfu, signed by several believers, said that Nathan, after having taken a ritual bath in the Ionian Sea, went to the synagogue and buried his head in the Torah scroll as he read from it, after which he stood silently for a quarter of an hour with his right ear next to the Torah shrine as if listening to a distant voice, his face transformed with an expression of ineffable joy. The next morning, which was the Sabbath, he preached to the congregation and told them with a solemn oath that 'God himself has appeared unto me and told me that the rabbi Sabbatai Sevi will be the Redeemer, and if this come not to pass then I shall have no portion of the God of Israel.'

At the end of March 1668 Nathan left Corfu with Samuel Gandoor and sailed for Venice, where they arrived before Passover. The circumstances of their arrival are obscure, other than that their entrance into the Jewish quarter of the city was held up for two days.

The Jewish quarter in Venice, the Ghetto, had been founded in 1516 in Cannaregio, one of the six *sestieri* of the city, in its north-western quadrant. The name comes from the Venetian word *geto*, or 'foundry', for the Jewish quarter was established on the site where the foundries for casting metal and making cannon had been located until the beginning of the sixteenth century.

The Ghetto was established to house Jewish refugees who had fled from the marauding troops of the League of Cambrai, the coalition that tried to destroy the power of the Venetian Republic. Early in 1516 the Venetian Senate decided to set up a compound for the Jewish refugees across from the old foundries, the Ghetto Vecchio, on the island known as Ghetto Nuovo. During the course of three days beginning on 29 March, representatives of the Senate escorted some 700 Jews into the houses around what is now Corte Ghetto Nuovo, thus establishing the first ghetto in Europe.

Three bridges linked the Ghetto to the adjacent isles of Cannaregio, and guards were stationed at the gates that gave access to these from within the Jewish quarter. These gates were closed an hour after sunset in summer and two hours after in winter, and they were not opened till dawn. All Jews were required to remain inside the Ghetto at night, and during the day they were required to wear distinctive badges when they went elsewhere in the city.

When the Ghetto was first created, most of its residents were Askhenazim from Germany, along with some Italian Jews from the south. As time went on they were joined by Sephardim from Spain, Portugal and the Ottoman Empire. In the spring of 1541 the Levantine Jews – those from the Ottoman Empire – received permission from the Senate to move into the more spacious accommodations in the Ghetto Vecchio. Then in 1633 the Senate approved a request from the Levantine and Ponentine Jews, those from Spain and Portugal, to move into what then came to be known as the Ghetto Nuovissimo. This established the bounds of the Ghetto until the end of the Venetian Republic in 1797, when Napoleon took the city. Soon after the French occupied Venice they revoked all anti-Jewish laws, and on 10 July 1797 the gates of the Ghetto were broken down, though many of the Jewish community continue to live there today.

During the days of La Serenissima the Jewish population in the Ghetto averaged about 2,000, reaching a peak of about 5,000 in the mid-seventeenth century. The Ghetto had six *scuole*, or synagogues, one for each of the various 'nations' that made up the Jewish community. There were also several *midrashim*, or rabbinic schools, the most notable being the Great Academy, so called to distinguish it from the 'Small Academy', the council of lay leaders of the Jewish community.

At the time of Nathan's visit the most famous Jewish scholar in Venice was the Kabbalist R. Moses Zacuto, a former Marrano who had broken with the Sabbatians after Sabbatai's apostasy. Zacuto has been called 'the Jewish Dante', a name stemming from his *Tofteh Aruch (Hell Prepared)*, published posthumously.

The chief rabbi of Venice at the time was Samuel Aboad, another former Marrano, who was also head of the Great Academy. Aboad was not a believer, but despite this he did not unduly repress the Sabbatians. His earliest recorded comment on the movement is a letter dated 18 February 1666. There he tells of astonishing rumours that believers in Italy were preparing to take the remains of their ancestors with them to the Holy Land, writing that 'the graves of them that sleep in the dust have been disturbed so as to remove the bones of the dead from their graves'.

Aboad was concerned that the Sabbatian movement would provoke the wrath of the Venetian authorities, and he tried to keep the enthusiasm of the Sabbatians in bounds so as not to split the Jewish community. The believers seem to have been predominately from the lower classes, led by some of the rabbinic scholars such as Moses Zacuto, at least until the time of Sabbatai's apostasy. When the Sabbatians called for mass penitence in preparation for the final redemption, Aboad went along with them, on the grounds that penitential exercises would in any event benefit the community. He advised caution 'until these things clarify themselves', meanwhile allowing the believers 'to persist in their repentance'. He went on to say that 'a penitential revival is good at any time, but the essential service [of God] is in the individual heart, walking humbly with God, examining one's conscience, and ridding oneself of all sins that delay the messianic event'.

The mass penitence that ensued in the Venetian Ghetto is reported by Baruch of Arezzo: 'The vast majority believed that God had visited His people to give them bread, that is, the bread of salvation. The sages and lay leaders decided, in joint session, to proclaim a great repentance the like of which has never been known before in this city.'

The rabbinic authorities in Venice came into conflict with the Sabbatians on 2 July 1666, after a meeting of the Small Academy, where the coded letter of 25 May from the believers in Istanbul was read, with its message that in their opinion Sabbatai was truly the Messiah. The elders of the council wanted the letter to be kept secret, but the news leaked out, leading the excited Sabbatians to demand that the forthcoming fast of the Seventeenth of Thammuz be proclaimed a feast day instead, to celebrate the coming redemption. The council responded on the eve of the Second of Thammuz (4 July 1666), proclaiming that the forthcoming Seventeenth of that month would continue to be observed as a fast day, and forbidding any further discussion of Sabbatai and the messianic movement. The order was obeyed, but only in public, for private discussions went on even more intensely than before:

The news of Sabbatai's apostasy shocked the believers in Venice, but many of them kept the faith nonetheless. They were encouraged by a letter from Samuel Primo, Sabbatai's secretary, signed by him 'at the behest of the messianic king'. The letter commanded the believers to spread the tidings of the messianic movement and to punish with severity anyone who spoke against Sabbatai:

For whithersoever the King's command and his faith come, ye shall proclaim the tidings of salvation and comfort, and hold fast to the stronghold of repentances . . . Behold Our Lord the King will give to you all riches and honour and glory, and especially to the righteous [believers] who smote that man who rebelled against the Lord of the universe [i.e. Sabbatai].

The letter concluded with a message of encouragment for the faithful: 'Rejoice in your King, your Saviour and the Redeemer of your souls and your bodies in heaven and on earth, Who will resurrect your dead and save you from Subjugation to the kingdoms and from the punishment of hell. These things are beyond the power of the mouth to utter.'

Sabbatai's apostasy led many Jewish communities to destroy all records dealing with the Sabbatian movement, as Samuel Aboad writes from Venice in a responsum dated 1674: 'they burned all the records and writing in which his [Sabbatai's] name was mentioned, in order that it should not be remembered. And that which we heard from the faraway cities we beheld ourselves in the cities of Italy.' Aboad states that many of those who had followed Sabbatai had repented of their belief in him and confessed, 'Woe unto us, for we have sinned.' He goes on to note that 'Also the rabbis of Constantinople . . . sent orders to the communities near and far . . . [to do away] with everything that has been written about that deceitful affair . . . that it should be forgotten and mentioned no more.'

According to Baruch of Arezzo, the rabbinic council in Venice threatened to excommunicate anyone who gave shelter to Nathan or even spoke to him. Nathan was informed of this by Samuel Aboad, who said that he would not be admitted to the Ghetto 'lest his presence cause some adversity'. Nathan responded by saying that he would not enter the city if he was not wanted there, but stating that he was on a divine mission 'to a certain place on behalf of the whole congregation of Israel'. Several of the believers with some political influence appealed to two of the Venetian nobility they knew, and one of the nobles invited Nathan to his palace, where he remained for two days and a night. The two nobles then succeeded in obtaining permission for Nathan to enter the Ghetto, along with Samuel Gandoor.

While Nathan was waiting to be allowed into the Ghetto he was visited by Moses Zacuto. According to Sabbatian sources, Zacuto admitted to him that his own Kabbalistic knowledge was inferior to that of Nathan, though he had studied the *Zohar* for thirty-eight years.

During the two weeks that he was in Venice, Nathan was interrogated by the rabbinic council, who however could not prevent the Sabbatians from flocking to see their Messiah's prophet and to talk with him. The rabbis eventually forced Nathan to sign a document repudiating his messianic prophecies and saying that he had been led astray by an evil spirit. They later published Nathan's 'confession', along with their own account of the affair.

The rabbis' account begins by saying that they had been humiliated by the things that had happened during the Sabbatian movement, which had disgraced Israel in the eyes of the Gentiles.

As far as the 'young man Nathan of Gaza' was concerned, they had tried to keep him from entering their community and causing scandal, but when this proved impossible they had been forced to take action to discredit the heresy he was preaching:

[Wherefore] before his departure on Monday the Twelfth of Omer [9 April 1668], we assembled together the rabbis of the yeshiva and the leaders of the community. We summoned him [Nathan] and he appeared before us, and when we examined him he could not give a satisfactory answer to any question, and shame covered his face and he could hardly speak.

The rabbis concluded by stating that they had refrained from excommunicating Nathan, whom they felt they had totally discredited, along with the Sabbatian movement.

The pamphlet included Nathan's signed confession, which denied the validity of his messianic prophesies: 'Whereas the rabbis of Venice have ruled that although I have seen the divine chariot as Ezekiel has seen it, and [heard] a prophecy to the effect that Sabbatai Sevi is the Messiah, yet I was mistaken and there was no substance in the vision. I therefore consented to their words and said my prophecy concerning Sabbatai had no substance.'

Nathan soon retracted this confession, saying that it had been made under duress. He wrote to the believers and told them not to give credence to the pamphlet and other communications sent out by the rabbis of Venice, 'since there is nothing in them'. He said that the Venetian rabbis were worthless men who pretended 'that they had investigated and examined the matter and found it to be nothing, as if they were masters of the assay'. The rabbis had asked him to perform a miracle, and he had said, as he always did, that this was not within his power. He informed them that he was on a sacred mission to go to an appointed place where he would perform a special *tiqqun* on behalf of Israel. The rabbis had then proclaimed that his prophecies were not true, 'and this is what their investigation amounted to', he said.

He went on to say that, though the rabbis may have felt triumphant in forcing him to sign a confession, he had nevertheless got the better of them, since everyone could see how I deceived them, to fulfil the verse [Psalm 18:26]: 'With the pure thou wilt show thyself pure; and with the froward thou wilt show thyself froward.' For I merely said that I had consented to . . . what they had ruled – in a matter which is not subject to rulings. They wished to persecute me . . . but for the grace of God . . . who destroyed their counsel, they could not even speak one hard word against me.

Nathan's followers in Venice and elsewhere reacted with hostility to the Venetian rabbis' pamphlet. One of the Sabbatians in Venice, Meir da Mestre, wrote a circular letter ridiculing the rabbinic council that had interrogated Nathan, and at the same time he urged the believers to continue their penitential exercises. Among the Venetian rabbis whom he derided was Moses Zacuto, who responded by saying that the Sabbatians were fools to believe in Sabbatai after his apostasy, and that they were endangering Italian Jewry by their behaviour.

Nathan and Samuel Gandoor then sailed from Venice to Finale Emilia, on the river Panaro north of Bologna, which was as far inland as they could travel by boat. Baruch of Arezzo writes that a crowd of Christians assembled on the banks of the Panaro, having heard news of Nathan's appoach, and when they saw him they shouted, 'Behold the Messiah of the Jews!' From there Nathan travelled overland via Bologna and Florence to Livorno, his itinerary once more being dictated by a celestial voice.

At that time the Jewish community of Livorno numbered more than 1,200, their forebears having been welcomed there in the previous century by the Medici. Unlike the Jews in Venice and elsewhere in Italy, those in Livorno were not confined to a ghetto, but lived together without restrictions in their own quarter of the town, where they built a house of worship known as the Great Synagogue. Sarah Sevi had lived in Livorno's Jewish quarter before leaving for Cairo to marry Sabbatai.

The majority of the Jews in Livorno were Sabbatians, the most notable being Moses Pinheiro, Sabbatai's friend and fellow student in Izmir. The opposition to Sabbatai was led by Joseph ha-Levi, who writes of how he was abused because of this: 'And I looked and there was no one to help . . . for not only the ignorant crowd, but the scholars too [were against me].' He later describes how the believers in Livorno reacted to Sabbatai's apostasy, separating into five different 'sects' according to how they interpreted his conversion, all of them still believing that he was the Messiah and would lead them to redemption. Sasportas quotes Joseph ha-Levi in his account of how Nathan of Gaza and other Sabbatian preachers were misleading the believers, persuading them that their Messiah had turned Turk to command the Sultan's army so that he could exact vengeance for the Chmielnicki massacres. Referring to Nathan as 'Satan', Sasportas writes:

And now these masters of lies are bestirring themselves again and have written that the Grand Turk has made him [Sabbatai] a commander of his army and has dispatched him with two hundred thousand men to make war in Poland, so as to fulfil the prophecy of Satan Ashkenazi of Gaza who had said that he [the Messiah] would revenge the martyrs of Poland.

Nathan remained in Livorno for about two months, making no public appearances but meeting in private with the believers who had gathered around Moses Pinheiro. He then departed for Rome, accompanied by Moses Capsuto, a wealthy merchant who for long was a leading spirit of the Sabbatian movement in Italy.

The Jewish community in Rome dated back to the first century BC, and was the oldest in Italy. During the early imperial era there were 50,000 Jews in Rome, almost 10 per cent of the total population, scattered in different quarters of the city: Trastevere, Campus Martius, Porta Capena, Subura, the Esquiline. In the thirteenth century the Jews began moving into the area around the Portico of Ottavia and the Theatre of Marcellus.

The synagogue known as the Scola Tempio was probably built soon after 1492, and by 1518 this was flanked by the Scola Nuova. By that time the expulsion of the Jews from Spain, together with the arrival of many others from elsewhere in Europe, had considerably increased the size of the community in Rome, resulting in the building of synagogues for the Catalans, Aragonese, Castilians, Sicilians, French and Germans. In 1555 a bull of Pope Paul IV forced the Jews of Rome to live segregated in a ghetto, and to have no more than one synagogue, to sell their real estate, to trade only in secondhand goods, and to wear the yellow cap as a badge. The community was able to circumvent the Pope's decree by building the Cinque Scole, which in one building housed five synagogues: the Tempio, Nuova, Catalana, Castigliana and Siciliana.

The ghetto was on the banks of the Tiber between Lungotevere Cenci, Via Catalana and Via Portico d'Ottavia, a labyrinth of at least eight narrow streets winding between five small squares of which the largest was Piazza Giudia, surrounded by a wall that had at first five gates and then eight. The Jews remained confined in this ghetto for more than two centuries, their numbers reaching about 4,000.

There is little evidence from which to gauge the strength of the Sabbatian movement in Rome, where the power of the Roman Catholic Church would have kept the believers from making any public display of their messianic feelings. One report from the city in 1666 notes that word of the appearance of the Messiah has led to the arrest of a rabbi and several members of his congregation, 'because of the impudence which they displayed as a result of this news'. The chief rabbi of Rome, Joshua Menaggen, wrote late in the summer of 1666 to Samuel Aboad in Venice, telling of his unhappiness with the behaviour of the Sabbatians, particularly their conversion of fast days to festivals.

There are several somewhat different versions of Nathan's visit. Baruch of Arezzo writes that Nathan journeyed to Rome 'in peace and returned in peace. But what he did and spoke there I do not know, and even if I knew I would not breathe a word of it.' According to Sasportas, Nathan went to Rome without revealing his identity, but the Jewish authorities learned of his presence and threatened to have him arrested, whereupon he shaved his beard and disguised himself before fleeing back to Livorno. There he told his supporters that he had been to Rome 'on a mission from his Messiah, and that he had performed his mission by throwing into the river [Tiber] an inscribed scroll – and yet one year and Rome shall be destroyed'.

A third version is given in a letter that Samuel Catalani of Ancona sent to his son Raphael on Corfu early in July 1668 – a report indicating that Nathan's mission to Rome had already taken on the qualities of legend. According to Catalani, Nathan's actions convinced everyone in the Jewish community in Rome that he was acting under divine instructions. Nathan had shaved his head and was dressed in finer clothes than he normally wore, as befitted an emissary to a great city. Nevertheless he and his companion, probably Moses Capsuto, spent the night in a hostel for penniless wanderers, beggars and lepers. This puzzled their fellow wayfarers, for they appeared to be wealthy merchants who could well have afforded far better lodgings. Capsuto, if it was he, told the other guests in the hostel that his companion was an Ashkenazim and could not speak their language, which was Ladino. The two travellers left the hostel before dawn and travelled to the papal Castel Sant' Angelo, which they circled 'around and around' for the whole of the day, during which time Nathan was lost in meditation.

Nathan's actions in Rome were evidently inspired by the talmudic tradition that the Messiah would live like an outcast with the beggars and lepers at the gates of Rome. This legend had previously motivated Solomon Molkho, a Marrano from Portugal, whose claim that he was the Messiah had led the Inquisition to burn him to death at Mantua in 1538. Molkho's symbolic visit to Rome as the Messiah is described in a biographical letter entitled *Hayyath Qaneh*, which was known to Nathan. Molkho writes that 'I entered the city and left my horse and fine apparel with the innkeeper, and told him that I had a ladylove in those parts whom I loved since days of old and ancient years, but her parents were hiding her where I could speak to her only in the rags of a beggar.' He asked the innkeeper to help him disguise himself as a beggar,

and I blackened my face and donned the filthy rags . . . and walked about despised and rejected of men, like a man of sorrows and acquainted with grief . . . and I went through the streets of the city until I came to the bridge over the Tiber near the Pope's fortress, where the beggars and sick are, and I remained among them like one stricken, smitten of God, for thirty days.

Catalani concludes his account by saying that Nathan and his companion left Rome an hour before midnight 'and travelled a distance of eight days within two days, and arrived here in Ancona. He remained here for eight days and departed joyful and with a glad heart. And wherever he went no harm befell the Jews and nothing became known to the authorities, although these places were swarming with informers and apostates.'

Catalani's account is different from that of other sources, who report that, after leaving Rome, Nathan returned for a while to Livorno before he left for Ancona, accompanied by Samuel Gandoor.

After Nathan's return to Livorno he wrote several notes to relatives and friends reporting on the successful completion of his mission to Rome. One of these notes was to his father, Elisha Ashkenazi: 'Blessings be to God to whom thanksgivings are due, and who has rendered all good unto me and has granted me strength and help to do his service and to unify his great name and to execute my intention.' Another was to Sabbatai's brother Joseph Sevi: 'I betook myself to the well-known great city [Rome], for this was the purpose of my voyage to Italy.'

Nathan wrote of his journey to Rome at greater length in a circular letter entitled 'Account of the Mission Accomplished by the Rabbi'. This circular, written in rhymed Aramaic and couched in almost incomprehensible Kabbalistic allusions, speaks of his descent into the dark abyss of the Roman *qelippah*, where he successfully fought against the forces of evil with the aid of the Messiah Sabbatai Sevi, 'whose Lamp shineth in the Levant'.

Joseph Hamis alludes to this letter in a sermon to his congregation on Zante. There he praises Nathan's courage in facing

an unprecedented danger, and surely he was protected by angels because he could not otherwise have escaped the mouth of the lion in a natural way . . . For he had to descend to a depth of the *qelippoth* and to cast himself thither, so as to fulfil [Psalm 91:13]: 'Thou shalt tread upon the lion and the adder, upon the young lion and the serpent shalt thou trample', as he no doubt did on that occasion.

Nathan also wrote to his followers in Venice in the same Delphic style, concluding with a prediction of the fall of 'the land of thick darkness', by which he meant Rome.

Nathan then left Livorno, accompanied by Samuel Gandoor, travelling back across Italy to Ancona, whose Jewish community was the second largest in Italy after that of Rome. They arrived on 21 June 1668, and remained eight days. They tried to conceal their identity from the Jewish community there, for, as Nathan had confided to Moses Pinheiro, he 'was not in the least afraid of the Gentiles, but only of the wicked among the Jews'. Nevertheless they were recognized by Jacob ben Sabbatai Kohen, who had seen them earlier that year on Corfu.

Kohen reported their presence to the rabbi of Ancona, the aged and blind Mahallallel Halleluyah, a distinguished Kabbalist and poet who had kept his faith in Sabbatai Sevi. The old rabbi approached them in his synagogue and bade them welcome, after which he and Nathan had a long discussion on Kabbalism and the messianic movement. Among the interesting points that emerged from this conversation was that Sabbatai was favourably disposed towards the Karaite Jews, some of whom had become his followers. Another was that Nathan's mission to Rome had been at the express command of Sabbatai Sevi, who had paid all the expenses. This emerged when the rabbi expressed his surprise that they did not ask for charity. Nathan replied that all their expenses had been paid by Sabbatai, who, according to Sasportas, had ordered them 'not to take a penny from any Jew because they were now going on a mission' for the Messiah.

At the end of their stay the old rabbi came down to the pier to see Nathan and Samuel Gandoor off, whereupon he and Nathan embraced and kissed as they said farewell, weeping on one another's shoulders. As Nathan's ship set sail, a sudden wind rose from the west as if by miracle and sped it across the Adriatic – or so wrote the rabbi, ending the account of his meeting with the man he believed to be the Messiah's prophet.

According to one Sabbatian source, Nathan and Samuel Gandoor disembarked at Ragusa (present-day Dubrovnik), on the Dalmatian coast. They seem to have remained there for some time, for there is no further word of their whereabouts until 17 August 1668, when they are known to have been in Durazzo (Durrës), the main port of Albania. On that day Nathan wrote to his friend David Yishaki, who was with Sabbatai in Edirne, telling him that he had completed his mission to Rome, 'where I have cast myself into the deep of the great abyss'.

The next stage in Nathan's itinerary took him southward by ship from Durazzo to Patras, and then to Navarino (present-day Pylos) in the south-western Peloponnese. From there he and his faithful companion Samuel Gandoor wandered across 'the length and breadth' of Greece, guided by a *maggid* until they came to Salonika. According to a Sabbatian source, Nathan remained there for six months, preaching to those who continued to keep faith in Sabbatai Sevi.

Thus did Nathan complete the strange mission to which he had been assigned by Sabbatai, whose intention was to wreak revenge on Rome, at least in the mystic Kabbalistic sense, for having destroyed the Temple in Jerusalem sixteen centuries before.

# 16. The Messiah in the House of Pharaoh

While Nathan was off on his mission to Rome, Sabbatai had been biding his time at Edirne Sarayı, where his nominal duties as the Sultan's gatekeeper took little of his energy.

After Nathan concluded his mission, Sabbatai may have gone to Salonika to meet him late in the summer of 1668. There is no definite evidence that they did meet then, but Tobias Rofe Ashkenazi, whose scant information on this period is generally reliable, says that when Sabbatai was in the Sultan's employ he visited the three largest cities in the area: Edirne, Istanbul, 'and sometimes Salonika'.

Thenceforth Sabbatai and Nathan met frequently, even after Nathan left Salonika to settle in Kastoria. One of their meetings in Salonika is mentioned by Moses ben Isaac ben Habib, a native of the city, and local Dönme tradition preserved the memory of Sabbatai's visits to Salonika and of his sermons to his followers there. His disciples in Salonika included Joseph Filosof, whose daughter would become Sabbatai's last wife. Nathan also gained many disciples in Salonika, which thenceforth became the centre of the Sabbatian movement.

Nathan found many believers when he moved in 1669 to Kastoria, whose numerous Jewish community consisted largely of wealthy fur dealers. While living in Salonika and subsequently in Kastoria, Nathan travelled widely among the Jewish communities in Thrace, Macedonia and Bulgaria. Wherever he went he found believers to whom he preached the doctrines of Sabbatianism, which he expounded in a work entitled *Sefer ha-Beriah, The Book of Creation*, published in 1670. This became the standard work of Sabbatian Kabbalah for the remainder of the seventeenth century, and, together with Nathan's other writings, it played an important role in the subsequent development of the movement and of the variant sects that split off from it. Nathan also kept up a widespread correspondence with believers elsewhere while in Kastoria, where for three years Israel Hazzan served as his secretary.

One of those with whom Nathan corresponded was Abraham Cardozo, who remained in contact with the Sabbatian inner circle even after Sabbatai's apostasy. Cardozo had defended Sabbatai by quoting arguments from the prophet Isaiah, who had predicted that the Messiah would at first be 'despised and rejected of men, a man of sorrows and acquainted with grief [Isaiah 53:3] . . . and we reckon him smitten of God. We do not understand that he bears our sins, that he takes upon himself our sufferings and wounds, and is punished for all of us, for our vanity and evil.'

Writing in 1668, Cardozo refers to a letter that was written to Nathan from a believer in Baghdad, who asked him for news about the Messiah of the House of Joseph. According to Cardozo, Nathan replied that 'he [Sabbatai] was here with us', but that 'many had removed their faith from him' because they could not understand his conversion to Islam.

Cardozo, in another letter, reports that the rabbis of Izmir said that if Sabbatai truly believed that he was the Messiah it was his sacred duty to 'sanctify the name of God' by suffering martyrdom. Leyb ben Ozer, writing in the same vein, said that one would have expected that, rather than convert to Islam, Sabbatai should have been willing to endure the most terrible torture 'and to permit his limbs to be torn from him one by one'.

Cardozo himself found it impossible to give an explanation for Sabbatai's apostasy, or for why he had asked some of his followers to convert to Islam. He could only call it 'a messianic mystery', saying 'and I for one am incapable of producing convincing proof'.

Meanwhile another prophet had emerged, a young rabbi named Sabbatai Raphael, from Mistra in the Peloponnese. This is probably the charlatan described by Paul Rycaut, who dates his appearance several years later than other, more reliable, sources. According to Rycaut, Sabbatai Raphael appeared in Izmir in January 1674 and claimed to be the Messiah, but the Jewish community,

being ashamed at first to bring another Messiah on the Stage, by help of money they accused him of Adultery, and produced a Sentence from the

Kadi, condemning him to the Gallies; in order unto which, and in proof of his good behaviour he remained some time in prison, in which interim he found means to clear himself of that Crime by open evidence to the contrary.

Rycaut goes on to say that the would-be Messiah 'had for the present escaped out of the power of the Synagogue, but not their Authority and money prevailed more than the Friends or Disciples of this Impostour; whom we will leave in prison, and *Sabatai* in the house of *Pharaoh*'.

The house of Pharaoh was Edirne Sarayı, the palace of Sultan Mehmet IV in Edirne, where Sabbatai had been living in comfortable captivity since the autumn of 1666. There his wife, Sarah, bore him a son in late 1667, and the boy was called Ishmael Mordecai. Nathan had prophesied the birth earlier that year, and also that the boy would be born already circumcised, as rabbinic legend held had been the case with Moses, but Ishmael Mordecai proved to be perfectly normal in this respect. According to Baruch of Arezzo, Sabbatai 'knew his wife after he put the pure mitre upon his head, and she conceived and gave birth'.

Sabbatai remained in touch with his followers even though he was in the Sultan's service at Edirne Sarayı. His continued contacts with Nathan of Gaza led the rabbis of Istanbul to complain that Nathan had not kept to his agreement, but there was nothing that they could do about this. Other disciples moved to Edirne to be close to Sabbatai, who seemed to be free to meet with them. Among them were several followers of Nathan – those whom Sabbatai had appointed as representatives of the Twelve Tribes of Israel. Samuel Primo, Sabbatai's private secretary, had moved to Sofia, but he came to Edirne frequently to meet with Sabbatai. Abraham Yakhini visited Sabbatai in Edirne and then returned to Istanbul without being asked to apostatize. Sabbatai's brother Elijah travelled to Edirne with his eldest son in the summer of 1667, but, although he joined his brother's entourage, he did not convert to Islam until 1671. Apparently Sabbatai at this time wanted to maintain the fiction that his apostasy was pretence. Later the inner circle of the Sabbatians formulated the doctrine that Sabbatai had converted to Islam as a definite stage in his emergence as the Messiah, his descent into the realm of the *qelippah*, which would require that his followers do the same. Meanwhile he played a double game, as is evident from the testimony of Tobias Rofe Ashkenazi, who reports that Sabbatai 'behaved like a rabbi as was his wont. Sometimes he prayed and behaved like a Jew, and sometimes like a Muslim, and he did queer things.'

About eighteen months after Sabbatai's apostasy he apparently experienced a 'great illumination', which seems to have come upon him during the Passover festival in 1668. Two Sabbatian documents give an account of this illumination, apparently written by disciples from Sabbatai's own words. One of these documents, now lost, was seen in Salonika in 1915 by the historian Solomon Rosanes, who found it when he was allowed to examine the secret Dönme archives. Rosanes describes it as a small tract entitled *Revelation*, beginning thus: 'Know ye that in the year 1668, as Our Lord AMIRAH was at his table celebrating the ritual of the Passover night, there appeared to him twenty-four thousand angels saying: Thou art our Lord, thou art our king, thou art our Redeemer.' The second document, entitled *Sahadutha de-Mehemnutha*, or *Testimony concerning the Faith*, has survived in several copies. It comprises an account in five chapters of Sabbatai's revelation during Passover in 1668, along with a commentary on the first chapter and a Sabbatian commentary on Psalm 19. The identity of the author of this tract is uncertain, but it has been suggested that he may be Solomon Laniado of Aleppo, who seems to have made a pilgrimage to Edirne in 1668 to see Sabbatai. The tract is written in the language of an apocalyptic vision, in which the author takes on the role of an observer of this heavenly encounter between God and Sabbatai.

According to the author, on the night of Passover, 1668, God let the Holy Spirit rest on Sabbatai Sevi, so that from that moment he would save and redeem Israel. But Sabbatai asked God to spare the Jews from the tribulations of the messianic age. Then God said to him, 'Thou hast more pity on my children than I do. Half the tribulations have already been discharged; let them take upon themselves the other part and do not suffer thyself.' Thereupon Sabbatai replied, 'Lord of the universe! Thou doest all this to save my honour, which has been profaned among some Jews since the day I went out into the field to reap the seed that had been sown among the nations. Behold, since that day I have gathered many sheaves which I have converted and which I have added from the Gentiles to Israel.' He continued, 'Let my own honour be profaned in order to increase the glory of God and of Israel, for they will all repent with a perfect repentance when they shall behold the thousands and myriads of Gentiles joining themselves to Israel.'

God, in the presence of the patriarchs, then said to Sabbatai, 'Even the reaper of corn cannot gather everything without losing a grain or two from every ear. I am the owner of the field, and the wheat is mine. I do not mind losing a few grains provided that thou harvest the wheat.' Sabbatai said to God, 'Give me leave', whereupon he called a bird to come and pick a grain. 'Then he killed the bird and took out the grain and sowed it and watered it with the sweat of the heavenly beasts, and it became a mighty tree that brought forth flowers and wonderful fruit. He took the firstlings of the fruit and gave it to God, who smelled it as the smell of the spices of Paradise.' Then Sabbatai said to God, 'If one grain can produce much marvellous fruit, how then can I redeem Israel in such a way that [no] souls should be lost?'

Thus the Messiah will not abandon even a single grain, and until they are all gathered in he will not consider his mission as completed and make redemption manifest. This was the doctrine that developed among Sabbatai's follower in Edirne: that there is a 'holy seed' even among the Gentiles, and that the Messiah descended into the realm of the *qelippah* to save every last grain.

Israel Hazzan, who was very close to Sabbatai in these years, writes thus of his master: 'Not one grain of wheat will be lost. This is why AMIRAH said that even if one person died and the birds ate his flesh he would command them to render it back and make it perfect again.' And Hazzan quotes Sabbatai in this regard: 'thus have I heard from his holy mouth: I can gather all the wheat and bring them together in one barn, and not one grain shall be lost. And if perchance a bird swallow a grain, I shall retrieve it from his mouth . . . for the purpose of the *tiqqun* of his mighty deeds is that not one soul of Israel shall be lost.'

The Chevalier de La Croix, who was in Edirne at the time, writes that on several occasions he saw Sabbatai walking about surrounded by a crowd of apostate Jews, 'who followed him to the synagogues where he preached conversion to Islam with such success that during the five years or so that the mission of this zealot for the religion of Mahomet lasted, the number of Turks [i.e. Jewish apostates] increased every day'.

The earliest report of apostasies by Sabbatai's followers comes from Leyb ben Ozer, who was told by travellers coming from Turkey that Sabbatians who had converted to Islam were trying to persuade other Jews to do the same, and that they had in fact 'drawn unto themselves many sinners'. Sabbatai himself became active in this effort after his 'great illumination' in 1668. According to a document belonging to Zalman Shazar, former president of Israel, and quoted by Gershom Scholem, Sabbatai commanded many of his followers

to appear before him, and he explained to them that everything had been ordained in heaven, as it was written in the *Pirqey de-Rabbi Eliezer* [a Kabbalistic prophetic work] that the Messiah would be swallowed among the Ishmaelites. He explained everything in accordance with his false Kabbalah, and had ready answers for everything and thus caused more than three hundred Jews to apostatize in the course of two or three months.

Paul Rycaut mentions these conversions in his account of Sabbatai's life in Edirne Sarayı, where he spent much of his time in theological discussions with Vani Efendi. As Rycaut writes, referring to the events of the two previous years:

These matters were transacted in the Years 1665 and 1666; since which *Sabatai* hath passed his time devotedly in the Ottoman Court, educated at the feet of the learned *Gamaliel* of the Turkish Lawe, (viz.) *Vanni* Effendi, Preacher to the Seraglio, or as we may term him, Chaplain to the Sultan, one so literate as to be esteemed the Grand Oracle of their Religion.

According to Rycaut, Sabbatai and Vani exchanged views on the Jewish and Islamic religions, each learning from the other. 'In this manner *Sabatai* passed his days in the Turkish Court, as some time Moses did in that of the Egyptians; and perhaps in imitation of him, cast his eyes often on the Afflictions of his Brethren.' Sabbatai continued to profess himself as the redeemer of the Jews. But, to give no scandal to the Turks, he declared, that unless his fellow Jews followed him into Islam 'he should never be able to prevail with God for them, or conduct them to the holy Land of their Forefathers'.

Rycaut says that

Hereupon many Jews flocked in, some as far as from *Babylon, Jerusalem*, and other remote places, and casting their Caps on the ground, in preference of the Grand Signior, voluntarily professed themselves Mahometans. *Sabatai* himself by these Proselytes gaining ground in the esteem of the Turks, had priviledge granted him to visit familiarly his Brethren.

According to Rycaut, Sabbatai, while visiting his fellow Jews, instituted the practice of 'circumcising their children the eighth Day, according to the Precept of *Moses*'. He also took the opportunity of 'preaching his new Doctrines, by which he had confirmed many in their Faith of his being the Messiah, and startled all; with expectation of what these strange ways of Enthusiasm may produce; but none durst publickly owne him, lest they should displease the Turks, and incur the danger of Excommunication from one, and the Gallows from the other.'

According to Israel Hazzan, whenever Sabbatai was in one of his ecstatic states he insisted that all those around him should convert to Islam. 'And this is why Rabbi Nathan warned us to keep away from AMIRAH as much as possible during his illuminations, for at such moments he wants all present to embrace the religion of Ishmael.'

Nathan, in a letter to his followers in Kastoria, includes a message from Sabbatai, who explains with enthusiasm why he abandoned traditional Judaism for Islam. 'Know ye . . . that I recognized with great clarity that the true God . . . has willed that I should come with all my heart into the Islamic religion, the religion of Ishmael, to permit what it permits, and to forbid what it forbids, and to nullify the Torah of Moses until the time of the End.'

Sabbatai goes on to say that it is important for the glory of God that he should bring into Islam all those to whom he would reveal the Mystery of His Godhead. He answers those who said that he had become a Muslim on the strength of a vision, and that when the illumination left him him he would regret what he had done. 'This is not so,' he insists, 'for I did this on my own, through the great power and strength of the Truth and Faith which no wind in the world and no sages and prophets can cause me to leave my place . . . Thus speaks the master of Truth and Faith, the Turco and Mesurman.'

Here Sabbatai seems to be referring to himself as a 'Turk' (*Turco*) and an 'Egyptian' (*Mesurman*). According to Moses Pinheiro, during these years Sabbatai used to sign his name as 'Turco', but, as Gershom Scholem points out, the same Hebrew letters can be read Kabbalistically as 'the mountain of God'. Scholem also points out that 'Mesurman' means 'one who has become "Egyptianized", that is, brought into the sphere of Misrayim, Egypt, which is a symbol for the power and realm of the *qelippah*, the power of evil'.

The letter above was probably written about 1668–9. Around that time Nathan met with Sabbatai and expressed his hope that he would soon reveal the Mystery of the Godhead not just to a select few but to a broader gathering of his disciples. Apparently even Nathan himself had not been among those to whom Sabbatai had communicated his later esoteric teachings on this subject. Sabbatai even accused Nathan of not having correctly understood his earlier teachings, and of having misrepresented them in his Kabbalistic writings. Sabbatai wrote a bitter letter about this to Nathan, dated the week of 20–25 October 1669: 'I will pluck the prey, the unripe fig out of your teeth as you have trespassed on my ban and have stolen and eaten and have made others eat in your wake, and have clothed yourself in seemingly refined garb which in truth are nothing but rags, and you have done evil to yourself and an injury to my soul.'

Nathan responded to this attack with complete submission,

declaring his absolute acceptance of Sabbatai's messianic mission and supreme authority. After that relations between the Messiah and his prophet continued to be as amicable as they had been before Sabbatai's outburst.

Israel Hazzan is a particularly important source of information about Sabbatai's behaviour during these years. He notes that when Sabbatai was in a state of illumination he continued, as in the past, to sing both sacred songs and Spanish *romanzas*, particularly his favourite, 'Meliselda', 'and the ignorant say that he is singing lewd songs'. Hazzan describes the transcendent heights to which Sabbatai was elevated during his Kabbalistic meditations: 'When AMIRAH practised solitude with his holy soul, he would unite his soul' to the four supernatural worlds of the Kabbalistic cosmos. 'And I beheld all this. Blessed be the Lord that I was vouchsafed to see his face when he practised this solitude.'

Hazzan also notes that Sabbatai had the highest regard for Mehmet IV, who apparently reciprocated this feeling, and he writes that 'the Grand Turk would enjoy a place of honour before AMIRAH even after the [Messiah's full] manifestation . . . and I have heard with my own ears that AMIRAH would not suffer anyone to curse him [i.e. the Sultan]'. Moses Franco, another Sabbatian believer, was told by 'Matrona' – undoubtedly Sarah – that the Sultan would be rewarded for his kindness to Sabbatai by great honour and the *tiqqun* of his soul.

Sabbatai and his disciples in Edirne were frequently visited by Nathan, and together they made preparations for the 'second manifestation' of the Messiah. This was to take place seven years after Sabbatai's apostasy, that is, in 1673–4, by which time Sabbatai would have finished 'collecting the seed that was sown among the Gentiles'. At first Sabbatai and his group would meet in the house of the wealthy believer Moses Kohen. Subsequently they assembled in the courtyard of Joseph Karillo, who, according to Israel Hazzan, had not yet converted to Islam 'in the presence of the Grand Turk'. Meir Rofe came to Edirne with three scholars from Bursa, he reports, 'and they and other great scholars sat with AMIRAH in the presence of the Grand Turk. Finally Sabbatai told them that God was like unto a glorious youth that resembled him [i.e. Sabbatai himself].'

Visitors came to Edirne from afar to see Sabbatai, some of them to talk with him, others content just to enjoy the beatific vision of the Messiah's person. One such pilgrimage is described in a letter which Solomon Kohen, in Volhynia, sent to his brother on 11 August 1672, after his return to Poland from a visit to Edirne. Kohen had been a rabbinic judge in Budapest for more than twelve years, but had left his post in order to 'see the face of Our Lord' in Edirne.

Kohen says that in Edirne he was with Sabbatai and Nathan as well as

other leading scholars who are still with Our Lord. And I beheld the face of the king in his shining radiance on the great festival of the Ninth of Ab until the Seventeenth of the month [16–24 July 1671]. There we beheld the most awe-inspiring things . . . For all his deeds are true, and he is without any doubt the true redeemer; we were with him continuously day and night for more than eight weeks.

Kohen reports of Sabbatai 'that when the great light is upon him he has no regular sleep, though he occasionally dozes, and his face shines with a great light. And now we hope that all things will become clear and evident, and the hidden things will become manifest. I also vouchsafed to pray with him several times.'

Kohen also spoke with Sabbatai's brother Elijah,

a very learned and extremely wealthy man who is several years older than Our Lord, and he told me all that had happened to his brother from childhood to this very day . . . I was also privileged to preach in the great Portuguese Synagogue in Adrianople in the presence of R. Nathan and other scholars (who were there with the consent of Our Lord), and later Our Lord himself came.

Kohen's letter closes with a plea to his brother, asking him to pray so that he too will believe that Sabbatai is the Messiah. 'My dearly beloved brother, whom I know to be God-fearing, pray fervently that thou mayest share the faith in Our Lord and merit the great goodness which God has reserved for those that fear him,

Josua Helcam, supposed commander of the Ten Tribes of Israel

Sabbatai Sevi leading the Jews to Israel

A chief rabbi in Ottoman Turkey          A Jewish woman in Ottoman Turkey

Nathan of Gaza leading the Jews from exile to Israel

A synagogue in Amsterdam

עטרת צבי

כימים ההם ובעת ההיא

אצמיח לדוד צמח צדקה

ועשה משפט וצדקה בארץ

תקון

והגית בו יומם ולילה

Sabbatai Sevi enshrined as the Messiah (above)
The Ten Tribes studying the Torah with the Messiah (below)

Sabbatai Sevi in prison receiving his followers

*Gallipoli on the Dardanelles,* by Joseph Mery, *c.* 1830

*Ottoman Edirne*, by Thomas Allom, 1838

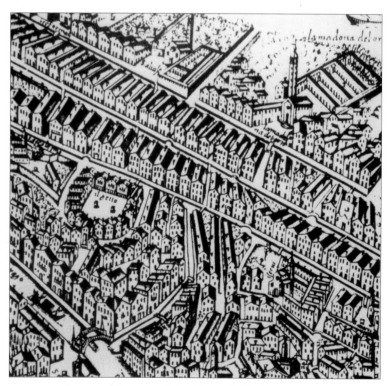

A perspective map of the Ghetto in Venice, 1677

*The Old Ghetto in Rome*, by L. Rossini, early eighteenth century

*Berat*, by Edward Lear, 1848

The chief dervish in the Mevlevihane
in Salonika, *c.* 1918

A dönme boy dressed as a dervish
in Salonika, late Ottoman era

An old *hanadji* praying with mourners in the Jewish cemetery in Salonika, *c.* 1918

for the faith in this matter is greater than the whole Torah . . . this our King and Lord is the true Messiah.'

Thus did Sabbatai pass his time in the House of Pharaoh, while his faithful followers waited and hoped for signs of the coming redemption.

# 17. Last Years in Edirne

Sabbatai had considerable freedom as the Sultan's chief gatekeeper at Edirne Sarayı. He could mix freely with both Jews and Muslims, and he often travelled from Edirne to Istanbul to meet with his disciples in the capital, who were led by his faithful follower Abraham Yakhini. He also met with unorthodox Muslims of the Bektashi and other dervish orders, participating in the religious ceremonies in their *tekkes* in both Edirne and Istanbul.

One notable dervish with whom Sabbatai was on intimate terms, according to Dönme tradition, was Niyazi Misri Dede, a renowned poet and mystic. Niyazi was born in the south-eastern Anatolian city of Malatya in 1617/18, the son of a Nakshibendi dervish. He joined the Halveti order of dervishes, but he often lived with the Bektashis, who revered him as a great poet and mystic. His fame as a Kabbalistic prophet came to the ears of the Grand Vizier, Fazıl Ahmet Pasha, who brought him to Edirne around 1670, when he would have first met Sabbatai. Later, when Niyazi was established as head of a Bektashi *tekke* in Istanbul, Sabbatai visited him there and was apparently initiated into the esoteric rites of the dervish brotherhood.

Sabbatai and Niyazi seemed to have a strong influence upon one another, which, given the extreme unorthodoxy of their views, could only take each of them even further from the accepted religious beliefs of Judaism and Islam. Niyazi, besides being a dervish (and a particularly unorthodox one at that – Cemal Kafadar describes him as a 'charismatic and often outrageous mystic'), was also rumoured to have secretly converted to Christianity.

The Bektashi sect would have particularly appealed to Sabbatai, for its heretical practices were similar to those of the Sabbatians, particularly the use of wine in its gatherings, where both men and women devotees came together in festivals, leading to the charge that they were engaging in sexual orgies. Mehmet IV was a Bektashi, as were all the sultans up to the end of the eighteenth century, and this may well have added to Sabbatai's interest in the sect.

Sabbatai continued his practice of creating new religious festivals and rituals for his followers. According to Israel Hazzan, 'he once sacrificed a dove, uttering with great devotion "an offering made by fire, of a sweet savour unto the Lord"'. He had changed the festival of the Ninth of Ab back into a fast in 1667, but he reintroduced it as a feast day in 1671 and proclaimed that all his followers should celebrate it for a whole week, like the Passover. But then the following year he abolished the feast and changed the Ninth of Ab back into a fast day.

Sabbatai experienced yet another state of illumination early in 1671 – one that would soon change the course of his life and of his messianic movement.

The source for this information is a recently discovered manuscript from the Dönme archives. This is a chronicle by Jacob Najara, the rabbi of Gaza, who spent the better part of 1671 in Edirne, during which time he was constantly with Sabbatai. The title of the manuscript is 'A Chronicle of what came to pass here, in Adrianople, from the day the distinguished scholar R. Jacob Najara arrived'.

Najara begins his chronicle with an account of a dream related to him by Sabbatai, 'who had been without illumination for a year and two months'. Sabbatai in his dream had fallen into a deep pit, from which he escaped by climbing up a rope thrown to him by his father and mother. Sabbatai did not interpret the dream for Najara, but it would seem that Mordecai and Clara Sevi had helped their son to make his way out of a deeply troubling quandary, and that was surely his ambiguous position as the Sultan's guest, with his messianic movement in a state of limbo. His subsequent actions show that he had indeed decided on a new course of action after his dream, which Najara dates to the Seventeenth of Sebat, that is 28 January 1671. Nathan, writing in 1672, refers to the Eighteenth of Sebat of the previous year as the anniversary of Sabbatai's renewal, meaning that his illumination had returned to him on the day after his dream.

Najara goes on to say that in their first meeting Sabbatai told him that most Jews would have to convert to Islam – or at least the chosen ones among his disciples. On the day before the feast of Purim, 23 February 1671, Sabbatai visited his brother Elijah, escorted by 'four of Vani Efendi's men'. Sabbatai said that he had experienced the most profound illumination of his life, and as a result he urged Elijah to convert to Islam immediately, along with his son. They then went together to the house of Vani Efendi, where Elijah and his son 'took the turban'.

Sabbatai and his entourage celebrated the feast of Purim at the house of Joseph Karillo. The next day Sabbatai rode about Edirne on horseback, surrounded by his disciples, and on the following Sabbath he presided over Jewish services in the Portuguese Synagogue as well as in a private home. The services were in both cases conducted quite openly, attracting the attention of many of the townspeople, including some Janissaries, but none of the Turks 'dared open his mouth', for Sabbatai and his disciples were under the Sultan's protection. That evening Sabbatai assembled those of his followers who were ready to convert to Islam – twelve men and five women – and on the following day he brought them to the imperial council chamber in Edirne Sarayı, where they all became Muslims. Sultan Mehmet, who had been observing the scene through a latticed screen, or *kafes*, then offered each of the converts a royal pension. But Sabbatai politely refused for his disciples, saying that they had converted through faith alone and without any thought of material reward.

A week later a Jew from Ipsala was persuaded to apostatize by Sabbatai, who told him to bring all the other Jews from his town to Edirne so that they too could be converted to Islam. On the following Sabbath, Sabbatai appeared in the Portuguese Synagogue with all his apostate disciples, leading the prayer service himself. He gave a long sermon in which he said that his interpretation of the messianic mysteries explained all the contradictions in Scripture and rabbinic tradition, after which he read passages from the Koran in support of his arguments.

On the Fourth of Nisan (5 March 1671) Sabbatai dictated letters to the leading scholars among his disciples in Istanbul, Bursa and Sofia, inviting them to meet with him in Edirne. His purpose was to persuade them to convert to Islam, but he told Vani Efendi and the Sultan that he could not predict the outcome of the discussion, since it depended on the divine illumination that would be granted to him.

On the Fifth of Nisan Sabbatai obtained a divorce under Muslim law from his wife, Sarah, to whom he had been married for nearly seven years. He justified his action by comparing himself to a Hebrew slave who had suffered for seven years in bondage to a bad wife who had been, as stated in a Jewish proverb, like 'leprosy to her husband'. Here Sabbatai quoted from Exodus 21:2, referring to the Hebrew slave: 'six years he shall serve: and in the seventh he shall go out free'. Nathan, who had never liked Sarah, wrote in a letter to Shemaya de Mayo, one of his circle, of how she had made life miserable for Sabbatai: 'The poison of the old serpent prevailed in her and she was constantly picking quarrels with him and sought to persecute him with all her might. She tried twice to put poison in his food, and, though no harm came to him, she persisted in her influence, and this was the real reason for the divorce.'

Nathan, in that same letter, writes that by the end of 1671 Sarah had borne Sabbatai a daughter, whose name and existence are otherwise unrecorded. Thus Sabbatai's decision to divorce Sarah must have been made before he knew that she was pregnant.

Sarah did not want to part with their son, Ishmael, who was three years old at the time of the divorce, and under Muslim law she was entitled to keep the child until he was seven. But Vani Efendi persuaded Sarah to give up the boy, who was brought to Sabbatai on the Seventh of Nisan. Sabbatai decided to have the boy circumcised on the following day, so that the lines of Leviticus 19:23–4 would be fulfilled: 'three years shall it be as uncircumcised unto you. But in the fourth year all the fruit thereof shall be holy.' The ceremony took place strictly according to Jewish rite, with the ten-year-old son of one of Sabbatai's apostate followers circumcised on the same occasion. Many Turks from the court at Edirne Sarayı were invited along with Sabbatai's disciples. Sabbatai circumcised his son himself, with Joseph Karillo acting as godfather. At the ceremony he gave his son the name 'Israel', but all subsequent references to the boy continue to call him Ishmael.

On the following Sabbath Sabbatai gave a sermon in the Portuguese Synagogue, reading first Leviticus 14:2, which begins with the words 'This is the law to be applied to a leper on the day he is purified . . .' He was undoubtedly referring to his recent divorce from his impure wife Sarah. His apostate followers accompanied him to the synagogue, but they were not permitted to partake of the feast, celebrating his divorce, that followed, though Sabbatai himself presided at it. The service and banquet were held quite openly, and again attracted the attention of crowds of townspeople, Turks included, with no one voicing any objection. At the end of the day Sabbatai conducted a traditional Jewish evening service in the Portuguese Synagogue, after which he rode on horseback around the town accompanied by thirty of the recent apostates, conspicuously holding a copy of the *Zohar*.

The scholars whom Sabbatai had invited to Edirne had by now arrived, the most prominent of those assembled being the rabbis Abraham Gamaliel, Joseph Karillo and Meir Rofe. Sabbatai's brother Elijah also joined them, although he was by no means a scholar. Nathan, who was then in the Bithynian town of Izmit (Nicomedia), was originally supposed to attend the meeting, but for some unknown reason he never received an invitation and was not present.

The meeting began in the *bash oda*, the imperial audience hall of Edirne Sarayı, in the presence of Sultan Mehmet, who was seated on his throne, with Vani Efendi and other Turkish notables in attendance. The proceedings were opened by Vani Efendi, who asked the Jewish scholars why they had come. They replied that they deeply respected Sabbatai Sevi, but that they did not understand why he had converted to Islam. Thus they had come to discuss the matter with him, and if they were convinced by his arguments they were prepared to follow his example. The rabbis were then brought to the Divan, the imperial council hall, where Sultan Mehmet retired behind the *kafes* of his private chamber, while Vani Efendi and the other Turkish officials sat back to listen to the debate.

The discussion that followed, which was conducted in Ladino, quickly degenerated into a heated squabble 'as in a talmudic school', according to Meir Rofe. This led one of the Turkish officials to suggest to Elijah Sevi that he intervene with his brother Sabbatai, so that the discussion could be carried on in a quieter and more dignified manner out of respect for the Sultan. Sabbatai would not hear of this, exclaiming in Turkish, 'Litigants shout in this Divan about a few aspers, so why should I not shout when it is a matter of the words of the living God!'

At the end of the discussion Sabbatai asked each of those present who had not yet converted to Islam if they were ready to do so now, but only two said that they were: Abraham Gamaliel and Joseph Karillo. According to Najara, the Sultan had ordered his chief executioner to put to death all those present who did not convert to Islam, but he relented, after which Sabbatai reassured them that they were under no pressure to apostatize. Sabbatai apologized to Mehmet for the fact that only two of his disciples had embraced Islam at this meeting, saying it was well known that the Jews were a 'stiff-necked people'.

Nathan's letter to Shemaya de Mayo also notes that, immediately after he divorced Sarah, Sabbatai announced that he intended to marry again. His new wife, he said, would be a Jewish girl and she would not convert to Islam, though she would wear Muslim dress. On hearing of this, Aaron Majar of Sofia offered his daughter as a bride to Sabbatai. Majar came to Edirne to discuss the match, but by the time he arrived Sabbatai had sunk into one of his states of deep depression and was unwilling or unable to talk about the matter. When he emerged from his depression Sabbatai suddenly announced that he would be taking back his divorced wife Sarah, which he did 'against the advice of all his friends', whereupon his illumination returned to him. But at the same time he said that at some future date he would marry the daughter of Aaron Majar. A marriage contract was drawn up and signed by Sabbatai and Majar on the Twenty-fifth of Sivan (24 May 1671), which Najara in his chronicle refers to as the day of the 'consummation of the blessed match'. Sabbatai, who was now once again in a state of full illumination, summoned all of those who had come to visit him in Edirne, including Najara, who writes that 'we beheld him in his beauty and strength, and we all fanned him with a fan in the manner of slaves to their master'.

The extraordinary state of mind of Sabbatai and his group at this time is communicated in a letter to Samuel Primo by an unidentified member of the inner circle in Edirne. The writer says that he feels himself to be 'in the garden of Eden' as he observes Sabbatai in the full light of the Messiah's illumination. He writes of Sabbatai's 'complete reversal from the holy side' on the Sabbath, implying that the Master was deliberately breaking the Sacred Law as part of his messianic evolvement of a new order before the final redemption. He notes further that at such times Sabbatai 'refuses to speak anything but the holy tongue [Hebrew], and this too only for the most urgent purposes'.

The unknown writer says of Sabbatai that 'he went to a place called Izurilak'. This is a corruption of 'Hızırlık', the name of a hill top north-west of Edirne where there was a dervish *tekke*. Hızırlık takes its name from Hızırellez, a mystical Muslim saint, whose name suggests that he is a reincarnation of the prophet Elias. The dervish *tekke* at Hızırlık was closed in 1642 when the locals complained that 'ungodly people' were congregating there. Mehmet IV reopened the *tekke* after he moved his court to Edirne, and he erected a *zaviye*, or hostel, to shelter those who, like Sabbatai, went there to visit the dervishes and take part in their ceremonies.

The writer says that after his visit to the *tekke* Sabbatai went to Edirne Sarayı accompanied by a Muslim cleric named Molla Mustafa and two or three of his apostate followers, one of whom was Moses Harari, who later reverted to Judaism, though secretly remaining a Sabbatian. Sabbatai behaved very oddly, sitting in the Grand Vizier's seat in the Divan and reciting from the Hebrew Bible. The palace guards tried to stop him, but since he was under the protection of the Sultan they refrained from touching him, and he mollified them with a bribe.

The writer notes that when Sabbatai was in a state of illumination, which often lasted for six days, 'all creatures appear to him as many flies', but 'when God hides Himself from Our Lord, he thinks nothing at all of his rank' and stays at home 'in order not to see the Jews, low and high alike'. Sabbatai emerged from his seclusion to celebrate the feast of Purim in the traditional Jewish manner, and was then in particularly high spirits. Soon afterwards he went with his brother Elijah and two other followers to the house of Ali Pasha, a high Ottoman official with whom he had established a close friendship. There he hosted a banquet at which kosher food and wine were brought from the house of his follower Moses Kohen.

Samuel Primo's correspondent notes that for three hours every day he met with Sabbatai, listening to him as he talked about such matters as 'the Mystery of the Godhead' and 'the God of Sabbatai Sevi'. At no point does he say that he himself was asked by Sabbatai to convert to Islam. He does note that on the Fourth of Adar *sheni* (the thirteenth month added in the leap year of the Jewish calendar), 3 March 1672, Sabbatai 'turned suddenly to the law of *hesed*', i.e. Islam. Thus it would seem that Sabbatai had decided to stop playing his double game, at least for the time being. Instead, he became a Muslim missionary among his own people, perhaps pressured into doing so by Vani Efendi.

The writer quotes two remarks by Sabbatai in this regard. The first was when Sabbatai, referring to his apostasy, said to him and his companions, 'Do not worry about this, for this is the will of God and I have to carry out His order.' The occasion of the second remark was a dinner at Sabbatai's home:

At the eve and exit of the Sabbath I ate with him in his house, and since yesterday the illumination returned to him anew. I am praying to God that this joy may manifest itself in the face of the sun, for he said to me: 'I have no satisfaction from anything, and I am not going to forsake the law of *hesed* [Islam], for through it there will be my redemption in the face of the sun.'

Meanwhile Sabbatai's followers for the most part kept their faith in him despite his apostasy and his renewed missionary effort on behalf of Islam. This is evidenced by a liturgical work known as *Hemdath Yamim*, which was used by the Sabbatians in Jerusalem as early as 1669. One of the prayers in this work addresses the Messiah 'who has descended into the abyss to gather the sacred sparks that have fallen into the *qelippah*', the Kabbalistic interpretation of Sabbatai's apostasy. The beginning of the prayer calls upon the

Messiah to emerge from the abyss to lead his followers, who still await him despite the calumnies of the non-believers:

Arise, messianic king, and behold the congregation of the Lord like unto a flock without a shepherd. How long wilt thou cast off and abhor, wilt thou be wroth with thine anointed, wilt thou make void the covenant of thy servant, profane his crown by casting it to the ground . . . so that all that pass by the way spoil him and he is a reproach to his neighbours?

The prayer closes with a plea to God for the return of the occulted messiah:

O Lord, turn not away the face of Thine anointed, and let Thy hand be established with him; and in Thy name shall his horn be exalted and be openly manifest to Israel Thy holy people, to save them that are sunk in the deep abyss, and to bring out of the darkness them that have been lost and polluted among the nations, to perfect the world in the kingdom of the Almighty, and the Lord shall be king over all the earth.

Israel Hazzan's commentaries on a number of psalms and other biblical texts shed some light on the esoteric world of Sabbatai and his inner circle in Edirne, particularly on the perplexing question of apostasy. Conversion to Islam was regarded as the burden that the elect of the inner circle had to bear, demanded of them by the Messiah so that they would share his terrible trial and *tiqqun*. Hazzan himself was spared this trial, but he makes it clear that he would have been ready to apostatize if Sabbatai had asked him to do so. Sabbatai made such demands during his periods of illumination, 'hitting out like a snake' at those around him, and Hazzan was fortunate enough not to be present on such occasions.

Hazzan's text implies that voluntary conversion to Islam was not necessary in the inner circle around Sabbatai. Those whom he directed to apostatize knew from Psalm 34:22 that 'none of them that trust in him shall be guilty', and hence no one who 'entered the crucible and forsook the Law of Moses in order to bring about the *tiqqun* of the world by taking the turban' would have to suffer for his action. 'They who took the turban at the behest of

# 18. Exile and Death

The intrigue that the rabbis of Istanbul had been plotting was put into action on 12 September 1672. Galland notes in his diary for that day that Sabbatai was arrested on orders from the aga of the Janissaries, 'together with the Muslims he had made Jews and that were with him'. The prisoners were then put in chains and sent to Edirne, after which nothing is heard of Sabbatai and his followers for three months.

The reference to Muslim converts to Judaism may confirm the comment made in the Sabbatian *Testimony of Faith* that many Gentiles had become believers, for these could have included Turks.

Galland heard nothing more about the case until mid-December, when a reliable informant told him that the orthodox Jewish rabbis of Istanbul had laid a trap for Sabbatai, giving a huge bribe to the *bostanji bashı*, the chief of the palace gardeners, who doubled as the palace guards. This official has been identified from a Turkish report as Boshnack (the Bosnian) Osman Pasha. The plot had been timed to coincide with the Sultan's absence on campaign, he and the Grand Vizier, Fazıl Ahmet Pasha, having left Edirne in June 1672 to lead the Ottoman army in an invasion of Poland. The campaign having ended victoriously, the Sultan and the Grand Vizier returned to Edirne in December of that year, when they found that Sabbatai was imprisoned.

The Grand Vizier, in a letter to the imperial council in December 1672, noted the report made to him by Osman Pasha that 'several disinterested Muslims had heard him [Sabbatai] utter blasphemies' and that they were prepared to testify 'and, if necessary, come to Edirne'. Galland, in a diary entry dated 15 December 1672, writes that the witnesses claimed to have seen Sabbatai 'wearing phylacteries and a Jewish bonnet [instead of a turban], surrounded by women, wine and several leaders [of his sect]'. The Chevalier de La Croix adds a detail to this in his memoir, writing that the *bostanji bashı* was making his rounds one night when he found Sabbatai and his followers singing psalms in a house in Kurucheshme, a village on the European shore of the Bosphorus. The allegations about wine, women and song lent support to the rumours that had long circulated about Sabbatai: that the arcane religious rites of his messianic movement involved sexual orgies.

Galland was told by a French-speaking Jew of Edirne named Mosé that Sabbatai's brother, probably Elijah, had petitioned the Sultan to have Sabbatai released. Mosé's report on the case indicated that Vani Efendi had also demanded that Sabbatai be set free. Mosé believed that Sabbatai could easily have obtained his release, but he seemed insistent on remaining in prison, and while he was in confinement the Grand Vizier ordered that the witnesses be brought to Edirne to testify against him. The Grand Vizier's letter summoning the witnesses reveals that he had now turned against Sabbatai, for he refers to 'the obstinate infidel who came from the Jews and received the turban, and who is now imprisoned in Edirne'. Though not mentioning Sabbatai by name, he notes that 'a complaint of persecution has been lodged with the Imperial Camp by the accursed prisoner who says "I am persecuted and treated unjustly."'

Galland writes of Sabbatai's case in his diary for 4 January 1673. Galland's informant told him that the witnesses against Sabbatai had been heard in Edirne, where he was sentenced to death, apparently because the judge had received a bribe of 4,000 piastres from the Jews of Istanbul. Galland also reports on the place and conditions of Sabbatai's imprisonment: 'He was imprisoned in Orta Capi, the prisoners of which are generally to be condemned. His execution, however, was postponed till after the month of Ramadan, when the Turks are careful not to shed blood. Even in this state Sabbatai obtained permission to visit the bath in order to be clean and pure as prescribed by the religion of the Turks.'

The place of Sabbatai's imprisonment referred to by Galland was Orta Kapı, the Middle Gate, the entrance to the Second Court of Topkapı Sarayı. The Orta Kapı gatehouse was the residence of the chief executioner, a post held by the *bostanji bashı*, and within it there was a cell reserved for those who had been sentenced to death. Those who occupied this cell were invariably beheaded by the chief executioner, who then displayed the severed head in a niche outside the gateway, where it remained for some days as an example of what happened to those who broke the Sultan's laws.

Galland's next diary entry on the case is dated 10 February 1673: 'the Jew Mosé told me about a month ago Sabbatai was banished to the Morea. The Grand Vizier would have put him to death, had it not been for the strong faction at court that supported him.' According to Sabbatian tradition, the 'strong faction' was led by the Queen Mother, Turhan Hatije, who intervened with her son to spare Sabbatai's life. The Sultan apparently remained very fond of Sabbatai, and so it was an easy decision to commute Sabbatai's death sentence and, instead, have him sent into exile.

Galland's identification of the place to which Sabbatai had been banished is vague and incorrect, since the Morea strictly speaking referred to the Peloponnese, although the term was often taken to mean western Greece and Albania. Santi Bani, ambassador of the Duke of Tuscany, reported on 19 January 1673 that Sabbatai had been banished to a place 'where there was none of his nation'. According to Leyb ben Ozer, Sabbatai had been exiled to Basan – 'where no Jew had ever set foot before'. This would be Elbasan, which is both a town and a region in central Albania but is nowhere near Sabbatai's actual place of exile. Leyb ben Ozer must have realized this, for he goes on to say that he never succeeded in finding out exactly where Sabbatai had been sent, for the rabbis in Istanbul had threatened to excommunicate anyone who spoke about Sabbatai Sevi, and as a result 'no good Jew would dare to inquire about this and to incur the penalty of the ban, while the believers invented all kinds of lies and confused one another'.

But in fact the place of Sabbatai's exile was known. La Croix, writing in 1679, says that Sabbatai was imprisoned in the fortress of Dulcigno in the Morea (actually in what was then northern Albania), and Tobias Rofe Ashkenazi remarks that the Turks kept him there to see what he would do next. Abraham Cuenque refers to Sabbatai's place of exile as 'a place far away at the end of the kingdom, where there are no Turks, but only uncircumcised [i.e. Christians]'. But travellers of the Ottoman period report that there was a substantial Turkish population in Dulcigno, though the town was predominantly Albanian, of whom the majority were Roman Catholic and the rest Greek Orthodox. There were also a large number of Gypsies and a whole quarter of black Africans, the latter having been brought there by the slave trade.

Dulcigno is known in Albanian as Ulqin, in Serbo-Croat as Ulcinj and in Turkish as Ülgün. The name 'Dulcigno' is Italian in origin, and was given to the town by the Venetians after they took it from the Serbs in 1421. The Venetians fortified the port and restored the Byzantine fortress that still encloses the old town. Dulcigno was captured in 1571 by the Turkish admiral Uluch Ali, later known as Kılıch Ali Pasha, and during the Ottoman period it degenerated into a lair of corsairs, cut off from its natural commerce in the Adriatic, suitable for nothing better than a place of exile. Edward Lear, writing in 1851 of the district of Shkodra (present-day Shkodër), just to the north-east of Dulcigno, remarks that 'They call this place the Siberia or exile of Turkey in Europe; and indeed it must be little less than banishment to those who have lived in Stamboul [Istanbul].'

Evliya Chelebi, who visited Ülgün in 1662, describes it as a 'fortress on the extreme frontier', administered by an Ottoman *voyvoda*, or provincial governor, along with a cadi.

The stone-built fortress is hexagonal in shape and is situated on the coast of the Gulf of Venice. It is well maintained and embellished with towers, ramparts, embrasures, loopholes and moats . . . Inside are the Mosque of Sultan Mehmet the Conqueror and small houses for the garrison troops . . . There are grain storehouses, armouries, water cisterns, and huge long-range battering guns. The castle warden resides in a loggia in front of the gate.

Evliya says that, in addition to the Turkish troops of the garrison, the fortress was guarded by 700 Albanian *gazis*, or warriors for the faith, 'brave and doughty soldiers all'. He notes that most of the Albanians were 'frigate men', that is to say, pirates, as is evident from his description of their activities:

There are 20 frigates in the harbour, as the fortress is situated on the coast. The Albanians here and from other towns take to their frigates and plunder infidel territory, burning and destroying, then return to Ülgün with rich booty and choice captives, and give one-tenth of the spoils to the *sancak-bey* [admiral]. When I was there, seven frigates had just returned full of booty from the infidel lands of Puglia [in southern Italy] . . . as well as 17 captives.

Such was the place to which Sabbatai Sevi was banished early in 1673.

The Turkish name of Sabbatai's place of exile was changed by the Sabbatians from Ülgün to Alqum, alluding to Proverbs 30:31: 'the king against whom there is no rising up' (in Hebrew, '*melekh alqum*'). This was probably an invention of Sabbatai himself, for in a letter of 1676, in which he signs himself as the king over all kings, and the anointed of the God of Israel and Judah, he notes that the letter was 'given at Alqum'.

Sarah was at first left behind in Edirne: although she wanted to go with her husband and to bring their son, Sabbatai refused to let her. There is no mention then or subsequently of their daughter, and it may be that she died in infancy. But after some months Sarah and her son, Ishmael, were allowed to join Sabbatai. Abraham Rovigo, the leader of the Sabbatians in Modena, said that he and his circle believed that the Messiah had to go into exile 'together with his wife, in order to make amends for Adam's sin, as it is written [Genesis 3:8], "and Adam and his wife hid themselves"'. But not long after her arrival Sarah died and was buried in Dulcigno, probably in 1674. Thus ended the remarkable career of the 'Wife of Whoredoms', who stayed by her exiled husband even after he rejected her, only to die in a remote corner of the Ottoman Empire where there is not even a gravestone to commemorate her existence.

Soon after Sarah's death Sabbatai decided that the time had come to formalize his marriage to the daughter of Aaron Majar of Sofia, to whom he had become engaged in the summer of 1671. He wrote asking Majar to bring his daughter to Dulcigno for the marriage, but he received word that the girl had been taken ill and died. He then wrote back to Majar and spoke of resurrecting the girl before long so that the marriage could be consummated. Sabbatai sent this letter with a Muslim mullah from Dulcigno, who also brought a message to Nathan and the other believers in Kastoria. When Nathan asked for news of Sabbatai, the mullah told him, referring to Majar's daughter, of 'the demise of the Lady and of the resurrection'. He went on to say that Sabbatai was hewing wood, cutting the big logs himself and leaving the smaller ones 'to Our Lord Ishmael'.

Ishmael was seven years old when his mother died, and it was only natural that he should come to be considered the heir apparent of the Sabbatian movement. Nathan had prophesied that through Ishmael the Gentiles would be spared in the final redemption, since God 'does not desire the destruction of his creation'. According to Israel Hazzan, who knew Ishmael during the years he was growing up in Edirne, 'the rank of Our Lord Ishmael will be like that of AMIRAH at the time of his anointing, for AMIRAH will be exalted beyond the comprehension of mortals, but "his seed shall be mighty upon the earth" [Psalm 112:2] and he [i.e. Ishmael] will be our Lord. For indeed AMIRAH had called him and told us [in Ishmael's presence]: This is your Lord.'

After the designation of Ishmael as 'Lord' and as heir apparent to the Messiah-king, the inner circle of believers began referring to Sabbatai as the 'Beloved'. Nathan, speaking of Sabbatai, instructed his followers 'to call him no longer Our Lord but Our Beloved'. Meir Rofe, in writing to Abraham Rovigo in this period, invariably refers to Sabbatai as 'Our Beloved' and not as 'Our Lord'.

Sabbatai may also have had with him in Dulcigno the son of the woman whom he had taken briefly from her fiancé in Istanbul. Although he continued to deny that he had ever touched this woman, he accepted legal responsibility for the son that she bore after she had been with him. The woman is not mentioned by the sources again after her marriage to Sabbatai, but her son may very well have remained with Sabbatai after he went into exile. Sabbatai, in one of his letters from Dulcigno, does mention a boy named Abraham, but other than that nothing further is heard of the youth.

After the death of Aaron Majar's daughter, Sabbatai made another attempt to find a new wife. This led him to write to one of his followers in Salonika, Joseph Filosof, a distinguished rabbinic scholar, whom he asked for the hand of his daughter Jochebed in marriage. Filosof consented to Sabbatai's request, knowing full well that the rabbinic authorities would come down hard on him for doing so. When the leaders of the Jewish community in Salonika dismissed him from the rabbinate and cut off his salary, Filosof responded with courage and dignity, according to Baruch of Arezzo, saying, 'I know what I am doing. The thing proceedeth from the Lord.' Referring to Filosof and his daughter Jochebed, Baruch goes on to write that 'he sent her, accompanied by his son, and the marriage took place in Dulcigno . . . according to the Jewish rite'. The son referred to here is Jacob Filosof, later known as Jacob Qerido, who would subsequently become one of the leaders of the Dönme movement. Sabbatai's new wife adopted the Muslim name 'Ayesha' at the time of her marriage, which was celebrated in the spring or early summer of 1675, though it is not known if her conversion to Islam took place then or later.

Sabbatai sometimes referred to Filosof as a reincarnation of Saul, and to his daughter as Mikhal, whereas at other times his new father-in-law is Mordecai and the girl is Esther. Writing earlier in 1675, Sabbatai addresses Filosof as 'Saul', saying, 'Give me thy daughter Mikhal as wife.' Writing in the spring of 1676, a year or so after the marriage, Sabbatai addresses Filosof as 'Saul, the elect of God, [who is] Mordecai, the son of Jair, the son of Shinei, the son of Kish, a Benjamite'. He then writes of 'my wife Hadassah Mikhal, who is Esther, my sister, my love, my dove, my undefiled, and her two sons Ishmael and Abraham'. Here Ishmael would have been Sabbatai's son by his late wife Sarah, whereas Abraham is probably the son of the girl he was with in Istanbul – the implication being that his new wife was looking after both boys as if they were her own children.

Sabbatai's letter to his father-in-law in the spring of 1676 is signed 'the Anointed of the God of Israel and Judah'. The letter is written in a spirit of great optimism, and Sabbatai expresses his hope that he and his family will soon visit Filosof in Salonika. This implies that Sabbatai was expecting that his exile would soon be ended, which may have prompted the references to forthcoming 'good news' in the correspondence of his disciples.

The first such reference is a letter written in the summer of 1675 to Abraham Rovigo in Modena from Meir Rofe, who was then in Livorno. Confusing the name of Sabbatai's father-in-law, Rofe writes that the 'Beloved' had married the daughter of Rabbi Florentin and that the prophet Nathan and Samuel Primo were planning to see him in Dulcigno. 'Surely it is not without reason that R. Nathan had resolved to visit him [now],' Rofe writes, remarking that he expected good news very soon, 'and then I shall return to my earlier abode with the Beloved'.

Rofe wrote repeatedly to Rovigo about Sabbatai, noting in one letter, 'as regards the Beloved, there is no news. If any good news should arise, I will let you know.' Later in the summer of 1675 Rofe wrote to Rovigo to say that Moses Pinheiro had received a letter from a believer who had spoken 'about the Beloved with his brother Joseph, and he told me there was no news at present but that he daily expected letters from his brother Elijah in Adrianople, who had notified him that he would soon have news for him from Our Lord and brother'.

Meanwhile Sabbatai had been biding his time in Dulcigno, receiving occasional visits from disciples and corresponding with other followers. One of those with whom he corresponded was Abraham Cardozo, who had written to him early in 1673 to say that Sabbatai was 'the anointed of the God of Jacob' and that the new messianic age would begin in the autumn of that year. When the autumn passed without an apocalypse, Cardozo sent off a batch of letters urging believers to be prepared for remarkable events that would occur in 1675. These letters caused a considerable stir, particularly in Amsterdam, where the well-known former-Marrano poet Daniel Levi de Barrios was so inspired by Cardozo's prophecy that he began mouthing prophecies himself, one of which is quoted by Sasportas: 'The signs of redemption will become manifest before the beginning of the Jewish New Year . . . all the Christians (and especially the ruler of Holland, Prince William of Orange) would become Jews . . . the king of France was Nebuchadnezzar . . . and the king of Spain was Hiram, the king of Tyre, and such like.'

Among those who visited Sabbatai in Dulcigno were members of his inner circle. Samuel Primo came to see him at least twice, on the second occasion leaving just before the arrival of Nathan of Gaza.

The nearest community of Sabbatians was in Berat, also known as Arnaut (Albanian) Belgrade, in south-central Albania, some 100 miles to the south of Dulcigno as the eagle flies. The most prominent member of the believers there was Isaac Albalag, a wealthy merchant who opened his home to travelling Sabbatians. Primo writes of his second visit to Sabbatai in a letter to Albalag dated 28 March 1675. He says that he has travelled from Sofia to Skopje (Turkish Üsküb), where he had been taken ill for ten days. While in Skopje he had received a letter from Sabbatai, who invited him to come to Dulcigno because he was in a state of illumination. Primo writes that on the following Monday he would be on his way to see the 'king in Alqum', and promises to pass through Berat on his return journey, in which case he will show Albalag Sabbatai's letter and other 'good tidings'.

Nathan writes of the prelude to his visit to Sabbatai in a letter to Shemaya de Mayo of Kastoria: 'Five weeks ago I left Sofia in order to travel to these parts, in the hope that I might find grace in the eyes of AMIRAH and be received by him. R. Samuel Primo preceded me by three weeks . . . and he is still standing before the Lord.'

Nathan goes on to say that Primo found Sabbatai to be in a depressed state, though he cloaks this in a Kabbalistic metaphor: 'But when he came he found him in the mystery of the fallen one. I waited for a fortnight in Durazzo and sent a messenger to ask permission, but he refused and I had to come thither to Belgrade [i.e. Arnaut Belgrade, or Berat] to wait until his great light will shine and I may behold his face.'

Abraham Cardozo, writing from Izmir to Meir Rofe, says that Nathan finally was invited to visit Sabbatai, whom he saw soon after Samuel Primo left. Cardozo indicates that the two visitors were planning to see the Sultan in Edirne, perhaps to ask that Sabbatai's forced exile be ended: 'The Beloved had written to his brother [Joseph Sevi] that in the winter of 1675 the great light did not cease. His brother was also informed that R. Nathan and R. Samuel Primo visited him and that they were together in great joy and preparing to go to the Grand Turk. May the Lord in his mercy announce to us tidings of salvation and comfort.'

According to Baruch of Arezzo, early in 1676 Sabbatai experienced one more period of 'great illumination, the like of which had never been before' and which led him to behave in a 'strange' manner that angered the Turks. Leading his followers in procession, Sabbatai marched to the Turkish quarter of Dulcigno and at midnight he climbed up the 'wall of the tower' (probably the ramparts of the ancient fortress), singing hymns and Ladino love songs. Later Dönme tradition explained this incident by saying of Sabbatai that 'he decided that the time of redemption had come, and that he was to manifest himself again in the sight of all living'.

At the end of Passover 1676 Sabbatai wrote a number of letters to his followers, 'given at Alqum', the only surviving one – addressed to the believers in Sofia – being a proclamation replete with biblical phrases suggesting that he is assuming aspects of divinity.

In the letter to Sofia, Sabbatai says that he 'made a serpent of silver and put it upon a pole'. In this he was playing the part of Moses, who, as is written in Numbers 21:9, 'fashioned a bronze serpent which he put upon a standard', using it as a talisman against the snakes sent by Yahweh to punish the Israelites for their blasphemy.

Sabbatai begins the letter with a greeting to his followers in Sofia, after which he says to them:

Behold I send an angel before thee to announce and tell you of all my glory . . . Beware of him and obey his voice, provoke him not . . . for I shall not forgive your transgression when God arises in judgement, and who is the god that can deliver you out of my hands, for beside me there is no God. But if thou shall indeed obey his voice and do all that I speak to you then I shall indeed go up and fill your treasures.

Sabbatai then concludes the letter in his usual bombastic style, writing, 'Thus saith the man who is raised to the heights of the

Father, the Celestial Lion and Celestial Stag, the Anointed of the God of Israel and Judah, Sabbatai Mehmet Sevi.'

Sabbatai wrote what proved to be his last letter in August 1676, requesting his friends in Berat to send him a *mahzor*, the festival prayer book, so that he could use it for the coming celebrations of Yom Kippur and Rosh Hashanah. The letter is signed with the same pompous titles as in the message he sent earlier that year to his followers in Sofia, ending with 'the Messiah of the God of Israel and Judah Sabbatai Sevi'.

On 5 September 1676 two visitors arrived in Dulcigno to see Sabbatai, their invitation having been brought to them by a Muslim mullah named Ali. The visitors were Joseph Karillo and another apostate follower, who may have been either Isaac Haber or Abraham Oheb. Six years later Karillo's companion gave Abraham Cardozo an account of their meeting with Sabbatai. He said that at the close of the meeting Sabbatai led him and Karillo to the beach south-east of Dulcigno, pointing along the shore as he spoke to them: 'Return every man to his house. How long will you hold fast to me? Perhaps until you can see beneath that rock on the coast?'

These were Sabbatai's last recorded words, spoken twelve days before his death on 17 September 1676. He died on Yom Kippur, the Day of Atonement, 5437. Dönme tradition holds that Sabbatai passed away at the time of the *ne'ilah* prayer that closes the service on the Day of Atonement – the time when rabbinic lore has it that Moses died. Sabbatai died just a month or so after his fiftieth birthday, and almost exactly ten years after his apostasy.

It appears that Sabbatai's inner circle kept his death secret for some time, probably because they were devastated by his demise and uncertain as to what it meant for the future of the messianic movement. More than a year passed before the news reached Italy, and then only vaguely and indirectly. The earliest extant record of Sabbatai's death is in a letter of 12 September 1677 from Meir Rofe in Livorno to Abraham Rovigo in Modena:

And now I will announce to you great news but keep it secret and for God's sake do not divulge it to anyone. A letter arriving from Sofia from

R. Samuel Gandoor says that it is true that the Beloved has been asked to the Celestial Academy on the very Day of Atonement. Let thy heart not be faint, and in another letter I shall write to you more about this matter.

Rofe then makes this Delphic comment to Rovigo concerning their departed Messiah: 'And you should ask a question how his words may come true after this, and why and for what reason this has happened, and whether this is a real death. Search this matter diligently and adjure the "master of the dream" to tell the truth, wheat without chaff, and let me know.' The 'master of the dream' referred to by Rofe is probably a *maggid* known to have manifested itself in the Sabbatian inner circle.

Rofe goes on to suggest again that Sabbatai's passing might be not a 'real death' but some form of messianic mystery which 'probably even the angels on high cannot grasp', for 'all matters concerning him are wondrous and mysterious from the beginning to the end, how much more this even'. He notes that Samuel Gandoor and the other members of the Sabbatian inner circle had imposed a ban of silence concerning the death of the Beloved, agreeing 'not to talk, let alone write to distant places . . . Even our master, the Holy Rabbi, the Holy Lamp [Nathan] whose light shines from one end of the world to the other, and from whom the great mystery [of Sabbatai's death] is possibly not hidden, is silent and does not want to speak for the time being.'

At the end of the letter Rofe notes that Elijah Sevi has taken Sabbatai's wife and children to Edirne. The children to whom he refers would have been Ishmael and Abraham. Ayesha eventually returned to the home of her father, R. Joseph Filosof, in Salonika, but there is no further mention of the two boys, whose fate is unknown.

Meanwhile the legend of Sabbatai's passing was beginning to take form. According to Israel Hazzan, when Sabbatai first realized that his end was approaching he prepared a seaside cave as his burial place, instructing those around him that he should be laid to rest there. The fully developed form of the legend was told a few years later by Baruch of Arezzo, who writes that on the eve of Yom

Kippur Sabbatai gathered around him his brother Elijah, his wife and the rabbis who were with him, after which he gave them final instructions concerning what to do when he passed away: 'Know ye that I shall pass away on the Day of the Fast of Atonement, at the time of *ne'ilah*. Carry me to the cave that I have prepared for myself near the sea, and on the third day my brother Elijah shall come to the cave.'

Baruch goes on to say that on the third day Elijah Sevi did as instructed and went to the cave, but found that its entrance was barred by a huge dragon. Elijah spoke to the dragon and said that his brother had told him to come there, whereupon the monster let him pass. When Elijah entered the cavern he found it empty, with not a sign of Sabbatai. As Baruch writes, 'Neither Our Lord nor anything else was in the cave, but it was full of light.'

Another version of the story of Sabbatai's passing is that he died and was buried in Berat. This story derives from Leyb ben Ozer, supported by the testimony of two chief judges of rabbinic courts, R. Joseph Almosnino of Belgrade and R. Sevi Hirsh Ashkenazi of Amsterdam, also known as Hakham Sevi. Gershom Scholem and most other twentieth-century Hebrew scholars rejected this version, whose principal proponent was Izhak Ben-Zwi, the second president of Israel.

Thus two variant traditions developed concerning the place of Sabbatai's death and burial, though the generally accepted version was that he had died and been buried in Dulcigno. The question of Sabbatai's burial place and other quandaries eventually deepened into insoluble mysteries, as the believers tried to come to terms with the passing of their Messiah. The inner circle soon developed a theology which had it that the apparent death of the Messiah was merely an occultation, and that at the appointed time he would return in all his glory for the final redemption. Their opponents mocked them for their vain hope, one of them saying, 'He is dead and buried. What more do you expect of him? Do you still cling to him?' But the Sabbatians held to the belief that their Messiah would return, quoting Psalm 142, the prayer of David 'when he was in the cave', which they believed to be a prophetic revelation of Sabbatai's occultation – particularly the last line of the psalm:

'Bring my soul out of prison, that I may praise thy name. The righteous shall compass me about; for thou shalt deal bountifully with me.'

# 19. The Messiah Occulted

While the other members of the Sabbatian inner circle tried to come to terms with Sabbatai's death, Nathan of Gaza remained silent, reduced to a state of profound despondency over the apparent collapse of the messianic movement.

Bitter quarrels among the Sabbatians led Nathan to leave Kastoria for Sofia. After he arrived there, probably in late 1676, he wrote what proved to be his last extant letter, addressed to 'my brethren and beloved that are in Kastoria'. He told of his unhappiness with the quarrels among the Sabbatians in Kastoria 'regarding redemption', and he commanded them 'on pain of excommunication' to 'keep one's mouth from speaking in this matter, either good or bad'. He paraphrased Lamentations 3:26 in his closing advice: 'It is good that a man shall both hope and quietly wait for the salvation of the Lord . . . thus speaketh he who seeks and pursues the peace of all Israel.'

By around 1678–9 the Sabbatians were beginning to agree on a new doctrine, which was that Sabbatai was not really dead but rather occulted from human view. According to a Sabbatian notebook written by a disciple of Hayyim Mal'akh, who was himself a follower of Samuel Primo, the doctrine of occultation was revealed to Nathan by a celestial *maggid*: 'AMIRAH was exalted and hidden, body and soul, on the Day of Atonement, at the time of *ne'ilah*. Whoever thinks that he died like all men and his spirit returned to God commits a grave sin. This was revealed by the holy R. Nathan to R. Samuel Primo, R. Samuel Gandoor, and the group of his close friends.'

Tobias Rofe Ashkenazi was astonished that even the most eminent scholars among the believers continued to keep faith after Sabbatai's death, which they explained as being 'mere illusion, for he was still alive, though hidden from the eyes of all living'.

Baruch of Arezzo took the view that during this occultation Sabbatai had gone off to join the Lost Tribes of Israel: 'Our Lord has gone to his brethren, the children of Israel, the Ten Tribes that are beyond the river Sambatyon, in order to marry the daughter of Moses. If we are worthy, he will return at once after the wedding celebrations to redeem us; if not, then he will tarry there until we are visited by many tribulations.' Baruch also notes that a rabbi in Greece was said to have seen 'Our Lord', who told him 'that he was departing this week for Tartary, which is the correct route to the river Sambatyon'.

Nathan lived until almost the end of his life in Sofia, where the heads of the Jewish community still kept faith in Sabbatai. Samuel Primo dwelt there as well, and they and other members of the inner circle perpetuated the doctrine of occultation and thus kept alive the flickering spark of the messianic movement. The Sabbatians in Italy were told by a believer who had been to Sofia that Nathan, while preaching in the synagogue there, had taken an oath that 'Sabbatai Sevi was the true Messiah and that there would be no other but he'.

During Nathan's last years in Sofia his Sabbatian devotional practices were duly recorded and passed on to his disciples in Salonika, most notably the rabbi Isaac Hannan. These records were surrounded by a nimbus of legends, one of which had it that when Nathan said his morning prayer a heavenly fragrance emanated from his room. Once, when the scent was unusually strong, Isaac Hanan's brother went up but was so overcome by the wonderful scent that he fainted. Nathan later explained to him that the souls of the saints in paradise came to his room when he said his morning prayers and normally wore their heavenly clothes, but on this day they had come without their garments and hence the fragrance which they exuded was unusually powerful.

During those last years in Sofia, Nathan made a number of liturgical innovations that subsequently became part of the Sabbatian ritual. He made, for example, several changes in the *yigdal*, the joyous hymn sung on the eve of Sabbath, giving it a messianic interpretation. He also composed a number of other hymns for the faithful, including a song of praise for Sabbatai

Sevi, beginning with this verse: 'How fearful, how highly exalted are you, Sevi's light! Priests and prophets does he beautify. In him is hidden the awaited gift. Who is like unto him, light of my heart, O great king, Sabbatai Sevi?. . . Thou eternal one above all worlds! My Messiah – he is my support! My king, my crown, my pride – Sabbatai Sevi!'

Another of Nathan's innovations came from his statement that 'a man who busies himself with matters pertaining to AMIRAH, even by telling stories only, is considered like one who studies the mysteries of the *merkabah*'. Later this statement was taken to heart by the Hasidim, who applied it to the telling of stories about their own saints, the *saddiqim*. This custom, which has always been considered an innovation of the Hasidim themselves, was actually acquired by them from the Sabbatians in following Nathan's command, his object being the perpetuation of Sabbatai's memory on the humble but most enduring level of folklore.

Nathan is known to have been still in Sofia through the first half of 1679, but in late summer or early autumn he decided that it was time to move on. A letter addressed to Mordecai Eisenstadt in February 1680, probably from Abraham Rovigo, reports that Nathan

had left Sofia for Salonika. Before his departure he had preached a sermon and exhorted the community to repent, saying that Sabbatai Sevi was surely alive and that he [Nathan] was going to meet him since he [Sabbatai] was now returning from beyond the river Sambatyon. He thus departed from Sofia to Turkey, and the people in Sofia are making great penitence.

By the time this letter was written Nathan had already passed away. He had died on Friday 11 January 1680 in Skopje, now the capital of Macedonia. Sabbatian legend has preserved the tradition that Nathan had arrived on a Friday from Kumanova, a day's journey north-east of Skopje on the road from Sofia. He immediately went to the house of the rabbi of Skopje, who would have been either Jacob Abulafia or Isaac Yahya, both of whom were followers of Nathan and possessed copies of his works. As soon as he arrived, Nathan asked that the gravediggers in the Jewish cemetery be sent to prepare his grave, since he knew that he was about to die and wished to be buried before the Sabbath. Nathan went on to say that his servant would arrive on Sunday, and that he too would die before that day was over. The legendary account of the prophet's passing goes on to say that 'While he was still in the rabbi's house he fell down and died, and the members of the congregation buried him with great honour. Also his servant arrived and died on the appointed day, and he was buried next to Nathan's tomb.'

A longer and more detailed account of Nathan's last days is contained in a work called *The Mystery of the Faith of Our Lord*, the Sabbatian notes of Benjamin Kohen and Abraham Rovigo compiled by Hayyim Segré. Segré notes that late in 1693 a visitor from Belgrade, a native of Sofia, had told him 'that as a young man he had been studying the Talmud with R. Nathan, and that he [Nathan] had been living in . . . Sofia for about thirteen [*sic*] years'. The visitor then described a last prophetic vision that Nathan experienced before he left Sofia on his final journey: 'One night he had a supernatural convulsion and was lying in a faint when the prophecy came to him. As soon as he recovered the rabbis came to ask of him what he had to tell.' Nathan told the rabbis that he had seen an enormous pillar in heaven, which he interpreted as the advent of a great war and terrible bloodshed. He prophesied that the Sultan would go to war against the Habsburg Emperor, but would be defeated. 'Within three or four years', however, the Grand Turk would gain the upper hand 'because Samael, the Prince of Evil, would help him, but at the same time the Messiah would make himself manifest'.

The story of Nathan's passing is told in the last paragraph of *The Mystery of the Faith of Our Lord*:

On the last night the meeting took place in the house of the wealthiest Jew in Sofia, and the rabbi [Nathan] asked them [Nathan's followers] to provide for the dowry of a poor girl, saying that this would be the last wo months, until the imperial army under King John II Sobieski of Poland defeated the Ottomans and forced them to flee in disorder. Kara Mustafa Pasha led the broken remnants of the Ottoman forces to Belgrade, where he was dismissed by Mehmet IV and then executed, his 'head rolling before the feet of the Sultan', according to an anonymous Turkish chronicler. The disaster at Vienna eventually led to the downfall of Mehmet IV, who was deposed on 8 November 1687 in favour of his younger brother Süleyman II. Mehmet was then confined to the infamous Cage at Topkapı Sarayı, the prison where the younger brothers of a reigning sultan were kept to prevent them from contesting the throne. Mehmet died in the Cage on 6 January 1693, the cause of his death being given by various chroniclers as gout, depression or poison.

By that time Vani Efendi had also died, so that by the end of the seventeenth century most of the principal figures in the drama of Sabbatai Sevi's apostasy had passed away. All but Sabbatai himself, his followers would say, for by then the doctrine of the Messiah's occultation was a matter of faith among the Sabbatians, who settled down to wait for his eventual Parousia, or Second Coming. And they could now wait with some hope, for Nathan's last prophecy would appear to have come true, with the downfall of Mehmet IV coming after a great war between the Sultan and the Emperor.

The other disasters prophesied for the 'last days' when the world would be turned upside down with the appearance of the Messiah were apparently now coming to pass, for besides the great war between the Sultan and the Emperor there were almost yearly visitations of the plague in Turkey as well as terrible fires in Istanbul, such as the one in 1680 that nearly destroyed all Galata. Then an eclipse of the sun cast the moon's shadow in a fleeting band across the city, temporarily turning day into night, convincing many that the end of the world was imminent.

Some of the Sabbatians reverted to orthodox Jewry after the death of Sabbatai, most notably his brother Elijah Sevi, who returned to Izmir and was accepted back into the Jewish community

time he would bother them as very soon he would enter b
Nobody understood what he meant by this bitterness, but he
on that same day for Üsküb and immediately on arriving there
and died.

Nathan had never converted to Islam, and so he wa
in the Jewish cemetery of Skopje. The tombstone on
grave was still standing until the Second World Wa
it was destroyed. The epitaph on his tombstone wa
graphed in 1917 and published by Solomon Rosanes in h
*of the Jews of Turkey and the Levant*. The epitaph refers tc
as the 'Holy Lamp . . . the master and rabbi Abraham I
Nathan Ashkenazi, may his soul rest in paradise, who w
to the Celestial Academy on Friday, the Eleventh of Set
year "The punishment of thine iniquity is accor
O daughter of Zion [Lamentations 4:22]."' (The qu
Lamentations contains a chronogram giving the year of
death.)

According to Rosanes, Sabbatians made an annual p
to Nathan's tomb on the anniversary of his death,
the occasion by reading the *Zohar* and having a feast i1
This pilgrimage continued until the early years of the
century, when the political turmoil in the Balkans and
sequent displacement of the Sabbatians brought the tradi
end.

Nathan's prophecy of a great war between the Sulta1
Emperor would seem to have been borne out by th
events. Fazıl Ahmet Pasha had died in 1676 and
succeeded as grand vizier by his foster brother, Kar.
Pasha of Merzifon. The new Grand Vizier eventually
Mehmet IV to mount a great campaign to capture Vienn.
Habsburgs, which the Ottomans under Süleyman the M
had tried but failed to conquer in 1529. The second
campaign against Vienna began in the early summer of 1(
Kara Mustafa Pasha led a huge army against the Habsbur
the Austrian capital under siege. But the defenders stoo

there. Sabbatai's other brother, Joseph Sevi, seems to have remained among the inner circle of those who had converted to Islam and kept the Sabbatian messianic tradition alive after the death of the one they continued to call the 'Beloved'.

Two major figures of the Sabbatian movement continued their activities into the first decade of the eighteenth century. One was Samuel Primo, Sabbatai's private secretary, who lived on until 1708, serving as chief rabbi of Edirne in his last years. The other was Abraham Cardozo, who succeeded Nathan of Gaza as the leading theologian and preacher of the messianic movement.

Cardozo was banned from Tripoli in 1673 by the rabbis there and went on to Tunis for a year, after which he left to join the group of believers in Livorno in the autumn of 1674. But at the end of May 1675 the elders of the community in Livorno forced him to leave, whereupon he went to Izmir, where for the next six years he was the leading spirit of the Sabbatians there.

The rabbis finally forced Cardozo to leave Izmir in the spring of 1681, and during the next sixteen years he moved in turn to Bursa, Istanbul, Rodosto (Tekirdağ, on the Sea of Marmara), Gallipoli and Edirne. While in Rodosto, Cardozo claims that he received letters from Sabbatai Sevi's widow, Ayesha. According to Cardozo, he met with Ayesha and she proposed marriage to him as 'leader of the believers', though nothing came of it.

Meanwhile Cardozo had issued a new prophecy, saying that redemption would come on Passover in 1682. Once again the appointed time passed without incident, but then in the next years there was a mass apostasy of Sabbatians in Salonika, giving rise to the sect known as the Dönme, or Turncoats. Cardozo strongly opposed this sect and wrote polemics against it. Nevertheless, Dönme literature is full of praise for Cardozo, who became a major influence on the developing Dönme theology. Cardozo also wrote in opposition to the ideas of Nathan of Gaza concerning the true nature of the Godhead, which he claimed was understood correctly only by himself and Sabbatai Sevi – a doctrine he published in a short work called *The Secret of Divinity*.

In 1686 Cardozo returned to Istanbul, where some Christian diplomats protected him from the hostile rabbis who condemned him and his disciples. He had been married twice and both wives had died, as had all his many children, most of whom had been killed by the plague. His opponents accused him of having illicit relations with women and fathering illegitimate children, although he was then nearing seventy. He was finally forced out of Istanbul in 1696 and moved to Edirne, but after three months he was forced to leave by Samuel Primo, who had become chief rabbi of the city.

He then moved to Rodosto, where he obtained a short tract entitled *Raza de-Mehemanutha* (*The Mystery of the Faith*), which, he claimed, Sabbatai Sevi had dictated to one of his disciples in Dulcigno at the end of his life. Cardozo describes the origins of this work, which agreed with his own teaching about the nature of the Godhead: 'When I was in Rodosto in 1697, a tract came into my hands entitled "The Mystery of the Faith" and written by a certain rabbi in Alqum at the instructions of Sabbatai Sevi. Its teaching is shining with wonderful wisdom and true faith, and there is no difference between it and my own teaching regarding the Mystery of the Godhead.'

Cardozo moved to Khios for a short while, and then settled in Crete, where he remained until around 1703. It is possible that he lived in the Jewish quarter of Khania, where there is known to have been a community of Sabbatians. By then he had issued a new prophecy: that Sabbatai Sevi would reappear in 1706 and lead all those who believed in him to Eretz Israel, the Holy Land. Cardozo made plans to go to Israel to await the Second Coming, moving to Haifa later in 1703. But the rabbis of Jerusalem and Safed refused to allow him to stay in their communities, and he was forced to move on to Egypt. He then settled in Alexandria, where in 1706 he was killed by his nephew during a family quarrel.

Cardozo's death came at just about the time that he had predicted for the Second Coming of Sabbatai Sevi. But Sabbatai did not reappear, disappointing his believers once again, though they could once more take comfort from their firm belief that he was still alive, albeit occulted by the celestial cloud that hid him from their view.

# 20. The Dönme and Other Believers

At the time of Sabbatai Sevi's death in 1676 the great majority of his followers, who called themselves *ma'min*, or believers, remained within the Jewish faith. During the previous decade, from the time of Sabbatai's apostasy in 1666, some 200 families had followed their Messiah into Islam, most of them in Edirne, Salonika, Istanbul, Izmir, Bursa and a number of other places in Asia Minor and the Balkans.

The apostates – the Dönme, or Turncoats – regarded themselves as an elect group who had been chosen by the Messiah himself. Outwardly they were good Muslims and had Turkish names, but privately they practised a messianic Judaism based on the teachings of Sabbatai Sevi and their interpretation by others of the inner Sabbatian circle, principally Nathan of Gaza. Their lives were governed by a set of 'Eighteen Commandments' supposedly dictated by Sabbatai himself, which were circulated among the Dönme as early as the 1670s. As Gershom Scholem points out, these repeat the Ten Commandments with marked Sabbatian variations, the prohibition of fornication being phrased ambiguously so as to resemble a counsel of prudence, which is not unexpected since the Dönme regarded the sexual restrictions of the Torah as abolished.

Other commandments regulated the behaviour of the Dönme with regard to Jews and Turks. The Dönme were required to observe the laws of Islam in public, though they were strictly forbidden to intermarry with true Muslims. They were also not allowed to use force in converting any of the other *ma'min* to the 'faith of the turban'. Regarding these believers who had not converted to Islam, one of the commandments states:

Announce to your comrades, who are *ma'min* who have not yet entered into the mystery of the turban, which is the battle [against impurity], that they keep both the external and the purely spiritual Torah from which they are to detract nothing until the time of the revelation [the ultimate redemption at the Parousia of the Messiah]. Then they will come under the Tree of Life and all will become angels.

After Sabbatai's death the centre of the Sabbatian movement shifted to Salonika. One reason for this was the presence there of Sabbatai's widow, Ayesha. After her return to Salonika, Ayesha proclaimed that her younger brother Jacob, known as Qerido, or 'the Beloved', was the reincarnation of her late husband. Jacob Qerido thereupon became the leader of a sub-sect of the Sabbatians in Salonika – a group that included his father, Joseph Filosof, the distinguished scholars Solomon and Joseph Florentin, and Abraham Barzillay, who had been a follower of Sabbatai since the days of their youth in Izmir.

During the early 1680s some of the leaders of this group experienced revelations, with Jacob Qerido emerging as a prophet. These revelations and prophecies led to a mass apostasy among the Jews in Salonika in 1683, a total of some 300 families converting to Islam en masse. There is some evidence that the Turkish authorities were involved in this mass conversion, which the leaders of the group announced in the presence of Sultan Mehmet IV. Smaller groups in Edirne and Istanbul followed the lead of those in Salonika, which remained the centre of the apostate Sabbatian sect, now for the first time known to the Turks as the Dönme.

A large number of Sabbatians retained their Jewish faith, even in Salonika, but there the Dönme group continued to increase through conversion and immigration, as they were joined by apostate believers from elsewhere in the Ottoman Empire and even abroad. Polish apostates joined them in the second half of the eighteenth century, and as late as 1915 there was a group of Dönme families in Salonika known as Lechli, or Poles. Although there were strict prohibitions about marriage outside their sect, Dönme tradition mentions a number of non-Jewish families of Turkish and Greek origin who eventually became members of their sect.

Jacob Qerido sought to demonstrate the sincerity of his conversion to Islam by making the haj – going on a pilgrimage to Mecca – though the original Dönme community in Salonika was very much opposed to this. Accompanied by several of his followers, Qerido left Salonika for Mecca in the early 1690s, but he died on the return journey, probably in Alexandria.

Opposition to the pilgrimage to Mecca was only one of several points of dispute between the original group of Dönme in Salonika and the one that had been headed by Qerido. This led to a schism in which the Dönme split into two groups. The original community of apostate Sabbatians were originally known as Izmirli, undoubtedly because they originated largely in Izmir, while later they were called Kapandsis. The followers of Jacob Qerido were known as Jacobites, or in Turkish as Jakoblar. Around 1700 a further schism occurred within the Kapandsis, some of whom split off to form a sub-sect under a new young leader, Baruchiah Russo, whose followers acclaimed him as the Divine Incarnation of Sabbatai Sevi. His father, Joseph Russo, had apparently been one of the early followers of Sabbatai Sevi and a disciple of Nathan of Gaza. After his conversion Baruchiah Russo was called Osman Baba. ('Baba', which in Turkish means 'father', is one of the names given to Muslim saints, another being 'Dede', or 'grandfather'.) His followers were known in Ladino as Konyosos and in Turkish as Karakash.

The Karakash were by reputation the most radical of the three Dönme sub-sects, and it was against them that Abraham Cardozo wrote the strongest of his polemics, particularly directed towards the doctrine of the divinity of Sabbatai Sevi and his reincarnation as Baruchiah Russo, alias Osman Baba. Russo died prematurely in 1720 and was succeeded as head of the Karakash sect by his son, who directed it until his own death in 1781. During the early 1720s the Karakash sent out missionaries to Poland, Germany and Austria, giving rise to branches of the sect in several places.

The Karakash differed from the other two Dönme groups in one important doctrine, in which the new messianic 'Torah of Emanations' (*Torah de-Azilot*) involved a complete reversal of values, the thirty-six *keritot*, or prohibitions, of the Torah being changed into positive commands. This change included sexual prohibitions, such as incest, which led to the charge that the Karakash were practising free love and ritual fornication involving incestuous sexual relations. Judah Levi Tuva, a Dönme preacher and poet of the late eighteenth century, gave a long sermon defending the abrogation of the sexual prohibition contained in the Torah. The Dönme holiday *Hag ha-Keves*, the Festival of the Lamb, observed on the Twenty-second of Adar, was a celebration of the spring equinox at which the Karakash were said to have engaged in ritual orgies, though there is no evidence to support this.

The earliest sources in Salonika agree on the relative social and economic status of the three Dönme sub-sects. The Kapandsis were largely professional people and merchants of the upper and middle class; the Jacobites were principally city officials and upper-level civil servants in Salonika; while the Karakash were artisans, shop-keepers and workers, including barbers, butchers, shoemakers and porters. During the early period, all the barbers of Salonika, being members of the Karakash sub-sect, gave different styles of haircut and beard trim to each of the Dönme groups, so that they were immediately distinguishable one from the other in the street.

Each of the three groups had its own secret place of worship in Salonika, and each had its own cemetery, while the orthodox Jews also had a burial ground. William Martin Leake wrote of the orthodox Jews of Salonika and the three groups of *ma'min* in his *Travels in Northern Greece*, published in 1835. Leake estimated that the population of Salonika at that time was 65,000, of whom 35,000 were Turks, 15,000 Greeks, and 13,000 Jews, the remainder being 'Franks' (Europeans) or Gypsies. A large number of those classified as Turks were actually *ma'min*, as Leake remarks in his discussion of the Jewish community in Salonika:

The Jews of Saloniki are descended from the largest of those colonies, which settled in Greece at the time of their expulsion from Spain at the end of the fifteenth century; but a considerable portion of them have become Musulmans since that time, though without them being acknowledged by the Osmanlis, and forming a separate class under the denomination of Mamins . . . among them are some of the wealthiest Turks at Saloniki . . . They go to mosque regularly, and conform to the Mahometan religion in externals, but are reproached by the other Turks with having secret meetings and ceremonies . . . They are said to be divided into three tribes, two of which will not intermarry with the third, nor will the latter give their daughters to the Osmanlis.

Estimates of the number of Dönme in Salonika differ widely. The earliest — that of the Danish traveller Karsten Niebuhr in 1784 — gives the number of Dönme families there as 600. The estimates of observers from the mid nineteenth century to the end of the Ottoman Empire in 1923 range from 10,000 to 15,000 individual Dönme in Salonika. The Dönme were officially classified as 'Turkish', and made up about half the Muslim population of the city.

Every Dönme had both a Turkish and a Hebrew name, the former for public use and the latter used privately in the family and in the community of the sub-sect. The Dönme were virtually all Sephardim in origin, so that their language was the Judaeo-Spanish known as Ladino, though most of them spoke Turkish and Greek as well. Their culture was Judaeo-Spanish, as evidenced by their surviving songs and poems as well as their folklore. There, as well as in their liturgical literature, there is hardly any evidence of Islamic influence.

At the beginning of the eighteenth century most of the Dönme knew Hebrew, which was the language of the Sabbatian liturgy. But as time went on knowledge of Hebrew decreased as the Dönme were cut off from rabbinic training, and the Ladino of their daily speech came to dominate both their profane and their sacred literature. Although the Dönme continued to say their prayers in Hebrew, most of them hardly understood the language. The extreme secrecy of the sect was such that until 1935 only two short Dönme prayers were known to the outside world. The secrecy was then breached when a Dönme family of the Kapandsis group donated a handwritten prayer book to the Hebrew University in Jerusalem. Gershom Scholem, who published the text of this prayer book in 1941, writes of its unexpected character, which was completely Jewish:

We were greatly surprised at the time to discover that we were here dealing with purely Jewish prayers . . . The mystical value of belief for these Sabbatians has replaced the real activity of fulfilling the commandments, which has become for them no longer possible or valid . . . No part of these prayers would make the reader even dream that these worshipers were Moslems.

Scholem then gives the full text of the Sabbatian credo, in which the most interesting parts are those that mention Sabbatai Sevi:

I believe with perfect faith that Sabbatai Sevi is the true King Messiah.

I believe with perfect faith that Sabbatai Sevi, may his majesty be exalted, is the true Messiah, and that he will gather together the dispersed of Israel from the four corners of the earth . . .

May it be pleasing before Thee, God of truth, God of Israel who dwells in the 'glory of Israel', in the three knots of faith which are one, to send us the just Messiah, our Redeemer, Sabbatai Sevi, speedily and in our days, Amen.

Most of the Sabbatians did not convert to Islam, even in Salonika, where there is evidence for the existence of believers who remained within the Jewish faith long after Sabbatai's death. Several prominent rabbis of Salonika and Izmir in the eighteenth century were secret followers of Sabbatai, while scholars who had studied with Nathan of Gaza or his disciples later became rabbis in important Jewish communities such as Ancona, Amsterdam and London, spreading the moderate Sabbatian doctrine of those who continued to remain within the fold of Judaism.

Another centre of Sabbatianism existed in Italy, first in Livorno, where Moses Pinheiro, Meir Rofe and others were active, and later in Modena under the lead of Abraham Rovigo, whose influence spread the movement into central and northern Europe. Rovigo settled in Jerusalem in 1701 and founded a yeshiva, most of its members being Sabbatians. The form of Sabbatianism that he and his followers practised differed from orthodox Jewish practice only in the secret celebration of the Ninth of Ab as a festival, and even this was sometimes abandoned. The same was true among other Sabbatians who had remained within the fold of Judaism, the only difference between their beliefs and those of the orthodox being their faith in Sabbatai Sevi and his eventual reappearance.

The Sabbatian movement also had followers among Ashkenazi Jews, who, after the death of Sabbatai, began to speculate that he may have been the Messiah ben Joseph rather than the ultimate Messiah of the House of David. This was the doctrine put forward in Prague in 1677 by Mordecai Eisenstadt, who for the next five years preached his version of the messianic movement in southern Germany and northern Italy.

Another prophet appeared at Vilna in Poland, a former silver-smith known as Heshel Zoref, who for the last three decades of the seventeenth century proclaimed that he was the Messiah ben Joseph and that Sabbatai was the Messiah ben David. He composed a vast work entitled *Sefer ha-Zoref*, which was meant to be the messianic version of the Torah. His last years were spent in Cracow, where he influenced the development of the Sabbatian Hasidim.

Parts of the works of Heshel Zoref came into the possession of Israel ben Elizer Ba'al Shem Tob, the founder of later Hasidism, who is reported to have said that Sabbatai Sevi 'had a mark of holiness, but Samael, the Prince of Evil, caught him in his net'. This statement originates with Leyb ben Ozer, who thus accounts for the failure of Sabbatai's messianic mission: 'Some said that the power of evil was rampant at that time and it was thus that he [Sabbatai] could work many things [i.e. miracles]. Others said that in the beginning there was in him the power of holiness, but that later the evil powers fastened themselves to him and the devil's work succeeded.' Even Nathan of Gaza had stated that as Sabbatai had entered the realm of the *qelippah* to restore its sanctity he could be called 'the King of Demons'.

Two other prophets arose in Poland. One of these, a former brandy distiller named Zadok, preached his version of Sabbatianism in Grodno (now Hrodna in Belarus) during 1694–6. The second, Hayyim Ma'lakh, preached his radical version of Sabbatianism in Poland and then went on to Edirne. He later joined up with another Sabbatian, Judah Hasid from Shidlov, and in 1696–1700 they formed the 'Holy Society of Rabbi Judah Hasid'. This was an extremely ascetic group of Sabbatians who emigrated to Palestine, there to await the Second Coming of Sabbatai Sevi, attracting many to their sect among both German and Polish Jewry. But Judah Hasid died shortly after reaching Jerusalem in October 1700, after which his group fell apart, several of his followers converting to Islam or Christianity, the rest of them returning to Poland, Germany and Austria.

Another important figure in the development of Sabbatianism in the eighteenth century was Nehemiah Hayon. While in Venice in 1713 Hayon published a work entitled *Oz le-Elohim*, a commentary on Sabbatai Sevi's last work on the mystery of the Godhead. Hayon claimed that he had received Sabbatai's work from a *maggid*, or, on other occasions, that he had found it in a copy of the *Zohar*. This led to a controversy that brought about for the first time a public discussion of Sabbatian theology among both Sephardic and Ashkenazi rabbis. The controversy revealed that a large number of rabbis were in fact secret adherents of the Sabbatian movement.

Meanwhile the Karakash sub-sect of the Dönme had gained footholds in Podolia, in Moravia and particularly in Prague. The leading rabbinic scholar in Prague at the time was Jonathan Eybeschuetz. It was he who headed the group of rabbis who on 16 September 1725 publicly condemned Sabbatai Sevi and issued a writ of excommunication against all Sabbatians. Similar condemnations were made in many other German, Austrian and Polish communities, calling on all Jews to denounce secret Sabbatians to the rabbinic authorities. This caused the Sabbatian movement to go underground for the next generation, particularly in Poland. Then in 1751 it was discovered that Jonathan Eybeschuetz himself was a secret Sabbatian, which caused an uproar throughout eastern Europe. His main opponent was Jacob Emden, whose polemical writings published in 1752–69 reveal how widespread Sabbatianism was at the time in Europe, as well as in the Ottoman Empire, most of the believers publicly denying their belief in Sabbatai although they kept the faith secretly.

Another branch of Sabbatianism emerged in eastern Europe under the leadership of Jacob Frank, who was born in 1726 in a village in Podolia. His father was an itinerant pedlar who often took Jacob on his journeys through the southern Balkans into the territory of the Ottoman Empire. Jacob Frank became a travelling trader and a caravan master, his journeys sometimes taking him to Salonika, where he was deeply influenced by the ideas of the

Karakash Dönme sect that had emerged under Baruchiah Russo. Eventually he founded his own sect, the so-called Frankists, in which he tried to create unity between the various Sabbatian groups that had developed since the death of Sabbatai Sevi.

Frank, who was believed by his followers to be a reincarnation of Sabbatai Sevi, was accused by his enemies of having conducted a ritual Sabbatian orgy. This led to the imprisonment of his followers, although he himself was allowed to go free because he claimed to be a Turkish citizen. He fled to Salonika, where he converted to Islam in accordance with the teachings of Baruchiah Russo. He then returned to Podolia, where he soon became the leader of the Sabbatians in eastern Europe.

After Frank and his followers were excommunicated from Judaism in 1756, he sought the protection of the Catholic Church in Poland. Frank and his wife were baptized on 17 September 1759, and many of his disciples followed his example, including more than 500 in Lvov alone. Thus the Frankists became a Dönme sect in eastern Europe, though in the guise of Roman Catholics rather than Muslims. But many of the leaders of the Catholic clergy in Poland were suspicious of Frank's motives, and on 6 February 1760 he was arrested, after which he was held in 'honourable imprisonment' in the royal fortress near Częstochowa, the famous Polish national shrine of the Black Virgin.

Frank remained confined in the fortress for thirteen years, directing the affairs of his sect from within the walls of his prison. A large number of his followers were allowed to settle around the fortress, within which they were reported to have engaged in ritual Sabbatian orgies. After the death of Frank's wife in 1770 his daughter Eva inherited her mother's title of 'Matronita', 'Holy Mother'. Frank elevated Eva to divine status, intimating that she was the illegitimate daughter of Catherine the Great, and that he was not her father but only her guardian, eventually identifying her with the Shekhinah, the Presence of God. Eva also inherited her mother's divine title of 'Gevira', 'Lady', which Frank had given to his wife to identify her with the Black Virgin of Częstochowa.

Frank's captivity ended in 1773, after the Russians captured Częstochowa and allowed him to go free. He and his entourage

moved to Brünn (present-day Brno) in Moravia, where he held court as if he were nobility, giving himself the title of Baron. He and his daughter went to Vienna in March 1775 and were received by the empress Maria Theresa and her son, the future Joseph II. Then in 1786 Frank moved on to Offenbach, near Frankfurt, where he lived in the same exalted manner until his death in 1791.

After Frank's death his daughter Eva became the head of the Frankist sect, which she directed in Offenbach as the Gevira until her own death in 1816. The scene at her court, a palace-temple known as Gottes Haus (God's House), is described in the memoirs of Moses Porges (later von Portheim), who in his youth had been sent on a pilgrimage to Offenbach from Prague, which had become the centre of the Frankist sect. He went to 'God's house', where the Gevira was enshrined as a living goddess, a portrait showing her in the 'adornments of the Holy Mother', the Virgin Mary. On the following day, as he writes, he was granted an audience with the Gevira herself:

How excited I was and how my heart beat! At last the door opened and I crossed the threshold. I dared not look the Gevira in the face, but fell to my knees before her and kissed her feet, for so I had been instructed. She spoke a few friendly words to me, praised my father and my decision to come here. When I withdrew, I deposited my wallet with the sixty guldens of silver and gold upon a table and left the room with my face towards the Gevira. The impression she made upon me was of grace and nobility. She had a friendly face which expressed kindness, delicate modesty and gentleness, and her eyes a saintly dreaminess. She was no longer young but created an effect of charm. Her hands and feet were splendid and beautiful. As I later learned I had pleased her.

After Eva's death the organization of the Frankists weakened, and they survived as a secret sect like the Dönme, marrying only among themselves. Most of the Frankists had not converted to Christianity, the converts being mostly those who had settled in Offenbach. Some of those who remained Jews were elevated to the nobility, such as the Hoenig family, and reached the highest levels of the Austrian imperial administration.

A large group of Frankist families from Bohemia and Moravia emigrated to the United States in 1848–9, some settling in New York City. It was customary for all these families to have in their possession a portrait of Eva Frank, the Gevira, whose image was venerated as a sacred icon. One of these icons was in the possession of Louis Brandeis, chief justice of the Supreme Court of the USA. Brandeis, the first Jew ever to sit in the US Supreme Court, was appointed by President Woodrow Wilson in 1916. He had undoubtedly received the icon of Eva Frank from his mother, Alice Goldmark, a descendant of one of the Frankist families of Prague who emigrated to the USA in the mid nineteenth century.

The Frankists of Prague and other communities in eastern Europe remained in secret contact with one another as well as with the Dönme in Salonika. These contacts were maintained despite the fact that some of the Sabbatians in eastern Europe had remained Jews while others had converted to Christianity or Islam. All of them still secretly revered Sabbatai Sevi as the Messiah, with the Frankists believing that the 'Beloved' had been reincarnated as Jacob Frank.

The closed world of the Dönme in Salonika opened up in the second half of the nineteenth century, when the young people of their community began to demand a European, i.e. French, education as well as closer relations with the Turkish people of the Ottoman Empire. The Dönme founded the Feyziye Schools, which were so superior to all other schools in Salonika that many who were not members of their community – including Orthodox Jews, Muslims and Christians – enrolled their children. Mustafa Kemal Pasha, later to be known as Atatürk, founder and first president of the Turkish Republic, was enrolled in one of the Feyziye Schools by his father. The school that he attended, the Terakki Lisesi, was founded by the Sabbatian Shemsi Efendi. Shemsi was reputed to be a member of the Kapandsis sub-sect of the Dönme, though he cooperated with the Karakash and hoped to bring together the three groups of believers through education. But Shemsi's ideas were too far in advance of his time, and he was expelled from the Dönme community of Salonika in 1912 and forced to move to Istanbul, where he died in 1917.

The desire of the Dönme youth to establish closer relations with the Turks of the Ottoman Empire led some of them to join the Young Turks, a movement dedicated to the reform and modernization of the Ottoman Empire. The political organization of the Young Turks, the Committee for Union and Progress, had its origins in Salonika, where young Dönme played an important part. Djavid Bey, one of three Dönme who served as ministers in the first Young Turk government in the Ottoman Empire in 1909, was a leader of the Karakash sect, being a direct descendant of Baruchiah Russo.

The Ottoman occupation of Salonika ended in 1912, when the city was taken from the Turks by a Greek army under Prince Constantine. A number of Dönme families fled from Salonika at that time, most of them moving to Istanbul. For the next six years Salonika was virtually under siege, first during the Balkan Wars of 1912–13 and then throughout the First World War, in 1914–18. The whole south-western part of the city was destroyed by a great fire in August 1917, ruining the old Greek, Turkish and Jewish quarters and most of their places of worship.

The First World War was followed by a war between Greece and Turkey, which ended in 1921 and was settled the following year by the Treaty of Lausanne. One of the terms of this treaty called for an exchange of minorities between the two countries, which was carried out in 1923. At the time of the population exchange there were some 15,000 Dönme in Salonika, almost all of whom were deported to Turkey. Most of the displaced Dönme settled in Istanbul, smaller numbers going to Edirne, Izmir and Ankara, the new capital of the Turkish Republic.

The few Dönme who remained in Salonika suffered the same fate as virtually all the Jews of the city in 1943, when the Germans shipped them off to concentration camps, where most of them died. Many of the Jews who survived subsequently emigrated to Israel, so that the Jewish population of the city today is only a small fraction of what it was in Ottoman times.

A number of other messiahs followed one another in turn during the last three centuries of the second Christian millennium, though none of them had so profound an effect on the Jewish world as that of Sabbatai Sevi.

The most recent of these messiahs was the Lubavitcher rebbe (righteous man) Menachem Mendel Schneerson, who was born in Russia in 1902 and died on 18 June 1994 in the Crown Heights district of Brooklyn, New York, where he had spent the latter half of his life after escaping from Soviet and then Nazi persecution. In 1951 he became head of the Hasidic Lubavich sect, whose messianic movement is called Chabad, an acronym formed from the Hebrew letters for wisdom, discernment and knowledge. Chabad has now formed an international system of schools and cultural centres, and publishes books and periodicals to promote the programme that the Rebbe began after he declared himself the Mosiach, or Messiah. The slogan of Chabad is 'Mosiach now!', which the Rebbe coined in 1951, saying that the responsibility of 'bringing about the coming of the Messiah' depended upon the labours of his followers, who fully expect him to return and lead them to the redemption for which they are paving the way.

And so the cult of another messiah flourishes while that of Sabbatai Sevi fades from memory, his sect apparently lingering on in name only among the descendants of his followers.

But was Sabbatianism only a fading memory, or was there perhaps a spark of the cult still alive, I wondered, as I set out on the last stages of my search for the Lost Messiah.

# 21. Waiting For The Messiah

I visited Salonika in the spring of 1999, looking to see what, if anything, remained of the presence of Sabbatai Sevi and his followers.

I went first to Molho's, the oldest bookshop in Salonika, owned by one of the few Jewish families who remain in the city. While browsing, I found two books about the Jews and Dönme of Salonika by my old friend, Nikos Stavroulakis. One of them was entitled *Salonika – Jews and Dervishes*. The other, which Nikos wrote together with Esin Eden, a well-known actress from a Dönme family in Istanbul, was called *Salonika: A Family Cookbook*. Both books gave me unexpected insights into the Jewish and Dönme past of Salonika in the Ottoman period, its few surviving monuments now almost forgotten and seldom visited, as if modern Greece wants to turn its back on this aspect of its history.

Most of the old synagogues of Salonika were destroyed in the great fire of 1917. One of those that survived was Kal Shalom, the oldest synagogue in the city, where Sabbatai Sevi worshipped when he first came to Salonika in the mid-1650s. At that time Sabbatai lived in the home of Joseph Florentin, one of the founders of the original Dönme sect. The Kal Shalom Synagogue and the Florentin house were still standing as late as 1930, but then they both vanished. The only Jewish monument that now remains from the Ottoman period is Yahoudi Hamam, the Jews' Bath, in the south-western sector of the city down by the site of the Byzantine port.

The largest extant monument of the Dönme community is Yeni Dzami, the New Mosque, built in 1902 by the Italian architect Vitaliano Pozzeli, and now a museum. There are also a few mansions built in the late nineteenth century by wealthy members of the Dönme community. Two of the finest of these neoclassical town houses were erected in the 1890s by the brothers Ahmet and

Mehmet Kapandzi, whose family name reveals that they were members of the Kapandsis sub-sect of the Dönme.

The Jewish cemetery, which dated back to the third century BC, was outside the walls of Salonika to the east. One of the three Dönme cemeteries was just beyond the Jewish burial ground to the north, while the other two were outside Yeni Kapı, the north-west gateway in the ancient city walls. Each of the Dönme cemeteries was used by one of the three sub-sects of the *ma'min*: the Kapandsis, the Jacobites and the Karakash. The most notable tomb in the Karakash cemetery was that of Baruchiah Russo, or Osman Baba, the founder of the Karakash sub-sect. The most prominent tomb in the Jacobite cemetery was that of Sabbatai Sevi's last wife, Ayesha, which was a place of pilgrimage until the first quarter of the twentieth century. One of those buried in the Kapandsis cemetery was Dervish Efendi, the leader of that sub-sect of Dönme in around 1800, whose name suggests that he may have been a member of one of the dervish orders, probably the Mevlevi, the famous Whirling Dervishes, who are known to have been on close terms with the Sabbatian *ma'min*.

At the beginning of the twentieth century there were some thirty-two *tekkes* of the various dervish orders in Salonika, the most numerous being those of the Mevlevi and the Bektashi. The largest and most richly endowed of these was the Mevlevihane, the main *tekke* of the Mevlevi dervishes, which was just outside Yeni Kapı, in the vicinity of two of the Dönme cemeteries. This was undoubtedly the *tekke* to which Dervish Efendi and other members of the Kapandsis sub-sect belonged, while the Dönme of the Jacobite and Karakash groups may have been associated with the Bektashi order.

The old Jewish and Dönme burial grounds began to disappear in 1927, when the University of Salonika was granted a large area of land outside the ancient city walls to the east. Within two decades nothing remained of these cemeteries, which were swept away along with all the dervish *tekkes*. Virtually the only images left of these places are the photographs in Nikos Stavroulakis's book on the Jews and dervishes of Salonika, which is based on a set of twenty-two photographs taken during 1916–18, probably by Hugh

Fawcett, a British officer with the Allied army of occupation. The photographs are about equally divided between the Mevlevihane and the Jewish cemetery, some of the latter images showing part of one of the Dönme burial grounds.

The photographs of the Jewish cemetery show a group of elderly women visiting the graves of departed loved ones, all of them wearing traditional costumes of the late Ottoman era. The women are accompanied by an old rabbi known as a *hanadji*, who was called upon to read the appropriate prayers for the dead when family members came to make their *kippaw*, or memorial visitation. It would appear that the Dönme retained this custom after they converted to Islam, for there are references to this *kippaw* being carried out in their burial grounds, though the *hanadji* would have been called a *hodja*, or teacher. One of the photographs shows an old woman leaving the grave after she has placed a small stone on the tomb, a talisman to ward off evil, a traditional Jewish custom that also seems to have been retained by the Dönme.

One of the photographs of the Mevlevihane shows the chief dervish, a biblical figure with a meticulously trimmed white beard, dressed in flowing black robes and wearing a black turban around the base of his cylindrical beige headdress as a symbol of his rank. Another photo shows part of the Muslim cemetery where the departed dervishes were buried, their tombstones topped with stone replicas of their headdress. Those of the Dönme who were members of the Mevlevi brotherhood may very well have been buried in the dervish graveyard rather than in the cemetery of their sub-sect. Here, in contrast to the bare ground of the Jewish cemetery, the tombs were shaded by cypresses, which seems also to have been the case in all three of the Dönme burial grounds. As Nikos Stavroulakis writes of the funerary symbolism of cypresses in Islam, 'There were, as was always the case around *tekkes* and cemeteries, a great number of tall and sombre cypresses. These trees were considered to mirror the virtues of the true and faithful Muslim: proud and erect before God, his head nodding in constant awareness of the Divine Will.'

The Salonika cookbook also gave me a fleeting glimpse into the vanished life of the Dönme. It turned out to be far more than a cookbook right from the beginning, for the introductory section by Nikos and Esin Eden gives a social history of the Salonika *ma'min*. Esin Eden acquired her menus from two old recipe books compiled by three generations of women in her family, going back to late Ottoman times. This provided a key to the lost world of the believers in Salonika, as Nikos writes in his introduction, explaining the difficulty he encountered in interpreting the cultural background of the recipes: 'The very secretive inner life of the Ma'min, for all purposes unknown to anyone who had not been initiated at marriage to a fellow Ma'min, made it difficult to uncover the ritual significance of many of the recipes or even to determine when they might have been served.'

He goes on to say that an even greater difficulty was the fact that these recipes grew out of a community that was 'Sephardi in origins, Jewish in certain surviving elements of ethnicity and religious culture but Muslim through adoption and Turkish by association'. 'And yet,' he concludes, 'and this was the crux of the problem, the Ma'min consistently avoided being too clearly any one of these. One might say that this is an improbable mix of cultures, but as the recipes prove, it existed, flourished and continues on though far from Salonika.'

Esin Eden's introduction gives the history of her family – Sephardic Jews who came from Spain to Salonika in the last decade of the fifteenth century. Her mother, Nutiye Eden, née Fuat, was born in Salonika in 1900 and died in Istanbul in 1981, after having spent 1928–39 in Brussels, where Esin was born, and from which the family fled to escape the Nazis. Though Esin did not set foot in Salonika until she was a mature woman, she felt that she knew its old way of life in Ottoman times through the customs perpetuated in her family, many of them associated with the special food that they ate in celebrating festivals or to mark the passing seasons.

Esin writes that theirs was neither exactly a conservative nor a religious family. 'As my mother grew older she would sometimes sit quietly in the evening reading the Koran or some pious book, but for the most part we did not celebrate festivals in an especially notable manner. There was a time in the early part of the year when lamb was not eaten and then suddenly "milk lamb" would appear boiled with tomatoes and parsley.' (The eating of milk-nourished lamb at that time of the year was a deliberate violation of orthodox Jewish dietary laws practised by the Dönme.)

Esin continues, 'Not everyone fasted during Ramazan but at the time of *iftar*, the daily evening breaking of the fast, some sort of sweet would usually appear, sometimes made of dates. As with everyone else *Asure* [a Turkish pudding] appeared during *Muharrem* [autumn] and was distributed to friends, relatives and the poor in great quantities.'

She also tells of some of ancient *ma'min* customs that her family practised: the poetic Sabbatian prayer that they recited when the first crescent moon appeared; the joyous song they sang at *kandils*, or Islamic holy days. As she writes:

For the new moon I was always taken out to see it and to recite a prayer that my mother taught me.

> O God I see the moon.
> O God I do believe.
> Let the moon be blessed by God,
> Inshallah [God willing].

At *Kandils*, even in Belgium, we would gather together and have special sweets and sing

> Butter money, candle money
> This night, festive oil lamp money.
> Like skewers in a row come the dervishes
> Lacking meat they ask for fishes.

The photographs in the book are particularly evocative, one of them showing Esin's mother as a girl dressed in Turkish costume, veiled to her eyes, another with her father wearing a fez, and one of her uncles as a child dressed in the long robe and cylindrical headdress of the Mevlevi dervishes. In the first chapter of the cookbook Nikos tells of the special affinity that the Dönme of Salonika had for the Mevlevi. He writes that 'The great Mevlevihane . . . had been of special significance to them, and many Ma'min were associated with it either directly as dervishes or as oblates. The last of the great composers of both music and poetry among the Mevlevi was Esat Dede, a Ma'min from Salonika who received his religious training as a dervish in Istanbul.'

Nikos goes on to note that for three centuries the Dönme of Salonika had made pilgrimages to the burial place of Sabbatai Sevi in Dulcigno, but that the breakup of the Ottoman Empire and the dispersal of the *ma'min* made it difficult for them to do so any longer. But apparently some of the *ma'min* somehow did manage to make these pilgrimages, for there is documentary evidence that pilgrims still visited Sabbatai's burial place until the second quarter of the twentieth century.

The downfall of the Ottoman Empire in 1923 dispersed the Sabbatian communities in the southern Balkans, and then the believers elsewhere in Europe were swept away in the Holocaust of the Second World War. The Jews of Turkey were spared the horrors of the Holocaust, as were the Dönme who had settled there after leaving Salonika.

When the Dönme first came to Istanbul in 1923 the population of the city was about 1 million, while in the 1995 census it was nearly 10 million. During those years the Jewish population of the city dropped from nearly 50,000 to about 30,000, mostly because of emigration to Israel. At the beginning of the Turkish Republic in 1923 most of the Jewish community was still living in their three old quarters, in Balat, Galata and Hasköy. During the latter half of the twentieth century most of the more prosperous Jews left their old quarters and moved to more modern housing in the new districts north of the Golden Horn or to Ortaköy on the European shore of the lower Bosphorus, though many still returned to Balat, Galata and Hasköy to worship in the old synagogues there. The oldest and most important of these is the Akrida Synagogue in Balat, founded in the first half of the fifteenth century by Jews from around Lake Okrid in Macedonia. Sabbatai is known to have preached in the Akrida Synagogue shortly before he was arrested by the Sultan's men in 1666. I mentioned this to the leader of the congregation when I last visited the synagogue in the summer of

1999, and he was well aware of the fact. But he did not want to speak about it, for the whole episode of the Sabbatian movement was still a sensitive subject among the orthodox Jews of Istanbul.

Just down the street from the Akrida Synagogue is the Mosque of Ferruh Kethuda, where in Sabbatai's time there was a lodge of the Bektashi dervishes. The lodge was headed by Niyazi Misri Dede, the 'charismatic and often outrageous mystic' who initiated Sabbatai into the esoteric rites of the Bektashi order. One of the unanswered questions in the story of Sabbatai Sevi involves the extent of his involvement with the dervishes, and another is whether he converted Niyazi to the Sabbatian sect. All religions would seem to have been the same so far as Niyazi was concerned, for he had already been accused of being a crypto-Christian, so conversion to the sect of a Jewish Messiah who had become a Muslim is not inconceivable.

The principal Jewish cemetery in Istanbul is on the hillside above Hasköy, where the Karaites also have a burial ground. One of those buried in the orthodox Jewish cemetery in Hasköy is Abraham Galanté, who devoted his life to a study of the Jews in Turkey, his particular obsession being to fill in the missing pages in the story of Sabbatai Sevi and his followers. I visited his grave in the spring of 1999, as I neared the end of my own quest to eliminate the same lacunae, some of which still defeated me.

After their resettlement in Turkey the Dönme quickly adapted to their new situation, developing a more open and modern way of life. Some of them became prominent in modern Turkey, making a name in business, academia, journalism or government, the most recent notable example being Ismail Cem, Foreign Minister in the government of Prime Minister Bülent Ecevit at the turn of the millennium.

During the past generation a few of the Dönme have started to marry outside their group for the first time, in keeping with their general tendency to blend in with the life of modern Turkey. This attempt at integration would appear to have been successful, for most of the Dönme are now distinguishable from other citizens of Turkey only by the last names that their families took when this was required by the modernizing reforms of the early Republic, the surnames 'Ipekçi' and 'Dilber' being the most common. The term 'Dönme' itself is now falling into disuse, since its meaning of 'Turncoats' or 'Apostate' is offensive, and instead they are now more generally called *Selanikliler*, or 'Those from Salonika'.

The Dönme have always been regarded with some suspicion in Turkey, particularly by Islamic fundamentalists, who do not consider them to be true Muslims. As a result they were included among other minorities who were subjected to the infamous confiscatory capital-gains tax known as the *Varlık Vergisi*, imposed in 1942.

The complex question of Dönme identity has recently been revived by Ilgaz Zorlu in his provocative book *Evet, Ben Selanikliyim* (*Yes, I am from Salonika*), where he describes the difficult situation faced by him and his fellow Turkish Sabbatians. Marc David Baer, in her review of this book, quotes Zorlu in this regard: 'Who are we, where are we from? Are we native, or do we feel as if we are foreign? Perhaps among all the other groups in Turkey expected to answer these questions, we are the people who have the most difficult time.' According to Baer, Zorlu tells of how every day as a group Sabbatians and Muslims 'live as if there is no difference between us, no distinction in religion, language, and custom, but in truth we belong to a secret community which only at home has protected and kept alive its own mystic structure with great zeal for three centuries'.

According to Baer, Zorlu says that all of the Sabbatians he interviewed insisted that 'We are not from Salonika!', evidently because they felt shamed by being identified as Dönme, which only deepened the secrecy of their community. Baer also notes that the anthropologist Leyla Neyzi reports a similar response from a Sabbatian whom she interviewed for her newspaper article '*Selanikli Kim?*' ('Who is from Salonika?'): 'My father told me never to say I am Salonikan [i.e. a Dönme] to anyone I did not know. This is a humiliating thing; people will belittle you. Because of this I was forced to learn of Sabbatianism not from my family but from books.'

All the Dönme one meets insist that Sabbatianism is no longer a living religion, although they do admit that some of the older people in their community still preserve some vestigial cultural remains of the beliefs and customs of their ancestors from Salonika.

Nevertheless, some Jewish scholars believe that the Sabbatian cult may still be alive, though the activities of the few who adhere to it are as closely guarded a secret as they were in times past. Gershom Scholem, in an essay on the Dönme published in 1960, refers to the accusations against them 'of practicing ritual fornication and free love in their secret gatherings', for which he says there is considerable evidence from contemporary sources. Dönme tradition itself, he says, 'affirmed in only thinly veiled fashion, the existence of orgiastic rituals which served as the high points of their religious life. As late as 1910 young Dönmeh confided to their Jewish fellow students that these celebrations were still practiced.' He also notes that 'In conversation with a respected visitor from Israel in 1942, a physician who had settled in Smyrna admitted that his grandfather had participated in ritual wife-swapping in Salonika.'

Scholem goes on to say that the continued existence of believing Sabbatians among the Dönme is attested down to the present day. He notes that in the spring of 1960 one of his informants, a Turkologist, reported on his conversations with the *hodja*, or religious leader, of the Karakash Dönme. This *hodja* had heard of Scholem and his associates in Israel, and he attributed their interest in the Dönme to the fact that they were secret Sabbatians!

When the Dönme came to Istanbul in 1923, many of them settled in Teshvikiye, one of the modern districts on the ridge above the European shore of the lower Bosphorus. Those who were practising Muslims went to the Teshvikiye Mosque, which is still used for conventional Islam worship by some of the Dönme community. Near this mosque there was also a 'temple' where the Dönme of the Karakash sect secretly worshipped, but this has now vanished. The Dönme bury their dead in their own cemetery in the hills above Üsküdar, on the Asian side of the Bosphorus. Their burial ground, which is in a place called Bülbül Deresi, the Valley of the Nightingales, is known as Selanikliler Mezarlığı, the Cemetery of Those from Salonika.

Most of the Dönme who were deported from Salonika in 1923 left by train for Istanbul, some of them stopping off in Edirne, which then had a substantial Jewish community. So, in the final stages of my search for Sabbatai Sevi, I once again visited Edirne, one of the places in Turkey that had changed least in the years since I first saw it.

During the Russo-Turkish War of 1878–9 Edirne was captured by the Russians, who then pushed on to the suburbs of Istanbul before they were stopped by the intervention of the Great Powers. At that time the imperial palace of Edirne Sarayı was destroyed, blown to pieces by explosives that had been set off by the Turks to prevent it from falling into the hands of the enemy. Edirne was recaptured by the Turks in 1912, during the Second Balkan War, and after the downfall of the Ottoman Empire it became part of the Turkish Republic, whose borders with Greece and Bulgaria are only a few miles beyond the city.

Edirne had a large Jewish population throughout the Ottoman period and into the early years of the Turkish Republic. There was also a community of Sabbatians here dating from the time of Sabbatai's residence in Edirne Sarayı, and their numbers increased after the population exchange of 1923. But then in the latter half of the twentieth century the Jews of Edirne began moving to Istanbul, as did the Dönme. By the end of the millennium there were only four or five Jewish families left in Edirne, their synagogue abandoned after an accidental fire a decade earlier. The Dönme are gone too, leaving not a trace of their existence in the town where their Messiah converted to Islam in 1666.

The ruins of Edirne Sarayı can still be seen on the island in the Tunca river known as Saray Ichi, the secluded site outside Edirne where the palace was first laid out by Sultan Murat II in the second quarter of the fifteenth century. The only building of the palace that has survived is a conical-capped tower known as Adliye Sarayı, the Palace of Justice, which was well restored in the 1970s after having been badly damaged in 1878. A few other buildings of Edirne Sarayı remain only as shapeless masses of ruins, including the palace hammam, where Sabbatai Sevi was taken to bathe after his conversion to Islam.

The railway line from Istanbul to Edirne has been rerouted in recent years to shorten the travelling time between the cities. The line was built before the Balkan Wars, which changed the boundaries between Turkey, Greece and Bulgaria, and until as late as the 1960s the train crossed back and forth between Turkey and Greece en route from Istanbul to Edirne. The rerouting has kept the line entirely within Turkey as far as Edirne, whose station has been moved from its original location in the process. Consequently the original station, a charming art-nouveau structure with a hotel and restaurant, stands all by itself a few miles from the centre of Edirne. It now belongs to the Turkish University of Thrace, which uses it as a residence for visitors and for festive occasions.

The Dönme of Salonika would have stopped here after they were deported from Salonika in 1923, a few of them getting off, most of them going on to Istanbul, where they arrived in the last days of the Ottoman Empire.

When I went to pay a sentimental visit to the old Edirne station, I recalled a story concerning Abraham Galanté, whose works on the history of the Jews in Turkey had been valued sources in my search for Sabbatai Sevi. Galanté did not succeed in completing the final stage of his own quest, which was to find the burial place of Sabbatai Sevi in Albania: his several attempts to travel there were all frustrated by the constant political unrest in the region. The closest he got, in the late 1950s, was the railway station in Edirne, where he alighted after a planned trip to Albania was suddenly aborted when the borders were closed after yet another political crisis.

While Galanté waited for a train to take him back to Istanbul, he noticed an old woman who was sweeping up in the waiting room, and singing while she worked. When she came closer he could hear that she was singing in Ladino, and then to his astonishment he realized that the song was one that the Dönme sang together to keep up their hopes in the long centuries of waiting for Sabbatai Sevi to return:

> Oh, my beloved's gone from me,
> God's chosen one, Sabbatai Sevi.
> Though fallen low and suffering smart,
> Yet he is closest to my heart . . .

Galanté questioned the woman, and learned that she was in fact a Dönme – one of the very few who still remained in Edirne. He asked why she was cleaning up in the waiting room, and she explained that she did this every day to make sure that it would be spotless when Sabbatai arrived. The Messiah had gone to his rest in Albania she explained, and when he returned he would surely come by train, picking up his faithful followers on the way to Istanbul, from where they would set sail for Jerusalem. She was waiting to join him, she said, and then excused herself to get on with her work, continuing her interrupted song.

# 22. The Last Journey

My search for Sabbatai Sevi had taken me around the eastern Mediterranean, visiting the places where he had travelled during the course of his messianic career. All that remained was to visit the country of his exile – a last journey that would take me to his final resting place.

I began planning my journey in search of Sabbatai Sevi's burial place two years before the end of the millennium. But all my plans were thwarted by political events: first the overthrow of the Berisha government in Albania and the anarchy that followed, then the war in Kosovo. And so as the new millennium turned up three zeros I began to feel that I would suffer the same fate as my predecessor Abraham Galanté, who passed away in 1961 without finding where the elusive figure I had come to call the Lost Messiah had been interred.

My planning was complicated by the fact that two eminent Jewish scholars differed in their opinions on the location of Sabbatai's last resting place. In a paper published in *Zion* in 1952, Izhak Ben-Zwi argued that Sabbatai had died and been buried in Berat, in southern Albania. Writing in the same issue of *Zion*, Gershom Scholem gave his reasons for holding that Sabbatai had passed away and been laid to rest in Dulcigno, which was then in the north-westernmost corner of Albania. Dulcigno, now known as Ulcinj, has since 1913 belonged to Montenegro, which is still part of former Yugoslavia, though moving towards independence. Ulcinj is on the Adriatic coast just across the border from Albania, but the only road into Montenegro at this point had been closed for some time because of the political situation. I thought that I might get to Ulcinj by a ferry from Bari or along the east coast of the Adriatic from Trieste, but the war in Kosovo and the flood of Albanian refugees across to Italy made this impossible for the time being.

During the interim I began pondering again the question of where Sabbatai Sevi had died and been buried. The Dönme of Salonika seemed to have had no doubt on this point, for on their pilgrimages to his grave they had gone to Dulcigno. Samuel Primo and Nathan of Gaza had visited him there in early 1675, as had Joseph Karillo and his companion on 5 September 1676, twelve days before Sabbatai's death.

But Leyb ben Ozer was told that Sabbatai had died and been buried at Berat, a story he heard from Joseph Almosnino of Belgrade and Sevi Hirsh Ashkenazi of Amsterdam, both of whom were chief judges of the rabbinic courts in their communities. According to Leyb ben Ozer, Almosnino's informant in this matter was 'a certain Turk who was with Sabbatai Sevi when he was ill and dealt with his burial'. As this account continues, 'Likewise our chief justice Hirsh, known as Hakham Sevi, testified that Sabbatai Sevi had died at Arnaut Belgrade and was buried on Yom Kippur. He was not buried with the Muslims, following his orders, which were indeed followed, that he be buried alone by the water. Jews do not live in that country at all.'

The last sentence in the testimony of Hakham Sevi is not true, for there was a Jewish community in Berat, many of whom had become followers of Sabbatai. In his last extant letter, Sabbatai had written to his disciples in Berat in August 1676, asking them to send him a prayer book for the Yom Kippur festival, the day on which he is supposed to have died. The Sabbatian community in Berat was headed by the wealthy merchant Isaac Albalag, to whom Samuel Primo had written before he visited Sabbatai in Dulcigno. If Leyb ben Ozer's story is true, Sabbatai would have been taken to Berat in his last illness, despite the rigours of the journey – perhaps because he would have had disciples to look after him there, whereas in Dulcigno there seem to have been no Sabbatians to care for him. There is no mention of whether Sabbatai's wife, Ayesha, went with him on his last journey, for Meir Rofe's testimony says that she and the children went with Elijah Sevi to Edirne but does not say if they stopped en route at Berat.

The legend that developed after Sabbatai's death had him dying in Dulcigno, and being buried in a seaside cave that he himself had

prepared as his last resting place. But, according to the legend, when Elijah Sevi went to the cave on the third day after his brother's death he found that it was empty. This was part of the Sabbatian cult – belief that Sabbatai was not really dead, but occulted from human view, to become manifest again at the time of his Parousia. And so the Dönme of Salonika would have fixed upon Dulcigno as the place of Sabbatai's death and the seaside cave as his grave, for this was in keeping with the myth of his occultation.

Sabbatai's wife, Ayesha, would have known that her late husband's tomb was in Berat, if Leyb ben Ozer's story is true, but it may have suited her purposes to go along with the legend that his shrine was in Dulcigno. In fact she may have been one of those who created the legend that Sabbatai had disappeared from his cave tomb in Dulcigno and was occulted from human view, whereas the real tomb in Berat, if Leyb ben Ozer is to be believed, might have been an embarrassment if her late husband's bones were eve exhumed.

There is no record of when the members of the Dönme beg; making pilgrimages to Sabbatai's supposed grave in Dulcigno, b it would have been after Ayesha returned to Salonika and declar that her brother Jacob was the reincarnation of her late husba the Messiah. Tradition has it that the Dönme in Salonika m pilgrimages to Dulcigno right until the end of the Ottoman per A few of them seem to have continued the custom even after Dönme were moved to Turkey. According to a 1965 Tel newspaper article referred to by Scholem, the 'Elders' of Dulci Ulcinj declared in May 1962 that anonymous foreign visitors to come and put stones and flowers on the grave of an unk 'holy man'. After that there is no mention of Sabbatai's tom I could only assume that it had been neglected and vanished pilgrims no longer came to Dulcigno.

By the time the first Dönme visitors arrived in Dulcigno t their pilgrimage, some years would have passed since Sa death. Thus there would have been time for the inner circl sect to have created an appropriate shrine in the seaside cav the legend had placed Sabbatai's burial. And so the pilgrim have worshipped their departed Messiah there, unaware

was buried elsewhere, at least if Izhak Ben-Zwi was correct in believing that Sabbatai passed away in Berat.

Ben–Zwi, in arguing that Sabbatai died and was buried in Berat, quotes the testimony of Rabbi Judah Jekuthiel Gruenwald, whose memoirs were published in Budapest in 1922. Gruenwald writes that he travelled to Albania late in 1918, after the end of the First World War, his goal being to find the grave of Sabbatai Sevi. He went first to Dulcigno and searched diligently for the grave, 'asking everyone, learned men, teachers and Muslim imams, but no one told me a thing'. Then finally he met an imam from Elbasan who told him that

Your prophet is buried in Albania . . . in the city of Berat which the Muhammedans call Arnaut Belgrade. At first I did not know at whom he was hinting; then it occurred to me that it might have been the person for whom I was looking . . . I went to Berat. During the two hours I spent in Berat I asked around until one learned man showed me the place where the Jewish Messiah had been buried, adding that the gravestone inscribed 'Mehmet Kapuji' [i.e. Mehmet the Gatekeeper – the title that Sabbatai held in the Sultan's palace] had been lost forty years earlier.

Ben–Zwi also writes of his interview with a young Albanian Sabbatian whom he met in Israel. The young man, whom Ben–Zwi refers to as Z. Ch., told him that he had been a member of a Sabbatian community in Tirana, the Albanian capital, comprising about forty believers, whose existence seems to have been unknown to Jewish scholars. The community worshipped in a synagogue in Tirana, and had a geniza where old Torah scrolls and important family documents were kept, but during the Italian occupation in the Second World War the place was robbed and the documents disappeared. The young Albanian told Ben–Zwi that from time to time he and other members of the community had made pilgrimages to Sabbatai's tomb in Berat. Ben–Zwi concludes his report on this interview by noting that the young Albanian's 'account was confirmed by an old Sabbatian, the late Dr Ismael Adn of Izmir . . . Dr Adn, who was born in Salonika, testified that he had once taken part in a visit to Sabbatai Sevi's grave in Albania.'

Local tradition holds that Sabbatai's tomb in Berat was still in existence until 1967. By then there were only about 200 Jews left in Albania, and within a few years all of them emigrated to Israel. There is no further mention of the tomb from that time on, and presumably it vanished.

Thus there was no reason for me to go to Albania, but I decided to go there all the same, and to Montenegro as well, for I wanted to see for myself the place of Sabbatai's exile and the site of his grave – such is the nature of obsession.

By the beginning of the new millennium the political situation in Albania and Montenegro had at least temporarily stabilized to the point where I could make plans to travel there with my wife, Dolores. We would be accompanied by Emin Saatci, an old Turkish friend who was fluent in Greek and could speak some Albanian. We booked a round-trip flight on THY, Turkish National Airlines, and on 27 April 2000 we flew from Istanbul to Tirana. As the plane crossed the southern Balkans I at last had my first glimpse of the snow-streaked mountains of Albania, of which Edward Gibbon had remarked more than two centuries ago that it was 'a country within sight of Italy less known than the interior of America'.

After our arrival we booked into a hotel and hired a car and a driver who spoke some Turkish, agreeing that he would take us first to Ulcinj, the old Dulcigno, and then to Berat. We had already made arrangements in Istanbul with the consuls of Albania and the former Yugoslavia, who had obtained permission for us to cross the border between Albania and Montenegro so that we could visit Ulcinj.

We started off the following morning. The first stage of our journey took us north to Shkodër, the regional capital of northern Albania. The town is situated at the south-eastern end of the lake of the same name, the largest in the Balkans, which crosses part of the border between Albania and Montenegro. Ulcinj is on the Adriatic shore south-west of Shkodër, approached by a road that leads out to the coast south of the lake.

Ulcinj had been a popular seaside resort until the beginning of the wars in Bosnia and Kosovo, but now there was not a tourist in sight. The locals were hopeful that tourism would begin to revive now that the Kosovo war was over, but this was being held up by the considerable tension with the Serbs over the issue of Montenegrin separatism.

The setting of Ulcinj is quite picturesque, with an old Turkish quarter dominated by a well-preserved fortress dating back to the medieval Byzantine period. The principal surviving tower of the fortress figures in one of the last recorded incidents of Sabbatai's life, when, according to Sabbatian tradition, 'he decided that the time of redemption had come, and that he was to manifest himself again in the sight of all living'. According to Baruch of Arezzo, Sabbatai was experiencing one more period of 'great illumination, the likes of which had never been before', leading his followers up to the 'wall of the tower', singing hymns and Ladino love songs. One of the songs that he would certainly have sung was 'Meliselda', and as I looked upon the towers of the old fortress I could almost hear Sabbatai singing in ecstasy:

> To the mountain I ascended
> To the river I descended
> Meliselda I met there,
> The king's daughter bright and fair.

Nothing that I had read of Ulcinj hinted of any extant monument in the town associated with Sabbatai Sevi: not a mosque nor a dervish *tekke* nor a Turkish cemetery. His only known Muslim acquaintance in the town had been Ali, the Muslim mullah who carried Sabbatai's invitation to Joseph Karillo and his unknown companion to visit him in Dulcigno. Ali was probably the imam of one of the local mosques, five of which have survived from Ottoman times, but there is no record of which one Sabbatai may have gone to during his three years of exile in Dulcigno. Ali may also have been the unidentified Turk 'who was with Sabbatai Sevi when he was ill and dealt with his burial' in Berat, according to Joseph Almosnino.

Most of the tourists who in times past came to Ulcinj were drawn by the long sandy beach that stretches eastward from the port, to within sight of Albania. Sabbatai had walked this way with Joseph

Karillo and his companion, pointing along the beach as he spoke to them, in what would be his last recorded words: 'Return every man to his house. How long will you hold fast to me? Perhaps until you can see beneath that rock on the coast?'

I looked eastward along the Adriatic coast, to where the mountains of Albania rose blue in the distance, but there was no rocky feature on the seaside that would fit the one in Sabbatai's last words. Nor could I find the seaside cave that he had prepared as his final resting place, but which his brother Elijah had found empty after he made his way past the dragon that was guarding the entrance. As Baruch of Arezzo wrote, 'Neither Our Lord nor anything else was in the cave, but it was full of light.'

So my pilgrimage to Ulcinj was in vain; but I had expected this, and so was spared disappointment. And I could at last rid myself of part of my obsession, for I had at least seen the place of Sabbatai's exile, the remoteness of which must have tried his soul.

We spent the night in Ulcinj and returned to Tirana the following day. During the drive I reflected that this was the route that Sabbatai would have been carried on in his last journey, to his final resting place in Berat, or so I now believed.

The next day we explored Tirana in a fruitless search for the old synagogue, which seems to have completely disappeared, along with the geniza where the records of the Jewish community had been kept for centuries. No one whom we asked could tell us where the synagogue was or had been, nor did they even know that Jews had ever lived in the city.

That evening we were invited to dinner by the Turkish ambassador, the Honourable Ahmet Rifat Ökçün, who was nearing the end of a five-year posting in Albania that he said was literally killing him. But he was obviously deeply interested in the country, and regaled us with fascinating stories of what he had learned about it and its people. He said that both the Greek Orthodox and the Roman Catholic Churches had been making great headway in Albania at the expense of Islam in recent years, after three decades in which all religions had been banned by the Communists. The last census before the banning of religion in 1967 had shown the percentages for the three major religions as 70 for the Muslims, 20 for the Orthodox and 10 for the Catholics, he said, whereas now he doubted whether the majority of the population really adhered to Islam. I asked him about the Jewish community, and he said that the only Jews now in the country were foreign businessmen, most of them Israeli, although he knew that some of these were native Albanians. As for Sabbatians, he had never heard of any during his tenure as ambassador.

He said that in 1967 the Communist dictator Enver Hoxha had destroyed all religious buildings in Tirana except for one mosque, one Roman Catholic church and one Orthodox church, leaving them as empty monuments of the benighted culture of pre-Communist times. We had visited the mosque earlier that day and found it empty except for the imam, who said that the number of faithful who came to the Friday noon prayer was far fewer than in the past.

After we left the Turkish Embassy, our drive back to the hotel took us past the Orthodox cathedral of Tirana, which was filled with worshippers, as was the outer courtyard and the wide boulevard for several blocks on either side of the church. It was the eve of Orthodox Easter, and as the church bells tolled midnight the Archbishop of Albania, speaking first in Greek and then in Albanian, proclaimed that Christ had risen, after which the crowd took up the cry and made it echo through the night across the city. This was the ecstatic celebration that the Sabbatians had longed for during the three centuries and more during which they had waited for the reappearance of their Messiah, or so I thought on the eve of the last stage of my search for Sabbatai Sevi.

We left early the following day for Berat via Durrës, a drive of eighty miles which first took us westward through the coastal plain and then south up into the foothills of the rugged mountains that comprise the rest of the country – High Albania – a world apart from the rest of the Balkans. The drive was very difficult, for the road was riddled with huge potholes, which had filled up with water from the torrential rain that had begun just as we set off and continued all day, with occasional cannonades of thunder and flashes of lightning, one of which illuminated the town of Berat in the valley ahead.

Berat is a remarkably preserved Ottoman town bisected by the Osum river, known also as the Beratino, which here cuts a gorge some 3,000-feet deep through the limestone rock between two precipitous pine-clad peaks, ramparts of Mount Tomorrit, which rises to almost 8,000 feet. The Osum cuts through the town, half-encircling a flat-topped acropolis rock towering some 600 feet above the river, its periphery ringed with the mile-long walls of an ancient fortress whose massive ramparts are studded with twenty-four defence towers.

During the early Ottoman period the Greek and Albanian Christian population of Berat lived within the walls of the fortress, while the Muslim town developed in the plain below the acropolis along the right bank of the river, in the quarter known as Mangalem. Later the Christians were evicted from the citadel and moved across to the hill on the left bank of the river, the quarter called Gorica. The two halves of the city were linked by a bridge over the Osum, which was restored in 1790 by the feudal lord Kurd Ahmet Pasha.

A census taken in 1583 records that there were 650 households of Muslims and 400 of Christians, indicating a population of 6,000–7,000. The census does not mention any Jews, though some Sephardim may well have settled here after they were welcomed to the Ottoman Empire by Sultan Beyazit II in 1492. Evliya Chelebi, who visited Berat in 1662, records that the town had thirty *mahalles*, or quarters, of which nineteen were inhabited by Muslims, ten by Christians, and one by Jews. The Jewish quarter was probably contiguous to the Turkish *mahalles* in the lower town along the right bank of the river.

Berat has more Ottoman monuments than any other town in Albania, not to mention a large number of beautiful old houses from the Turkish period. The mosques survived only because the Communist government designated Berat as a museum city. The earliest of these monuments is Xhamia Mbretit, the Mosque of the Ruler, which stands in the south-west corner of Berat's main square. This is an imperial mosque erected by Beyazit II, probably in 1492, when the Sultan personally commanded a campaign in Albania. According to Evliya Chelebi, Beyazit built four other structures as part of the *külliye*, or pious foundation of his mosque.

These were a *medrese*, or theological school, a hammam, or public bath, a *mesjit*, or small mosque, and a *tekke*, a lodge for the Halveti order of dervishes. All these structures are still standing and in good repair, with the imperial mosque once again serving as an Islamic house of worship after having been closed for three decades.

The most interesting of the auxiliary structures in Beyazit's *külliye* is the *tekke*, which was rebuilt in 1790 by Kurd Ahmet Pasha, and restored after its reopening in 1997. The entrance porch, which faces the mosque, has a very attractive portico of round arches carried on five columns of white marble. The entryway at the left end of the porch leads to the largest of the two chambers into which the *tekke* is divided – the *semahane* – the room where the dervish ceremonies were performed, with a balcony to the left as one enters reserved for the women devotees. The ceiling and upper walls of the *semahane* are beautifully decorated with paintings of floral motifs, with the woodwork panels gilded and adorned with inlay of sea-tortoise shell and mother–of–pearl.

The inner room of the *tekke*, to the right of the *semahane*, originally served as the *türbe*, or tomb, of Kurd Ahmet Pasha and his son Mehmet Kemalettin. But the tombs were removed in the cultural revolution of 1967 and the *türbe* was converted into a school for Communist indoctrination of young people. When we entered the *türbe* we found a class in session, with six teenage girls attending a chemistry lecture given by a bedraggled gentleman of about forty who said that he had formerly been a professor at the university in Tirana. The young Egyptian cleric who ran the school told us that a purely religious training in Islam was no longer sufficient to prepare young men and women for life, and so he and his colleagues had introduced secular subjects to the curriculum as well. The girls told us that they were hoping to enter the University of Tirana, one saying that she wanted to study chemistry, while the others were planning careers in medicine, law, economics, business administration and literature. They were also studying English, and one of them said shyly that we were the first foreigners to whom they had ever spoken in that language.

I spoke to the mullah who was in charge of the mosque and the *tekke*, asking him about the graveyard that had been part of Sultan

Beyazit's *külliye*, for, as I had only recently learned, this was where local tradition placed the tomb of Sabbatai Sevi. The mullah pointed out two old tombs on the west side of the courtyard between the mosque and the *tekke*, saying that these were the only funerary monuments that remained from the graveyard, the others having been destroyed in 1967. We went to look at the inscriptions on the two tombstones, both of which were memorials to women in the family of Kurd Ahmet Pasha, which was probably why they were spared, for he was renowned in Albania as a benevolent despot under whom Berat had prospered.

My belief that Sabbatai was buried here was based on the tradition of the local Sabbatian community, which was that his tomb was beside the river, and the graveyard of Sultan Beyazit's mosque was the only cemetery in Berat which fitted that description. Also, local Muslim tradition had it that his grave had been cared for by the dervishes of the Halveti *tekke*, who believed that Sabbatai was a local *baba* or *dede*, the name given to Turkish saints. The dervishes would probably not have known that Sabbatai was an apostate Jew, and even if they had it would not have mattered, given the catholicity of their religious views. What is more, when the Sabbatians of Berat buried Sabbatai here they would have made no indication on his funerary monument that he was not a Muslim, so to all appearances it would have been the *türbe* of a Turkish holy man.

So finally I had found the last resting place of the Lost Messiah – at least to my own satisfaction, though there was no concrete proof that my theory was correct, no textual reference or inscribed tombstone on the site of his grave. Nor was I a believer, who might stand at the supposed site of the tomb and hope that the Messiah would one day end his long occultation and reappear, to lead the *ma'min* to redemption. Nevertheless, I would seem to have completed my quest, having followed in Sabbatai Sevi's footsteps all the way from his birthplace in Izmir.

As I stood before the site of what I believed to be Sabbatai's tomb, completely drenched by the pouring rain, a deafening clap of thunder exploded above me and then the *tekke* was suddenly illuminated by a flash of lightning. It was a kind of Sabbatian epiphany, I thought, with some wry amusement – a tribute to the persistence of my search. Then in that mood I recalled a poem that had been written three centuries ago by an unknown Sabbatian in Italy.

> The king in his splendour will now appear
> wreathed in the crown of kingship
> to give the righteous justice and, without fear,
> the eastern kingdoms subdue and grip.
> For the poorest of folk he'll bring the truth near,
> for the holy seed who to the Law adhere.
> O God, grant Sabbatai Sevi grandeur.
> Return, rebuild your dwelling pure.

But somehow Sabbatai continued to elude my grasp and to draw me on, for there were still missing pages in his story and questions about the present state of his messianic movement that I had not fully answered.

A few days after my return to Istanbul I paid a sentimental visit to the Kohen Sisters' Bookshop, the old Jewish bookshop where I had first learned of the existence of Sabbatai Sevi. The owner told me that he was a nephew of Eliza Kohen, who had died more than thirty years ago. All the rare books that I had once seen here had long since been sold, he said, and it was only a matter of time before he would have to sell the shop itself or convert it to another use, for it was losing money. The shop was part of a world that no longer existed, he commented sadly, and I could only agree, as I said goodbye and left, feeling as if I was closing a door on my own past.

I strolled down through the old Jewish quarter in Galata and then took a ferry across the Bosphorus to Üsküdar on the Asian shore. At the ferry landing there I took a taxi up through the Valley of the Nightingales to the district of Selamsız, a strange name meaning 'Without Greetings'. This brought me to the Selanikliler Mezarlığı, the Cemetery of Those from Salonika, which I had not visited since the early days of my quest.

The Cemetery of Those from Salonika is unlike any of the many other burial grounds of Istanbul, be they Jewish, Christian or

Muslim, in that there are no symbols on the funerary monuments to indicate the religion of the deceased – no Jewish star of David, no crucifix, no Islamic star and crescent.

A number of the tombstones bore the family name 'Kapanci', the Turkish form of 'Kapandsis', the name given to the original Dönme sect in Salonika. Many bore the names 'Dilber', 'Ipekçi' and 'Koyuncu', the most common family names among the Karakash sect of the Dönme. One stone was inscribed with the name 'Filosof', that of the family of Sabbatai Sevi's last wife, Jochebed, later known as Ayesha, whose brother Jacob Qerido had given his name to the Jacobite sect of the Dönme.

Many of the older tombstones had inscriptions recording that the deceased were born in Salonika and died in Istanbul. The most notable of these was the tombstone of Shemsi Efendi, the teacher of Atatürk. The older inscriptions were in the Arabic script used in Ottoman times, while the later ones were in the Latin alphabet adopted by Turkey in 1928. The birthdate on the older tombstones was usually given in the Muslim calendar, i.e. AH, after the Hegira, Muhammad's flight from Mecca to Medina in AD 622, whereas the dates of deaths after the Turkish calendar reform of 1926 were given in the Gregorian calendar. Thus there were stones such as one I saw that recorded the date of birth as 1283 (AD 1866) and the date of death as 1930.

I was surprised at the number of inscriptions recording places of birth other than Salonika. One recorded that the deceased was born in 1888 in Ioannina, which, so far as I know, is the only evidence of a Sabbatian community there, more than two centuries after the death of Sabbatai. Others of those buried were from Albania, Macedonia, Bulgaria, Syria and Egypt, as well as towns in central and eastern Turkey, having been displaced from their homes by the population movements that followed the collapse of the Ottoman Empire, all of them finding their last resting place here in the Valley of the Nightingales on the Asian shore of the Bosphorus.

A Dönme friend of mine had been buried here some years before, and I wandered around until I found his grave. His tombstone, like all the others around his grave, had no emblem or inscription to indicate whether he had been a Muslim, Jew or Christian, the only information recorded being his name and dates of birth and death. His epitaph was conventional and gave no clue that my departed friend, though nominally a Muslim and by ancestry a Sabbatian, had actually been an atheist.

During the hour or so that I spent wandering through the cemetery I saw a number of people visiting the graves of family members, some of them praying in the Muslim manner, head bowed and hands apart. I had been told that, when the Karakash were buried here, the funeral service was first conducted by a Muslim imam, but that after he had left a Sabbatian funeral rite was conducted by a Dönme *hodja*. I asked the caretaker about this, but he disclaimed any knowledge of such a practice. But when the mother of a Dönme friend of mine was buried here recently the prayers for the dead were recited by an imam whom I learned to be a Mevlevi dervish, and I supposed that this was how the Sabbatian funerary custom was perpetuated.

Then I saw an old woman praying at her family tomb, and when she finished she kissed the horizontal tombstone and rubbed it fondly with her right hand. Before leaving she bent to pick up a pebble, which she placed carefully on the tombstone, just as the old women had done in several photos in Nikos Stavroulakis's book on the Jews and dervishes of Salonika. The pebble was a talisman to warn off evil, an ancient custom that the Dönme had preserved from their Jewish ancestors – one that in fact predates Judaism, Islam or Christianity.

On a number of the tombstones I found curious epitaphs that seemed to express a deep longing for redemption, without actually saying so in words: 'I am longing for the God I love, here I wait for Him.' None of the inscriptions made any mention of Sabbatai Sevi, nor of his supposed reincarnations as Jacob Qerido or Baruch-iah Russo, even on the oldest tombstones, for the Dönme had to keep their secret in the grave just as they did in life, remaining silent about their faith in the Messiah who had led them into Islam, waiting for their saviour to emerge from his long occultation, their graves shaded by cypresses and now, in early May, sprinkled with the pink blossoms of Judas trees.

And so I left them in peace and departed from the cemetery,

Carpi, Solomon Joseph, *The History of Sabbatai Sevi*, ed. Nahum Brüll (Vilna, 1879)

Coenen, Thomas, *Ydele verwachtinge der Joden in den Persoon van Sabethai Zevi (Idle Expectations of the Jews shown in the Person of Sabethai Sevi)* (in Dutch: Amsterdam, 1665)

Courmenin, Louis Deshayes, Baron de, *Voyage de Levant . . .* (2nd edn, Paris, 1632)

Currie, Jean, *Rhodes and the Dodecanese* (3rd edn, London, 1981)

Dankoff, Robert, and Elsie, Robert, *Evliya Çelebi in Albania and Adjacent Regions (Kosova, Montenegro, Ohrid)* (Leiden, Boston and Cologne, 2000)

Derin, Fahri Çetin, *Abdurrahman Abdi Paşa Vekayinamesi, 1648–1692 (Chronicle of Abdurrahman Abdi Pasha, 1648–1692)* (in Turkish: Istanbul, 1993)

Eden, Esin, and Stavroulakis, Nikos, *Salonika: A Family Cookbook* (Athens, 1997)

Eldem, Edhem, Goffman, Daniel, and Masters, Bruce, *The Ottoman City Between East and West: Aleppo, Izmir and Istanbul* (Cambridge, 1999)

Evelyn, John, *The History of the Three late famous Impostors, viz. Padre Ottomano, Mahomed Bei, and Sabbatai Sevi . . . the suppos'd Messiah of the Jews* (London, 1669)

——, *The Diary of John Evelyn*, ed. E. S. de Beer (Oxford, 6 vols., 1955)

Evliya Chelebi, *Narrative of Travels*, trans. Joseph Von Hammer (London, 1834)

Fortis, Umberto, *Jews and Synagogues: Venice, Florence, Rome, Leghorn: A Practical Guide* (Venice, 1973)

——, *The Ghetto on the Lagoon: A Guide to the History and Art of the Venetian Ghetto (1516–1797)* (Venice, 1988)

Freely, John, *The Western Shores of Turkey* (London, 1988)

——, *Istanbul: The Imperial City* (London, 1996)

——, *Inside the Seraglio: Private Lives of the Sultans in Istanbul* (London, 1999)

Galanté, Abraham, *Nouveaux documents sur Sabbetai Sevi: Organisation et us et coutomes de ses adeptes* (Istanbul, 1935)

——, *Histoire des Juifs de Turquie* (Istanbul, 9 vols., 1940)

Galland, Antoine, *Journal d'Antoine Galland pendant son séjour à Constantinople (1672–73)*, ed. Charles Schefer (Paris, 2 vols., 1881)

Goffman, Daniel, *Izmir and the Levantine World, 1550–1650* (Seattle and London, 1990)

Goitein, Solomon Dab Fritz, *A Mediterranean Society: The Jewish Communities of the Arab World as Portrayed in the Documents of the Cairo Geniza* (Berkeley, 1967)

——, *Letters of Medieval Jewish Traders* (Princeton, 1975)

Goldberg, David J., and Rayner, John D., *The Jewish People: Their History and Their Religion* (London, 1987)

Gövsa, Ibrahim Alaettin, *Sabatay Sevi* (in Turkish: Istanbul, undated [1939–41])

Hathaway, Jane, 'The Grand Vizier and the False Messiah: The Sabbatai Sevi Controversy and the Ottoman Reform in Egypt', *Journal of the American Oriental Society*, Vol. 117, No. 4 (October–December 1997), pp. 665–71

Johnson, Paul, *A History of the Jews* (London, 1987)

Kafadar, Cemal, 'Self and Others: The Diary of a Dervish in Seventeenth Century Istanbul and First-Person Narratives in Ottoman Literature', *Studia Islamica*, Vol. 69 (1989), pp. 121–50

Karmi, Ilan, *Jewish Sites of Istanbul: A Guide Book* (Istanbul, 1992)

Kiel, Machiel, *Ottoman Architecture in Albania (1385–1912)* (Istanbul, 1990)

Knolles, Richard, *The Lives of the Othoman Kings and Emperors* (London, 1610)

Kochan, Lionel, *Jews, Idols and Messiahs: The Challenge from History* (Oxford, 1990)

Kritovoulos, *History of Mehmed the Conqueror*, trans. Charles T. Riggs (Princeton, 1954)

La Croix, Chevalier de, *Memoire . . . contenant diverses relations très curieuses de l'Empire Ottoman* (Paris, 1684)

Leake, William Martin, *Travels in Northern Greece* (London, 1835; reprinted Amsterdam, 1967)

Lear, Edward, *Journal of a Landscape Painter in Albania* (London, 1851)

Lenowitz, Henry, *The Jewish Messiahs: From the Galilee to Crown Heights* (New York and Oxford, 1998)

Levy, Avigdor, *The Sephardim in the Ottoman Empire* (Princeton, 1994)

——, ed., *The Jews of the Ottoman Empire* (Princeton, 1994)

Lewis, Bernard, *Christians and Jews in the Ottoman Empire* (New York, 1983)

——, *The Jews of Islam* (Princeton, 1984)

Lewis, W. H., *Levantine Adventurer: The Travels and Missions of the Chevalier d'Arvieux, 1653–1697* (New York, 1962)

Leyb ben Ozer, *The Story of Shabbetay Zevi*, ed. Sh. Zucker and R. Plesser (in Hebrew: Jerusalem, 1978)

Liebes, Yehuda, *Studies in Jewish Myth and Jewish Messianism*, trans. Batya Stein (New York, 1993)

Mandel, Arthur, *The Militant Messiah, or, The Flight from the Ghetto: The Story of Jacob Frank and the Frankist Movement* (Atlantic Highlands, NJ, 1979)

Migliau, Bice, and Procaccia, Micaela, with Silvia Rebuzzi, *Lazio Jewish Itineraries* (Venice, 1997)

Neyzi, Leyla, '*Selanikli Kim?*' ('Who is from Salonika?') (in Turkish), *Gazete Pazar*, Istanbul, 5 October 1997, p. 15

Ortayli, Ilber, 'Ottoman Modernisation and Sabetaism', in *Alevi Identity* (Istanbul, 1999)

Özendes, Engin, *Edirne: The Second Ottoman Capital* (Istanbul, 1999)

Papagiannopoulos, Apostolos, *Monuments of Thessaloniki* (Salonika, undated)

Pettifer, James, *Blue Guide Albania* (2nd edn, London, 1996)

Porter, Ruth, and Harel-Hoshen, Sarah, eds., *Odyssey of the Exiles: The Sephardi Exile 1492–1992* (Tel Aviv, 1992)

Rodrigue, Aron, ed., *Ottoman and Turkish Jewry: Community and Leadership* (Bloomington, Indiana, 1992)

Rosanes, Solomon, *History of the Jews of Turkey and the Levant* (in Hebrew: Jerusalem and Sofia, 6 vols., 1933–4)

Russell, Dorothea (Lady Russell Pasha), *Medieval Cairo and the Monasteries of the Wadi Natrun* (New York and Toronto, 1963)

Rycaut, Paul, *The Present State of the Ottoman Empire* (4th edn, London, 1680)

Sasportas, Jacob, *The Fading Flower of Sevi*, ed. Isaiah Tishby (in Hebrew: Jerusalem, 1954)

Scholem, Gershom, 'A Prayer Book of the Dönme from Izmir', *Kiryat Sefer*, Vol. 18 (in Hebrew: Jerusalem, 1941), pp. 298–312, 398–408; Vol. 19, pp. 58–64

——, 'Where did Sabbatai Sevi Die?' (in Hebrew), *Zion*, Vol. 17 (1952), pp. 79–83

——, *The Messianic Idea in Judaism* (New York, 1971)

——, 'Shabbetai Zevi', in *Encyclopaedia Judaica*, Vol. 14 (Jerusalem, 1972), pp. 1219–51

——, *Sabbatai Sevi: The Mystical Messiah*, trans. R. J. Zwi Werblosky (Princeton, 1977)

——, *Kabbalah* (London, 1978)

Shaw, Stanford J., *The Jews of the Ottoman Empire and the Turkish Republic* (London, 1991)

Stavroulakis, Nikos, *Salonika – Jews and Dervishes* (Athens, 1993)

Thevenot, Jean de, *Travels of Monsieur de Thevenot in the Levant*, trans. A. Lovell (reprinted London, 1971)

Tishby, Isaiah, *Paths of Faith and Heresy: Essays and Studies in Kabbalistic and Sabbatian Literature* (in Hebrew: Jerusalem, 1964)

Vacalopoulos, Apostolos E., *A History of Thessaloniki*, trans. T. F. Carney (Thessaloniki, 1963)

——, *History of Macedonia, 1354–1833*, trans. Peter Megann (Thessaloniki, 1973)

Veinstein, Gilles, *Selanik [Salonika] 1850–1918* (in Turkish: Istanbul, 1999)

Vickers, Martha, *The Albanians* (London, 1995)

Young, Martin, *Corfu and the Other Ionian Islands* (3rd edn, London, 1981)

Zilfi, Madeline C., *The Politics of Piety: The Ottoman Ulema in the Postclassical Age (1600–1800)* (Minneapolis, 1988)

Zinberg, Israel, *A History of Jewish Literature, Vol. V: The Jewish Center of Culture in the Ottoman Empire*, trans. and ed. Bernard Martin (Cincinnati, 1974)

Zorlu, Ilgaz, *Evet, Ben Selanikliyim (Yes, I am from Salonika)* (in Turkish: Istanbul, 1998)

# Index